Equal Opportunity Theory

Dennis E. Mithaug

SAGE Publications
International Educational and Professional Publisher
Thousand Oaks   London   New Delhi

For information address:

 SAGE Publications, Inc.
2455 Teller Road
Thousand Oaks, California 91320
E-mail: order@sagepub.com

SAGE Publications Ltd.
6 Bonhill Street
London EC2A 4PU
United Kingdom

SAGE Publications India Pvt. Ltd.
M-32 Market
Greater Kailash I
New Delhi 110 048 India

Printed in the United States of America

Library of Congress Cataloging-in-Publication Data

Mithaug, Dennis E.
    Equal opportunity theory / Dennis E. Mithaug.
        p.   cm.
    Includes bibliographical references (p.) and index.
    ISBN 0-7619-0261-9 (cloth: acid-free paper).—
ISBN 0-7619-0262-7 (pbk.: acid-free paper)
    1. Equality.   2. Social justice.   I. Title.
HM146.M57   1996
305—dc20   96-4430

This book is printed on acid-free paper.

96 97 98 99   1 10 9 8 7 6 5 4 3 2 1

Sage Production Editor: Michèle Lingre
Sage Typesetter: Andrea D. Swanson
Sage Cover Designer: Candice Harman

Equal

Opportunity
Theory

4

In Memory of Ellen Sager

Contents

List of Figures

Introduction

Equal opportunity theory resolves the discrepancy between the *right* and the *experience* of self-determination. It locates the cause of this discrepancy in the lack of capacity and opportunity among individuals whose personal, social, and economic circumstances are beyond their control. By claiming that every member of society deserves an optimal chance of securing the good in life, the theory explains our collective responsibility for ensuring fair prospects for all. The theory shows that when prospects for self-determination are distributed fairly, they are equally optimal for all. Although one person's pursuits will be different from another person's, prospects are nonetheless comparable because all individuals have roughly the same chance of pursuing or not pursuing, of fulfilling or not fulfilling their own ends *over the long term*.

This means that inequality is a problem of unequal prospects for engaging and succeeding in self-determined pursuits. When prospects for pursuing the individually defined good in life are not distributed equally among members of a society, the ideal of liberty for all is jeopardized. In all countries of the world, including the United States, this is the case. Substantial numbers of individuals fail to engage and succeed in their own pursuits and as a consequence, lose control over life's circumstances. The persistent pattern of failure they experience leads to a loss of hope and a growing sense of helplessness and despair that destroys the very basis of their self-respect. They become victims in a cycle of personal, social, and economic decline that debilitates and erodes their capacity for improving their own prospects for life. These individuals need and deserve help to reestablish their experience of self-determination.

Equal opportunity theory justifies social redress on behalf of less well situated individuals by claiming that (a) all persons have the right to self-determination, (b) psychological and social conditions of freedom cause some individuals and groups to experience unfair advantages in determining their future, (c) declines in self-determination prospects for the less fortunate are due to social forces beyond their control, and (d) as a consequence of these declines, there is a collective obligation to improve prospects for self-determination among less well situated groups. The collective action proposed by the theory is to optimize prospects for self-determination among the less fortunate by improving their *capacity* for autonomous thought and action, by improving the *opportunities* for effective choice and action, and by optimizing the *match* between individual capacity and social opportunity by eliminating obstacles and constructing opportunity that encourage more frequent expressions of self-determination.

This book establishes a foundation for understanding this discrepancy between the right and the experience of self-determination, and then it describes how policies derived from equal opportunity theory regulate social opportunity toward the experience of equal liberty for all, including those individuals with the least optimal prospects for self-determination throughout life—people of color and people with disabilities. Chapter 1 presents the logical and philosophical basis for equal opportunity theory; Chapter 2 presents the theory's psychological foundations; Chapters 3 and 4 present the social and judicial background for equal opportunity theory; and Chapter 5 shows how the optimal prospects principle derived from the theory decreases the discrepancy between the right and the experience of self-determination for children and adults with significant physical, mental, social, and economic disadvantages. The concluding chapter discusses the implications of this new theory of redress for measuring progress toward fairness in liberty for all and for resolving the apparent contradiction between the quest for fairness and the quest for excellence.

Chapter 1 considers four answers to the question of what constitutes a fair chance in life for all individuals, including the least advantaged members of society. The first comes from the dominant social stratification ideology that equates a fair chance with an equal opportunity—the assumption being that in the United States equal opportunity is widespread. Consequently, the misfortune of others is due to their failure to take advantage of opportunity available to all. A second answer comes from Rawls's theory of justice, which claims equal opportunity means equal shares in the surplus created by fair and just institutions of cooperative endeavor. This conception yokes the outcomes of the most advantaged with those of the least advantaged in a contingency that ensures benefits for all regardless of their status or position in the group. A third answer comes from Nozick's theory of justice as entitlement, which takes fair chance to mean unfettered expression of power to self-determine, restrained only by the minimal state when that expression infringes on the self-determination of others. According to this view, social redress on behalf of the least advantaged is not possible because it requires unjust transfers of resources from those who earned them justly through their own self-determined effort.

The chapter concludes by explaining that equal opportunity theory improves on these theories because it takes into account the three-factor causal sequence affecting prospects for self-determination—capacity, opportunity, and outcome. Variation in capacity and opportunity affects and is affected by outcomes of self-determined thought and action. This causal interaction yields cycles of cumulative advantage and disadvantage that adversely affect prospects for self-determination for individuals already experiencing significant constraints in their personal capacity and social opportunity. Equal opportunity theory justifies the amelioration of these cumulative disadvantages to improve prospects for self-determination for least well situated individuals.

Chapter 2 claims that Rawls's theory cannot solve the declining prospects problem because application of the difference principle actually erodes the very basis of self-respect Rawls claims is the primary good resulting from a just social order. This is because prospects for self-determination through cooperation depend on a match between individual interests and group opportunities. Individuals enter and leave cooperative relationships and groups form and dissolve according to this correspondence. When social redress fails to improve connections between the two, it fails to alter prospects for self-determination for individuals or to ensure progress toward cooperative gain for groups. It also renders itself inadequate for improving conditions of the least advantaged in that it undermines the very basis of self-respect, which is producing one's own gain in accordance with *individually determined* needs, interests, and abilities rather than receiving gain from others in accordance with *other-determined* needs, interests, and abilities as Rawls's difference principle would require.

Equal opportunity theory solves the problem of cumulative decline in prospects for self-determination for less well situated groups by explaining how variation in individual capacity to adjust to group circumstance affects and is affected by variation in optimalities of opportunity defining those social conditions. Although individuals can optimize adjustments and maximize gain toward their ends under a wide range of opportunity optimalities, they will experience grossly different levels of self-determination in the process. This is because an optimal adjustment to a suboptimal condition often requires accommodation to external demands that is contrary to one's self-determined pursuits in life. This is not true for people who enjoy optimal opportunities. For them, optimal adjustment usually accommodates self-determined pursuits. These differences are greatest at the margin of opportunity optimalities in which interaction between capacity and circumstance is egregiously *constraining* as in the case of people with unusual mental, physical, and social disadvantages and in which that interaction is extremely *emancipating* as in the case of people with unusual mental, physical, and social advantages.

What is also interesting about these contrasting adjustments is that the two groups are *equally likely* to maintain their status in life. Extremely favorable and extremely unfavorable optimality conditions produce similar levels of adjustments but dissimilar levels of self-determination. For individuals experiencing suboptimal opportunity, self-regulated problem solving to improve one's adjustments is unlikely because the risk of failure is greater than the potential for gain, and for individuals experiencing optimal opportunity, problem solving to improve adjustments is unlikely because existing adjustments already produce gain toward personally determined ends. In neither condition are individuals likely to adjust differently—to change their thoughts or actions to improve their situation in life. Consequently, their prospects for self-determination will remain unchanged as well. People in suboptimal circumstance will continue to work in the service of ends determined by others, whereas people in optimal circumstance will continue to work in the service of their own, self-determined ends.

For individuals with suboptimal opportunity, prospects for self-determination decline to the extent that external circumstance determines what actions are necessary just to survive, much less to live according to a self-defining plan. These people experience little self-determination and are unlikely to improve prospects on their own. The opposite is true for people with favorable circumstance; they get what they want and need in life simply by thinking and acting as they have in the past. Consequently, their prospects for self-determination approach a maximum, whereas prospects for self-determination for individuals with suboptimal opportunity approach a minimum.

Equal opportunity theory builds on this understanding of how prospects for self-determination depend on optimalities of opportunity—that people at the margins of opportunity optimalities have contrasting levels of self-determination and that they are unlikely to change their patterns of adjustment or their prospects for self-determination *on their own*. The implication is that because opportunity conditions similarly discourage individual initiative and risk taking at both ends of the optimality continuum—a scale of cumulated advantage that locates one group in the lowest stratum of the social structure and the other group in the highest stratum—then responsibility for success or failure in determining one's direction in life cannot be attributable to individual effort alone. We cannot, therefore, conclude that one group is more self-determining than another because it engages in more effective or efficient problem solving to meet personal goals. Another equally influential factor affecting prospects for self-determination is optimality of opportunity. The reason one group's prospects for self-determination minimizes whereas another group's maximizes is because prospects for self-determination are a function of capacity-opportunity interactions. Consequently, social redress to ameliorate the injustice caused by the experience of suboptimal opportunity should focus on this causal connection rather than on the distribution of gain resulting from this connection—for example, through Rawls's difference principle. It should focus on increasing capacity, opportunity, and the match between the two. This approach would optimize prospects for self-determination for all, including those least well situated in society.

Chapter 3 explains why Nozick's theory of entitlement fails to account for how the undesirable consequences of unrestrained self-determination of the few diminishes optimalities of opportunity of the many. In societies where power and wealth accumulate at the top and poverty and pervasive helplessness concentrate at the bottom, a condition of freedom as power prevails. Under these circumstances, there is no universal right to self-determination because all expressions of freedom depend on one's location in the social structure that is coincident with accumulated social and economic advantage. Rawls recognizes this threat of unregulated natural freedom even in countries such as the United States that were founded on the principle of equal liberty (see Rawls, 1971, p. 72). But Nozick's theory does not. Application of principles of entitlement supervised by a minimal state would lead to the same ill-treatment of the less fortunate that slaves and disabled people have experienced throughout history. Consequently, his theory is inadequate in determining what is fair treatment for persons disadvantaged by their personal, social, and economic conditions.

The chapter claims Nozick's theory is insensitive to the effects of accumulated advantage on prospects for self-determination because Nozick assumes individuals to be solely responsible for the advantages and disadvantages they experience. Consequently, they are entitled to what they get. Another, equally robust explanation is that the evolution of optimalities of opportunity creates cycles of success and failure that lead to unequal distributions of advantage among any population of actors. According to this view, an individual's good fortune is a function of interactions between personal capacity and socially defined optimalities of opportunity that create social drift toward increased optimalities of opportunity for those with greater accumulated gain (success) and decreased optimalities of opportunity for those with accumulated loss (failure). The ultimate effect of these self-perpetuating cycles of distributive advantage is a structure of *differential optimalities* that defines a society's system of social stratification. Once established, this structure, not individual initiative, distributes prospects for self-determination to the advantage of the most advantaged and to the disadvantage of the least advantaged.

Chapter 3 explains the emergence and persistence of social stratification by showing how interactions between individual capacity and social opportunity stratify optimalities of opportunity. The three factors responsible for these effects are individual ability to manage resources to produce gain toward desired ends, the presence of social and environmental opportunity to control the means for producing desirable gain, and the outcomes of previous gain pursuits. Individuals who get what they need and want in life have these three factors working in their favor. They manage their resources effectively and efficiently in producing gain toward their ends, they have opportunities for controlling the means necessary for gaining toward their ends, and the outcomes obtained from previous pursuits place them in advantageous positions for subsequent pursuit. These factors interact to accelerate advantage by increasing optimalities of subsequent opportunity for those in favored situations and to accelerate disadvantage by decreasing optimalities of subsequent opportunity for those in unfavorable circumstances.

Chapter 3 describes how this process works over time to create gross discrepancies in personal, social, and economic circumstances that diminish prospects for self-determination for people who are poor and who are disabled. The implication for fair chances is that, although various structures of differential opportunity are the *outcome* of a multitude of individually determined pursuits as claimed by Nozick, they are also the *cause* of unfair distributions of opportunity optimalities among that same multitude of individuals, as claimed by Rawls. The effect of the end state distribution is that those in higher positions in the social structure consistently experience more favorable opportunities for self-determined pursuits than those in lower positions. Those lowest in the hierarchy of cumulative advantage suffer most. Their prospects for getting what they need and want constitute unfair chances for the self-determined life.

Nozick's theory of entitlement fails to take into account this social selection effect. His theory considers only the personal construction effect produced when individuals manage their personal resources as effectively and efficiently as they can to reach ends they want. If this were the only factor for success of individual pursuits, his theory would be adequate in adjudicating fair chances. But it is not. Social selection also affects success by increasing optimalities of opportunity for some and decreasing optimalities of opportunity for others. Social selection works in all situations and is independent of individual effort. So individuals can no more take credit for the better opportunities usually associated with their status in life than they can be responsible for lower optimalities of opportunity associated with a lower status in life. Both end state conditions are arbitrary from a moral point of view in that they function independently of individual capacity and effort.

Chapter 3 traces the effects of unrestrained freedom during three transformations in sociopolitical power, beginning with hunting and gathering, which was organized according to each tribe member's individual capacity to produce gain for himself or herself and his or her tribesmen. During the 10,000 years that followed that period of relative egalitarianism, the evolution of freedom as power yielded social organizations based on gross differences in advantage between members of the human group. One reason for this change was the shift in human adaptation from nomadic to sedentary means of production because the effect of this change was an acceleration of production in gain and, at the same time, a reinvestment of surplus gain to optimize ever more challenging opportunity. A secondary consequence of this increased productivity was the surplus gain and advantage that came to be associated with positions in the division of labor. For the first time, occupying a position in the physical and social environment had a greater effect on one's access to productive gain and prospects for living the good life than one's personal ability to produce desired gain.

Social selection theory explains how these factors created inequality in social life by showing how variations in the optimalities of individual adjustments and the optimalities of their opportunities interact to accumulate gain or loss for different members of the group. The selection effect occurs when the same individuals have optimal opportunities to optimize adjustments within a group's division of labor, and when they use this advantage to produce surplus gain for themselves and their families. This differentiation in advantage accelerated during the transformation to sedentary modes of production because it placed individuals in structured relationships with each other, which meant that the *same people* would now interact with the *same optimalities of opportunity* to create a stratification of opportunities and outcomes favoring those in more favorable positions.

The moral problem with this structuring of opportunities was that it favored individuals according to their positions rather than according to their capacities. This, in turn, had the effect of enhancing the capacities of those in favorable positions so they could maintain control over those favored positions, and it had the opposite effect for those in less favorable positions because it tended to diminish their capacities so that they could never improve their positions. This was a natural consequence of freedom as power. It permitted the acceleration of advantage for some and the acceleration of disadvantage for others. It created unequal prospects for freedom within the group.

Chapter 4 explains how the modern ideal of freedom as right evolved from the ancient experience of freedom as power, and how this connection between freedom as right and freedom as power continues to affect ideologies justifying the distribution of opportunities for self-determination today. Following the breakdown of ancient systems of social stratification after the fall of the Roman Empire, a new social order emerged in the West. This new order justified the distribution of opportunities and outcomes among members of the feudal community by basing the distribution of opportunities and outcomes according to expectations for mutual benefit through exchange. Under this system, freedom became a right through negotiations between equally powerful actors. So as the decentralization of power increased during the Middle Ages, new power holders legitimated their holdings by using their positions of influence to establish contractual relationships with other power holders who agreed to respect those rights in exchange for reciprocal respect for their holdings. The resulting contracts legitimated control over positions and gain accumulations attached to those positions. In this way, what was negotiated as right due to an initial advantage in exchange stratified opportunities and outcomes as in the ancient past. What was different, however, was the method of justification. For the first time, the *social* contract, with its connection with human nature and natural law rather than ancient tradition legitimated by divine authority, decided who deserved what opportunity to produce gain in the community.

By the beginning of the modern era, the beneficiaries of this new ideology were individuals with newly acquired sources of economic power. They used this new belief in contractual rights to pursue their own ends during the Industrial Revolution where they further enhanced their capacity by gaining technical control over the means of producing goods and services that were in demand throughout the industrial world. The ideology of freedom as right for all persons helped them argue for their own interests against the feudal nobility who still had sufficient resources to maintain their positions of power and advantage in the community. The new ideology also encouraged others to expect more from the new social order as well. In fact, it tended to raise expectations for everyone, including those lacking the experience and the right to self-determination. In this sense, basing the right to freedom on a social contract claimed to be anchored in human nature and natural law turned out to be fundamentally destabilizing because it provided no basis for excluding those *who lacked* the capacity or opportunity to determine their own way in life. Consequently, any individual or group could perceive their situation to be discrepant from the ideal of freedom for all and demand restitution to ameliorate the discrepancy. And they did.

The ideal of freedom for all raised expectations among all members of the new order, including those least advantaged in society, and this produced the discrepancy between the ideal of freedom for all and the reality of freedom for some. The discrepancy, in turn, created different 19th-century theories to explain away or to offer recommendations for its amelioration. Theories of individual determinism, for example, identified the individual as the principle force in the production of variation in opportunity and outcome among members of the community and, as a consequence, claimed that the discrepancy was justified although perhaps unfortunate for those experiencing it. Theories of environmental determinism claimed that the forces of nature caused some individuals and groups to adjust more successfully than others and as a consequence, there was little that could be done to ameliorate the problem over the long term, because the course of natural and social evolution was inexorable. Theories of collective determinism identified the group as being responsible for inequality and claimed that collective intervention on behalf of the least advantaged was justified to equalize the differences between them and the most advantaged.

The difficulty with each of these modern solutions to the discrepancy problem was that they were based on a conception of causality that was unicausal and unidirectional, a condition we know to be contrary to experience. By emphasizing one source of influence rather than multiple sources, each theory yielded recommendations about what ought to be that contradicted what history tells us. For example, we know that we have a hand in determining our future, that we act on our social and physical environment to make it more or less favorable for securing what we want. We also know that the social and physical environment often limits our capacity and our opportunity to succeed in life and that sometimes these limitations seem to be unfair. So the problem of justifying social redress comes down to understanding how our capacity and our opportunity interact to affect our prospects for self-determination.

Equal opportunity theory reflects this understanding. It claims *interaction* between the environment, the individual, and the group ideology is responsible for those changes in social life we attribute to "sociocultural evolution." The theory goes beyond this attribution, however, suggesting that when these interactions lead a community of actors to agree that the right to self-determination should be extended to all its members, then that community has an obligation to back that claim and agreement by ensuring optimal prospects for self-determination for all. In other words, the collective claim for fairness in liberty for all creates a *social obligation* to give every individual a reasonable chance of living the self-determined life. In this sense, the claim itself serves as a motivational force for social redress when some members of the community experience a discrepancy between the right and the experience of self-determination.

Chapter 5 describes two conditions in the 20th century that resulted from this interaction between the environment, the individual, and the group ideology, and that led to the development of a social redress principle to reduce the discrepancy between the right and experience of self-determination. The two conditions were (a) a perceived discrepancy between the right and the experience of self-determination among persons least well situated in society and (b) a redistribution of sociopolitical power favoring those persons. Chapter 5 shows how the presence of these conditions affected the development of social redress for persons of color and people with disabilities. In both cases, when there was a moral claim justifying a fair distribution of rights to self-determination *and* when there was an accumulation of resources held by these two groups that enabled them to act on their own behalf to renegotiate the social contract, then the community responded favorably to their claim for redress by taking action to reduce the discrepancy.

The propositions of equal opportunity theory are based on the historical observations of Chapters 3 and 4 suggesting that discrepancies between rights and experiences of self-determination will be present in all societies espousing the ideal of freedom for all because freedom as power will always control the evolution of social relationships. To ameliorate this persistent problem of inequality in the distribution of the experience of freedom, the theory recommends redress through capacity building and opportunity restructuring. The propositions that follow summarize the reasoning behind this recommendation, which is based on the collectively affirmed ideal that "all individuals have the right to self-determination."

Equal Opportunity Theory

1. All individuals have the right to self-determination.
2. All societies have some individuals who lack the capacity to self-determine.
3. All societies generate unequal opportunities to self-determine.
4. Consequently, some individuals do not experience the right to self-determine because they lack the capacity and opportunity to do so.
5. Therefore, all societies should optimize prospects for self-determination among these least advantaged members by increasing their capacity and improving their opportunity to self-determine.

This theory of social redress has greater intuitive appeal than either of the theories offered by Nozick or Rawls in that it is based on the assumption that *fair prospects* (meaning fair chances) for self-determination are what the average person wants and expects in life. In fact, this expectation for social redress has not changed from when William Graham Sumner (1961/ 1883) recommended it:

> Instead of endeavoring to redistribute the acquisitions which have been made between the existing classes, [claiming that] our aim should be to *increase, multiply, and extend the chances.* Such is the work of civiliza- tion. Every old error or abuse which is removed opens new chances of development to all the new energy of society. Every improvement in education, science, art, or government expands the chances of man on earth. (pp. 144-145)

Moreover, this expectation, along with the desire of the average person to control those circumstances in life that affect the prospects of personal pursuits, has not changed substantially in the 150 years since Tocqueville's *Democracy in America* (Gans, 1988, p. 1). Gans's study of American individualism explains the expectation for a fair chance according to what the average middle American wants, which includes

> liberation from unwelcome cultural, social, political, and economic con- straints, but also [they want to be free] from lack of economic as well as emotional security. . . . Whenever possible, they hope to be free to choose goods, services, and ideas, especially those relevant to the process of self-development, so that they can learn their own needs and wishes and begin to be able to achieve as many as reasonably possible. Nonetheless, for most, popular individualism still involves a prior step, *obtaining personal control over the general environment* so as to minimize threat and unwanted surprise, and in order to lay the groundwork for self- development [italics added]. (p. 2)

This focuses our attention on the link between the desire for control and the desire for a fair chance. It forces us to think about how our sense of control affects the estimation of our chances of taking advantage of our opportunities. If we turn the logic around, it helps us understand that our prospects (or chances) for self-determination are based on our sense of control over the circumstances of life. It also compels us to conclude that as our sense of control increases, our estimation of our chances for suc- cess—our prospects for self-determined pursuits—increases. Finally, it sensitizes us to the converse: As our sense of control decreases, our prospects for self-determination decline, too. Chapter 5 shows how social redress in the last half of the 20th century has evolved toward improving these *chances or prospects* for self-determination for all persons, including those least well situated in society. It traces this development for persons of color and for individuals with disabilities through various capacity building and opportunity restructuring policies designed to improve prospects. The hope of the original effort was to provide these two left out groups with the same chance of experiencing the American ideal of life, liberty, and pursuit of happiness as that afforded other Americans. It was to provide these two groups with that *middle range* of opportunity optimalities that encourages individuals to believe in themselves and in their opportunities sufficiently to engage those opportunities to produce results that change unfavorable circumstances to favorable circumstances for getting what they want.

Chapter 5 argues that this approach to redress was more effective than Rawls's difference principle could have been because it attempted to affect the root cause of declining prospects for self-determination among members of least well situated groups—the lack of a sense of control over life's circumstance. The ideal of equal opportunity that drove the social policies of the 1960s and 1970s was built on findings in *Brown v. Board of Education* and from Coleman's 1966 study on equal educational opportunity that *the lack of control in life* was responsible for underachievement among African American children (see Coleman, 1990, pp. 75-120). The chapter explains that this approach to redress ended up being less successful than expected because it failed to focus on the match between an individual's capacity and opportunity.

The optimal prospects principle fulfills the ideal of equal opportunity by correcting this oversight. It promotes this match between capacity and opportunity by focusing on the *interaction between them.* The principle is sensitive to the empirical fact that when either capacity *or* opportunity to self-determine is diminished or constrained, the probability of self-determination diminishes; when the prospects of engaging in self-determined pursuits decline, fairness in liberty for all is threatened. The optimal prospects principle is based on an understanding of how individuals interact with opportunity to improve their chances of getting what they need and want in life. When opportunities are *just-right challenges*—when they offer the right amount of risk for the gain expected—they will be pursued. *All persons,* regardless of who they are, where they come from, or whether they have a disability or a disadvantaged background, will think and act on just-right opportunities *repeatedly* to learn what they need to learn and to adjust what they need to adjust to reach the ends they most desire. In other words, all persons have the ability to regulate their thoughts, feelings, and actions in pursuit of ends that define themselves as *self-determining persons—that define themselves as being free.*

The concluding chapter identifies the major implications of this revised policy to be (a) suggestions for measuring progress toward fairness in liberty for all and (b) the elimination of the apparent conflict between the desire for fairness and the quest for excellence. The measure of progress toward fairness suggested by equal opportunity theory requires a change in what it means to be a person and what it means to have an opportunity. Whereas in the past, a person's capacity to adjust to life's circumstances was seen as invariant, today it is seen as variable, depending as it does on one's *acquisition or loss of various resources* during different transactions with the environment. Likewise, with the concept of opportunity that was once conceived as independent of the person and determined by the environment. Now, it is conceived as interdependent and variable with the person and the environment, depending as it does on the optimality value Person attaches to it in judging prospects for various self-determined pursuits.

Finally, the apparent incompatibility between equality, liberty, and excellence dissolves (a) when we understand that fairness is a *means* for self-determination and that excellence is an *outcome* of that self-determination and (b) when we understand that the condition needed to achieve fairness in liberty for all is the same condition that promotes excellence. This is because fairness is present when individuals engage opportunities for self-determination, and all people are likely to engage opportunities for self-determination when their opportunities are optimally challenging. In other words, the pursuit of excellence occurs "naturally" when all actors are fully engaged in optimally challenging opportunity for pursuing their own ends in life.

Fair Chances

What most people expect in life is a fair chance to pursue their own plans (see Gans, 1991, pp. 2-5, 36-38). They do not want guarantees for the best in life, nor do they want unfair discrimination to frustrate pursuits that may prove successful. What they want is to be treated fairly and to have the same chance of determining their own directions and pursuing their own interests as others. Unfortunately, this expectation is more reasonably stated than practically fulfilled in most societies of the world. Historically, the opportunity to pursue one's own version of the good life has favored small groups of privileged elites who have benefited from labor of the masses. Today, gradual amelioration of gross differences between the few and the many has raised hopes that fair chances for determining the direction and content of one's life can be guaranteed to all and that universal rights to self-determination can be achieved (Humana, 1992).[1]

These expectations for a fair chance in life are reflected in the United Nations *human development index,* which monitors progress toward improving the longevity and literacy of different peoples of the world. The index identifies disparities in life prospects as measured by opportunities and outcomes people experience in different regions, ethnic groups, and income classes. Its intent is to encourage use of surplus wealth to improve prospects for self-determination among the least advantaged and to improve their lives so they have more options. This means getting resources to the people who most need them by increasing the level of democracy, by equalizing prospects for self-determination among the least advantaged, and by preventing development aid and investment from being concentrated in the hands of the politically powerful (Lewis, 1994, p. A6).

The United States ranks 8th in the world on the human development index and 11th on the *human freedom index,* which compares the freedoms actually enjoyed. On gender equality, for example, the United States ranks first in affirming women's right to stand for election, second in the percentage of women holding economic, political, or legal decision-making positions, second in the percentage of those who are in the armed forces, and fourth in the percentage of those who are lawyers (Wolff, Rutter, & Bayers, 1992). But even in the United States, getting what you want in life varies by gender, ethnicity, and the presence of physical or mental disability. If you are female, from a minority group, and have a disability, your chances of pursuing the life you want is less propitious than if you are a white male without a disability. Women earn 65% of male income; African Americans and Hispanics earn 58% of what whites earn and are three times as likely to live below the poverty level (Wright, 1990, pp. 287-288). Presence of a mental or physical disability lowers employment rates to 33%, with 67% willing but unable to find work. For those with jobs, compensation is only 67% of what nondisabled workers earn (Shapiro, 1993, p. 27-28).

So the disturbing reality is that many U.S. citizens experience personal, social, and economic circumstances that adversely affect their prospects for achieving a personally meaningful and satisfying life. This demands explanation. Why do these people suffer from unfortunate conditions throughout life? One answer claims that unequal prospects are the result of failure to take full advantage of the fair chances available to everyone. This view is shared by many Americans, even in times when everyone experiences hardship. In 1980, for example, when 8 million Americans were out of work, 70% of the public considered economic prospects for the poor to be good or very good, whereas two thirds believed their prospects to be the same as or better than the average American (Schwarz & Volgy, 1992, p. 11). The public also believed lower economic outcomes for the poor resulted because they were not thrifty, they lacked effort, ability, and talent, so they deserved what they got. These attitudes have not changed. In 1989, a Gallup poll found that 64% of the public believed economic conditions of the poor were due to lack of effort (Schwarz & Volgy, 1992). Rothman (1993) calls this the *dominant stratification ideology,* which argues the following:

1. There are abundant economic opportunities.
2. Individuals should be industrious and competitive.
3. Rewards in the form of jobs, education, and income are, and should be, the result of individual talent and effort.
4. Therefore, the distribution of inequality is generally fair and equitable. (p. 57)

Another explanation for persistent misfortune is that the United States does not provide a fair chance for all. The claim of fair chances is simply a myth born of philosophies from people such as Benjamin Franklin who said, "If they are poor, they first begin as Servants or Journeymen; and if they are sober, industrious, and frugal, they soon become Masters, establish themselves in business, marry, raise Families, and become respectable Citizens" (quoted in Rothman, 1993, p. 33).[2] Nineteenth-century author Horatio Alger (1834-1899) popularized the same message in books such as *Ragged Dick, Luck and Pluck,* and *Tattered Tom,* describing how underprivileged youth succeeded through honesty, diligence, and perseverance.

So the claim of equal opportunity goes back centuries, adding credence to the social stratification ideology that if you work hard you will succeed, and if you do not, you deserve to fail. Of course, experiences of the poor, people of color, and individuals with disabilities belie this claim. For them, the rags-to-riches story is just that—a story. The discrimination, denied opportunity, and diminished prospects for participation in community life that they experience is unlike anything most Americans will ever face. Today, at least, we are sensitive to the effects of these debilitating personal, social, and economic circumstances. Perhaps this is because we have 40 years of experience with social policies that contradict assumptions underlying this popular ideology. After all, the emergent equal opportunity principle reflected in these policies is based on an assumption that fairness in the distribution of educational and occupational opportunity is necessary for every American to have a reasonable chance at success and happiness in adult life.

Fairness in Equal Opportunity

Since *Brown v. Board of Education* ruled in 1954 that segregated educational opportunity unfairly diminished prospects for school achievement for African American children and, as a consequence, limited their chances of success as adults, equal opportunity has become the guiding principle for assessing fairness in social policy. A decade after *Brown,* Congress passed the Civil Rights Act requiring the commissioner of education to investigate educational inequality in American schools. In the decades following Coleman's study, which affirmed the extent of disadvantages experienced by African American students, schools across the United States commenced programs of desegregation—voluntarily and in response to court mandates—to correct inequalities caused by the "separate but equal" doctrine. By the 1970s, the equal opportunity principle also covered children and youth with disabilities. Public Law 94-142—the Education for All Handicapped Children Act of 1975—guaranteed all students with disabilities a free and appropriate public education. This created a new legal theory for guiding treatment of those least well situated in society—people with disabilities (Rothstein, 1990).[3]

Today, application of the equal opportunity principle extends to adult opportunity. The Individuals With Disabilities Act of 1990 connects school and work by providing assistance to students in transition to the community, and the Americans With Disabilities Act of 1991 prohibits discrimination and other obstacles in the way of equal opportunity, full participation, independent living, and economic self-sufficiency. This expands self-determination entitlement from birth to adulthood and creates disability policies that are unique in the world and in the history of civilization.

Derivatives of this evolving pattern of social redress to correct inequalities of opportunity have sensitized policymakers to the plight of other less well situated groups as well. Recently, groups such as the "forgotten half" who drop out of school or who leave the system for employment in American business and industry with only a high school diploma have become targets for opportunity rectification. For them, prospects for the good life over the long term have become progressively less auspicious than their counterparts who pursue college degrees and access to high-paying jobs in the professions.[4] Social reform measures are also being considered for welfare mothers, another less well situated group failing to make the transition to social and economic well-being and respect in the community. But here there is less concern with opportunity and more concern about responsibility. This comes from different assumptions about what is just opportunity and outcome under conditions of long-standing dependence on governmental subsistence support. Even though most experts agree welfare dependence will not decrease under existing circumstances, rationales for different policies evoke different theories about what is fair.[5]

What is different about the treatment of these four groups is attribution of responsibility. The assumption driving intervention on behalf of the first three groups is that *through no fault of their own,* they are less well situated personally, socially, and economically; consequently, they are in need of governmental assistance. Individuals with disabilities are unable to correct their disabling condition without help; children of African American descent are not responsible for their disadvantaged background brought on by past generations in slavery; youth who do not go to college but who seek work in business and industry are not responsible for the lack of decent-paying jobs available to them when they leave school. But welfare mothers are presumed to be responsible for their situation and for its solution. Notions about what is fair suggest that they should not remain on welfare forever and that the government should provide disincentives for the status quo as well as incentives for behaviors that will escape poverty and dependence.

So it is of interest here how the plight of these less well situated populations evoke different assumptions about cause, responsibility, and justification for help. Exempting African Americans, people with disabilities, and youth aspiring for non-college-degree careers from responsibility while affixing responsibility to welfare recipients raises questions about the theory or theories of justice that justify these different moral judgments. What are they and how do they discriminate between those who deserve noncontingent social support for self-determined behavior and pursuit and those who deserve contingent incentives and disincentives to rectify their behaviors and pursuits?

Two theories come to mind here—Rawls's theory of justice as *fairness* and Nozick's theory of justice as *entitlement.* Rawls's theory recommends social intervention on behalf of the less well situated because all personal, social, and economic advantages are morally arbitrary. Hence, *all four groups* are eligible for social support because no one is morally responsible for the plight they experience. Nozick's theory recommends social intervention on behalf of the less well situated only through charitable acts of individuals because *none of the four groups* is morally deserving of what they do not possess. Any transfer of goods from the well situated to the less well situated violates principles of justice as entitlement, which claims individuals deserve only what they earn through legitimate acquisition and transfer of holdings.

RAWLS'S THEORY OF JUSTICE

John Rawls (1991) argues that because people do not earn their intelligence any more than they earn their disability, they do not deserve to be unduly rewarded for intelligent activity that brings great wealth, nor do they deserve to be punished for unintelligent activity that guarantees poverty. Instead, they deserve an equal share of the collective surplus resulting from cooperation. Because individuals come together in contractual agreement to guarantee long-term safety and mutual benefit, each has an equal right to that surplus,[6] regardless of conditions of natural physical and mental capacity. Human institutions are fair and just to the extent they distribute cooperative surplus to correct and compensate for nature's random dispensation of advantages and disadvantages in life. Because all individuals benefit more through cooperation than from working alone, they deserve equal shares, unless an alternative distribution is more beneficial for everyone.

Under Rawls's rules for the just social order, no one is left out because of nature's lottery. Persons with abilities and disabilities benefit alike from cooperative gain, as do persons with less ample social and economic resources. Social cooperation in just institutions is similar to a family in which each shares the success of others. In circumstances in which exceptional fortune justifies giving one a greater proportion of the cooperative surplus, everyone still benefits in some proportion. No one is sacrificed for the good of the whole or for the good of some fraction of the whole. Rawls argues that rational persons who are free to construct principles of justice based on this conception of cooperation for mutual advantage would agree on two principles to guide their construction of fair and just social institutions—one principle guaranteeing equality in the assignment of rights and duties in the group and the other tolerating social and economic inequalities to the extent that they benefit all members of the group (Rawls, 1991):

> I shall maintain instead that the persons in the initial situation would choose two rather different principles: the first requires equality in the assignment of basic rights and duties, while the second holds that social and economic inequalities, for example inequalities of wealth and author-

ity, are just only if they result in compensating benefits for everyone, and in particular for the least advantaged members of society. These principles rule out justifying institutions on the grounds that the hardships of some are offset by a greater good in the aggregate. It may be expedient but it is not just that some should have less in order that others may prosper. But there is no injustice in the greater benefits earned by a few provided that the situation of persons not so fortunate is thereby improved. The intuitive idea is that since everyone's well-being depends on a scheme of cooperation without which no one could have a satisfactory life, the division of advantages should be such as to draw forth the willing cooperation of everyone taking part in it, including those less well situated. (p. 15)

His system of mutual benefit through fair distribution of cooperative surplus rectifies persistent inequality in liberty and opportunity, income and wealth, and the bases of self-respect. It prevents unregulated conditions of initially equal natural freedom from evolving toward inequality.[7] It accomplishes this by creating institutions that regulate toward the goals of equal liberty and fair distributions of inequality according to principles that divide the problem of inequality of opportunity and outcome into two parts, one addressing the problem of equalizing freedom and the other addressing the problem of distributing social and economic inequalities (Rawls, 1991):

1. Each person is to have equal right to the most extensive basic liberty compatible with similar liberty for others.
2. Social and economic inequalities are to be arranged so that they are both (a) reasonably expected to be to everyone's advantage, and (b) attached to positions and offices open to all. (p. 60)

The purpose of social redress is to make equal opportunity *fair,* to ensure that those suffering personal, social, and economic disadvantages have the same prospects for pursuing their life plan as others better situated at the starting gate. It is to correct the problem of holding positions open to groups of disadvantaged persons only to have them denied access because they lack skills, attitudes, and experiences necessary to compete successfully for the positions. It makes "open" positions "live" options for persons previously denied access. Fair equal opportunity means *equal prospects.* Rawls (1991) calls this the liberal interpretation of social redress:

The thought here [about the principle of fair equality of opportunity] is that positions are to be not only open in a formal sense, but that all should have a fair chance to attain them. Offhand it is not clear what is meant,

but we might say that those with similar abilities and skills should have
similar life chances. More specifically, assuming that there is a distribution
of natural assets, those who are at the same level of talent and ability, and
have the same willingness to use them should have the same prospects of
success regardless of their initial place in the social system, that is,
irrespective of the income class into which they are born. In all sectors of
society there should be roughly equal prospects of culture and achievement for everyone similarly motivated and endowed. The expectations of
those with the same abilities and aspirations should not be affected by their
social class. (p. 73)

Although fair equal opportunity is a step toward social redress, it is
not sufficient from the moral point of view because it leaves unregulated
sociocultural bias resulting from expressions of natural talent and ability
arbitrarily bestowed by nature. In that no one deserves the abilities or
disabilities given them by nature, they do not deserve the opportunities and
outcomes derived from those arbitrary gifts, either. So Rawls adds the
difference principle to fair equal opportunity that yokes the success of the
most advantaged with the nonsuccess of the least advantaged, arguing the
following:

> Higher expectations of those better situated are just if and only if they
> work as part of a scheme which improves the expectations of the least
> advantaged members of society. The intuitive idea is that the social order
> is not to establish and secure the more attractive prospects of those better
> off unless doing so is to the advantage of those less fortunate. (p. 75)

In combination, fair equality of opportunity and the difference principle operationalize the second principle of justice as fairness, which is to
arrange social and economic inequalities so they are to everyone's advantage and are attached to positions and offices open to all. The difference
principle addresses regulations on behalf of universal advantage and the
fair equal opportunity principle addresses regulations to open positions and
offices to all. Rawls calls this combination "democratic equality."

NOZICK'S ENTITLEMENT THEORY

Rawls's theory makes sense if you accept his conception of social
cooperation as interdependent activity for mutual benefit. It is less appealing, however, if you define mutual advantage as a situation in which
independent actors engage in bilateral exchanges to satisfy different indi-

vidual interests. After all, a good portion of the American experience, present as well as past, is predicated on these less cohesive versions of social cooperation in which independent and collateral social action presume substantial autonomy of individuals acting as their own agents in aggregate rather than cohesive relationship. Under these conditions, fairness in the distribution of benefit depends more on what individuals bring to the relationship than what emergent surplus is produced for common distribution due to coordinated activity. In exchange, there is a presumption from the outset that Person will produce benefit X for Other who will reciprocate by producing benefit Y for Person. The relationship is fair to the extent both gain in proportion to what they give. In other words, they deserve what they receive because they earn what they receive by giving something to get it. Person *earns Y* by giving Other *X,* and Other *earns X* by giving Person *Y.* This is fair and just, and it is the argument put forth in Nozick's entitlement theory.

Fairness as entitlement claims primacy for the individual's right to think and act independently. It is based on a conception of an autonomous being that is (Nozick, 1974)

> able to formulate long-term plans for its life, able to consider and decide on the basis of abstract principles or considerations it formulates to itself and hence not merely the plaything of immediate stimuli, a being that limits its own behavior in accordance with some principles or picture it has of what an appropriate life is for itself and others. (p. 49)

For Nozick, autonomous actors have primacy over groups, institutions, and states. In fact, the only reason for ceding any authority to such entities is to constrain actions of other beings from infringing on that autonomy. Hence, Nozick[8] (1974) argues for the minimum state:

> Our main conclusions about the state are that a minimal state, limited to the narrow functions of protection against force, theft, fraud, enforcement of contracts, and so on, is justified; that any more extensive state will violate persons' rights not to be forced to do certain things, and is unjustified; and that the minimal state is inspiring as well as right. Two noteworthy implications are that the state may not use its coercive apparatus for the purpose of getting some citizens to aid others, or in order to prohibit activities to people for their *own* good or protection. (p. ix)

The notion of autonomous individuals being obliged by membership in a group to share their success with the less fortunate is unjust and unfair, a conclusion that contradicts Rawls's theory of justice. According to entitlement theory, the only basis for helping the less fortunate is through *voluntary* transfer of goods and benefits from those who have more to those who have less. There is no legitimate external entity for accomplishing this transfer either. Unauthorized redistribution of social goods is wrong because it violates what one is entitled to receive from his or her own production or from his or her legitimate exchange with others. Nozick conceives the autonomous actor as the principle unit of action and benefit in a loosely connected social network of exchanges initiated and consummated through voluntary, self-determined associations. Society and its institutions are not exemplars of cohesive, closed systems of social cooperation as conceived by Rawls. Hence, the surplus gain Rawls claims is available for redistribution through cooperative activity is really traceable to individual effort and ownership (Nozick, 1974):

> Is it now impossible to disentangle people's respective contributions? The question here is not whether marginal productivity theory is an appropriate theory of fair or just shares, but whether there is some coherent notion of identifiable marginal product. It seems unlikely that Rawls' theory rests on the strong claim that there is no such reasonably serviceable notion. Anyway, once again we have a situation of a large number of bilateral exchanges: owners of resources reaching separate agreements with entrepreneurs about the use of their resources, entrepreneurs reaching agreements with individual workers, or groups of workers first reaching some joint agreement and then presenting a package to an entrepreneur, and so forth. People transfer their holdings or labor in free markets, with the exchange ratios (prices) determined in the usual manner. If marginal productivity theory is reasonably adequate, people will be receiving, in these voluntary transfers holdings, roughly their marginal products. (p. 187)

Nozick's society is composed of autonomous actors freely interacting with each other to fulfill plans for meeting their needs and interests in accordance with their various capacities and motivations for effective thought and action. Under these conditions of freedom, there can be no central entity collecting and distributing products according to supercooperative rules of justice. There can only be actors determining what they need and want, deciding how to get it, developing plans for acquisition, initiating action, following through, getting results, evaluating consequences, making adjustments, and then trying again. Self-determining individuals, not cooperative groups, are units around which judgments of fairness and justice must be made. Nozick (1974) explains that we are not in the position of children who have been given portions of pie by someone who now makes last minute adjustments to rectify careless cutting. There is no central distribution, no person or group entitled to control all the resources, jointly deciding how they are to be doled out. What each person gets, he gets from others, who give to him in exchange for something, or as a gift. In a free society, diverse persons control different resources, and new holdings arise out of the voluntary exchanges and actions of persons. There is no more a distributing or distribution of shares than there is a distributing of mates in a society in which persons choose whom they shall marry. The total result is the product of many individual decisions which the different individuals involved are entitled to make. (pp. 149-150)

Accordingly, justice as entitlement specifies only three principles: (a) those defining circumstances under which a good or holding can come under the control of a person (to be held), which Nozick calls the *principle of justice in acquisition;* (b) those defining circumstances under which a good or holding can legitimately change hands from one holder to another, which Nozick calls the *principle of justice in transfer;* and (c) those circumstances that justify rectification for injustices occurring in which either of the first two principles is violated, which Nozick calls the *principle of rectification.* Justice occurs when all holdings are held or transferred in accordance to these principles, as summarized in the following (Nozick, 1974):

1. A person who acquires a holding in accordance with the principle of justice in acquisition is entitled to that holding.
2. A person who acquires a holding in accordance with the principle of justice in transfer, from someone else entitled to the holding, is entitled to the holding.
3. No one is entitled to a holding except by (repeated) applications of 1 and 2. (p. 151)

Nozick argues that individuals have Lockean rights to make decisions about what they will do with their own labor and the products of that labor. As a consequence, any infringement or abridgment of labor or, by extension, its resultant property is a violation of the right to self-determination because it abrogates decisions about how one is to use her own resources to satisfy personal needs and interests. To permit such invasions of personal decision making is to give others control over oneself, to become, in a sense, the slave of another (Nozick, 1974):

Seizing the result of someone's labor is equivalent to seizing hours from him and directing him to carry on various activities. If people force you to do certain work, or unrewarded work, for a certain period of time, they decide what you are to do and what purposes your work is to serve apart from your decisions. This process whereby they take this decision from you makes them a *part-owner* of you; it gives them a property right in you. Just as having such partial control and power of decision, by right, over an animal or inanimate object would be to have a property right in it. (p. 172)

The product of your labor is rightly yours because you already *have* it. You may not deserve it in any moral sense, but you are entitled to keep it because no one else is more entitled to what you have created.[9] If you are entitled to the product of your labor, then you are entitled to your personal assets in the same way. All natural assets, labor, and its products connected in this causal chain, therefore, are yours (Nozick, 1974):

A. If people have X, and their having X (whether or not they deserve to have it) does not violate anyone else's (Lockean) right to entitlement to X, and Y flows from (arises out of, and so on) X by a process that does not itself violate anyone's (Lockean) rights or entitlements, then the person is entitled to Y.
B. People's having the natural assets they do does not violate anyone else's (Lockean) entitlements or rights.
   Therefore,
   1. People are entitled to their natural assets.
   2. If people are entitled to something, they are entitled to whatever flows from it (via specified types of processes).
   3. People's holdings flow from their natural assets.
   Consequently,
   4. People are entitled to their holdings.
   5. If people are entitled to something then they ought to have it (and this overrides any presumption of equality there may be about holdings). (pp. 225-226)

Fairness as entitlement, therefore, is freedom to exchange products of one's labor according to the principles of acquisition and transfer. Nozick's summary phrase for this is "from each as they choose, to each as they are chosen," which assumes a social world built on freely constructed transactions between autonomous actors pursuing their own life plans.[10] Fairness here does not mean equality. It does not imply, for example, that final distributions of social exchange be equal or conditionally unequal according to some normative principle. Fair outcome depends on fair process. If acquisitions and transfers of holdings are fair, then outcome distributions are fair too—even though they result in social and economic inequality. In consideration of equal opportunity then, opportunities are holdings that Person acquires by creating or exchanging with another who has the desired opportunity. Person acquires and transfers opportunities as any other resource. The bottom line is that no resource—including an opportunity resource—can be transferred without consent of the holder of that resource. The equal opportunity problem as conceived by Nozick comes down to the following:

> There are two ways to attempt to provide such equality [of opportunity]: by directly worsening the situations of those more favored with opportunity, or by improving the situation of those less well-favored. The latter requires the use of resources, and so it too involves worsening the situation of some: those from whom holdings are taken in order to improve the situation of others. But holdings to which these people are entitled may not be seized, even to provide equality of opportunity for others. In the absence of magic wands, the remaining means toward equality of opportunity is convincing persons each to choose to devote some of their holdings to achieving it. (Nozick, 1974, p. 235)

Freedom and Equality

So the antinomy between freedom and equality remains.[11] The discrepancy between the right and the experience of freedom for all continues unresolved. On the one hand, there is the dominant social stratification ideology that denies a discrepancy problem because failure to express the right to self-determination always follows those who lack talent, effort, and persistence. If you lack these traits, you deserve to fail. On the other hand, there is the equal opportunity principle implied by *Brown,* which challenges this view, as well as the conclusions drawn from theories of justice by Rawls and Nozick. The principle challenges any social policy that ignores circumstances associated with people that limit prospects for self-determination.

The equal opportunity principle bases these challenges on the empirical fact that variation in personal capacity and social opportunity affects success in life. This recognition of interaction effects between capacity and circumstance highlights difficulties in using Rawls's theory of justice as fairness or Nozick's theory of justice as entitlement to resolve the discrepancy between the promise and the reality of fair chances. The difficulty with justice as fairness has to do with Rawls's use of the difference principle to adjust all inequalities for the benefit of the less well situated. Application of that principle actually *decreases* prospects for self-determination because it increases dependence on social and economic benefits that are provided *independently* of individual needs for just right opportunities to fulfill self-determined interests and abilities. This undermines the basis of self-respect, which is an essential good in Rawls's just social order.[12] In other words, Rawls's emphasis on collective security rather than individual self-development threatens the very autonomy and self-respect he claims parties to the original position (in formulating a just society) would want to avoid.

Nozick's theory of entitlement does not create this problem. In fact, its priority is protecting the autonomy of individual thought, action, result, and consequence. Whereas this emphasis on personal autonomy sanctifies self-development and ensures self-respect in a way that Rawls's theory does not, it fails to check unregulated cumulative effects of categorically protected self-determined acts that gain advantage of resource and opportunity for the few to create gross inequalities of social circumstance that the equal opportunity principle attempts to redress. It is here that application of Nozick's entitlement theory creates rather than resolves the discrepancy between the promise and the reality of fair chances. Nozick's theory denies the justice of ameliorating any personal, social, or economic circumstance causing a decline in life prospects for any individual or group.

Although he agrees suffering is unfortunate, he still holds that the misfortune of others does not justify taking resources from those who have acquired them fairly and giving them to the less fortunate who would not be acquiring them fairly. Rawls's rational restructuring toward greater equality is unjust because it takes holdings from those who earned them to give to those who did not. Nozick's theory of entitlement promotes self-determination by guaranteeing connections between personal initiative and rewards, but it denies legitimacy for any external intervention that weakens or strengthens an individual's personal, social, or economic circumstances.

So the dilemma for determining what is fair remains. Both theories of justice argue convincingly from different horns of the dilemma about whether social intervention on behalf of the less well situated is justified. Rawls's justice as fairness recommends social redress for their benefit, and

Nozick's justice as entitlement recommends rectification only through voluntary transfers from persons well situated to persons less well situated. Governmental intervention on behalf of children and youth who are disabled and who are socially and economically disadvantaged is justified by Rawls's justice as fairness but not by Nozick's justice as entitlement. Public charity is the only redress for the least advantaged under justice as entitlement because governmental opportunity and outcome transfers are fundamentally unjust.

Where does this leave compensatory social policy whose legitimacy comes from the equal opportunity principle? Does it leave justification with the theory of justice we apply? Or does it depend on how different conceptions of justice balance the treatment of freedom and equality? For example, when freedom as power is the basis for justice—as in Nozick's entitlement theory—the emphasis is on individual *capacity* to self-determine a course of action to justify success and failure in life. Consequently individuals are entitled to their own pursuits and morally responsible for results they produce through those pursuits. Any external entity intervening in the process is an infringement of this capacity to self-determine. But when equal freedom for all is the basis for justice, as in Rawls's justice as fairness, the emphasis is on rectifying inequalities created by variability in individual capacity and opportunity to self-determine. The focus shifts from the individual pursuit to comparative opportunity and outcome of different pursuits—how they are distributed among a population of actors. This perspective judges fairness as a function of equality of opportunity and outcome rather than of freedom from obstacles to self-determination.

Nozick and Rawls emphasize different components of the freedom condition to create alternative conceptions of justice, one focusing on individual freedom and the other on rights of all to that freedom. The first deals with individual initiative, responsibility, and desert under the notion of freedom as power, and the latter deals with equal opportunity and entitlement under the notion of freedom as right. Neither deals fully with justice as a balance between freedom *and* equality. Weinreb (1987) explains it the following manner:

> In highly developed, modern societies, public policies and practices are critical aspects of self-determination and other determination. It is a mistake, however, to regard the principles of liberty and equality as prior and independent. They acquire their normative content by reference to the content of justice, without which they merely describe what is the case. The relationship is reciprocal; they in turn give content to the idea of

> justice. Within a human community, in which the reach of positive law is
> unlimited, justice is realized as liberty and equality. Very likely because
> of our practical concerns, it is easier to work from liberty and equality to
> justice, rather than the reverse. But justice comprises the others; it is the
> larger idea, and the more fundamental. (pp. 248-249)

The Nozick and Rawls theories offer partial solutions to the problem
of freedom and equality. Nozick's solution emphasizes the *individual* and his
or her capacity, responsibility, and desert in the process of self-determination,
whereas Rawls's solution emphasizes the collective responsibility of
the *cooperative group* for ensuring all persons an equal right to self-
determination. But neither is a complete formulation. Again, Weinreb
(1987) explains it:

> The theories of Rawls and Nozick are as convincing as they are because
> each of them elaborates one aspect of the complete idea of justice and
> excludes the other. Since the constraint that is finally introduced in the
> other direction is so much more limited than what our actual practices
> suggest, it may appear to be obviously consistent with justice and not to
> require argument. Nevertheless, the failure of each theory as a general
> theory of justice becomes evident when they are placed side by side. Both
> play the same game; and one does not succeed more than the other. The
> constraints introduced to resolve the antinomy of justice have themselves
> no general theoretical basis. In the end, the specific boundaries drawn by
> Rawls and Nozick between what constitutes a person and what is merely
> circumstantial are not abstractly more just than any other; all that can be
> said for them is that they serve plausible and, from opposite points of view,
> minimal utilitarian goals. (p. 240)

The failure of the two theories to meet the standard for general theory
of justice is due to their singular focus on one component of the justice
problem—individual responsibility for freedom to the exclusion of collective responsibility for equality for Nozick's theory of entitlement and
collective responsibility for equality to the exclusion of individual responsibility for freedom for Rawls's justice as fairness (Weinreb, 1987):

> Rawls' argument leads to the complete displacement of desert by entitle-
> ments according to his principles, all that a person is and has being at the
> disposal of the community for the equal benefit of all. The full implication
> of Nozick's argument leads to the unlimited extension of desert, "mine"
> meaning simply anything I can get and keep [freedom as power]. In both
> cases, the implication has to be avoided, because neither entitlement

without desert nor desert without entitlement satisfies the idea of justice. (pp. 239-240)

For Rawls, the concept of person is diminished in significance and the concept of the group enhanced to maximize entitlement, and for Nozick the concept of person is fully inclusive of events and resources causally linked to personal decision and action and the concept of person is fully maximized through freedom as power (capacity). But between these half conceptions of the just social order lies the principle function of justice, which is to adjudicate balance between one person's freedom as power and another person's freedom as right. For justice is nugatory when freedom as power for some expands to oppress freedom as right for others or when demand for equal freedom for all expands to diminish individual capacity for freedom of some. Response to this pragmatic need for a conceptual distinction between freedom as power and freedom as right is how a just and moral order is formed.

Freedom and the social circumstances that expand and constrain its expression reflect actions of individuals and groups whose experiences operationalize the meaning of freedom and equality. On the one hand, individuals experience capacity and opportunity to choose and enact choice in pursuit of personal needs and interests, and on the other hand, groups of actors experience protection from denial or infringement of their capacity and opportunity for experiencing comparable levels of self-determination. So for any social condition there are *freedom conditions* unique to individual needs and interests in self-determined pursuits and *opportunity conditions* defined by the intersection of one person's rights to express self-determination and other persons' obligations to respect and provide opportunities for those expressions. In other words, *freedom as power* and *opportunity rights* entitling the expression of that power are locked in *interdependent relations* that demand boundaries that both separate and join Person and Other.

Reduced to these elemental states, the problem becomes one of interaction between capacity and opportunity for self-determination, as Table 2.1 illustrates. Column 1 presents the essential components of freedom as self-determination with "Autonomy of X" in row 1 representing the autonomous thinker and actor, "Freedom from Y" in row 2 representing potential obstacles to X's pursuit of self-determined ends, "Freedom for Z" in row 3 representing opportunities available to X to pursue self-determined ends, and "Results A-W" in the last row representing the results of X's self-

Table 2.1　Interaction Between Capacity and Opportunity to Self-Determine

Column 1 *Self-Determination*	*Column 2* *Initial State Capacity* *to Self-Determine*	*Column 3* *Opportunity* *to Self-Determine*	*Column 4* *End State Capacity* *to Self-Determine*
Row 1: Autonomy of X	Initial state of mental and physical abilities to choose and enact choice to satisfy needs and interests in life	Awareness of an unmet goal and presence of a plan for producing gain to meet that goal	End state of mental and physical abilities to choose and enact choice to satisfy needs and interests in life
Row 2: Freedom from Y	Initial state of obstacles of social status and cultural competence that prevent choices and actions to satisfy needs and interests in life	Presence of social status and cultural competence circumstances that prevent specific choices and actions from producing expected gain toward an unmet goal in life	End state of obstacles of social status and cultural competence that prevent choices and actions to satisfy needs and interests in life
Row 3: Freedom for Z	Initial state of opportunities of social status and cultural competence that allow choices and actions to satisfy own needs and interests in life	Presence of social status and cultural competence opportunities that allow specific choices and actions to produce expected gain toward an unmet goal in life	End state of opportunities of social status and cultural competence that allow choices and actions to satisfy own life
Row 4: Results A-W	Initial state of experience in producing gain toward satisfying needs and interests in life	Results of specific choices and actions to produce an expected gain toward an unmet goal in life	End state of experience in producing gain toward satisfying needs and interests in life

determined pursuits. This is a compete description of the freedom condition, including as it does all the essentials of the freedom condition as set down by MacCallum.[13]

Laying out the freedom condition in this manner identifies the three-part causal sequence that determines successful and unsuccessful expressions of self-determined action, which includes (a) the *capacity* of person for autonomous thought and action (autonomy of X), (b) the *social circumstances* describing constraints (freedom from Y) and opportunities (freedom for Z) for expressions of autonomous thought and action toward self-determined ends, and (c) *results and consequences* of self-determined thought and action.[14] From here, it is evident that variation in any factor will affect subsequent conditions of freedom by expanding, contracting, or maintaining levels of expression and outcome. On one hand, increased capacity will affect social circumstances by enabling Person to overcome obstacles and seize opportunities that produce good results, and on the other hand, improved social circumstances for Person will affect his chances of producing beneficial results that in turn will enhance his autonomy for subsequent self-determined thoughts and actions.

Columns 2 through 4 in Table 2.1 describe changes in the freedom condition from an initial state of capacity to self-determine in column 2 to a final state of capacity to self-determine in column 4, with an intervening opportunity to self-determine represented in column 3. Row 1 traces Person's capacity for autonomous thought and action through those three phases. Rows 2 and 3 represent initial, intermediate, and final phases of the social circumstances constraining and facilitating autonomous thought and action, and row 4 shows the disposition of outcomes before, during, and after self-determined choices and actions.

Table 2.1 shows how the freedom condition changes from initial to final states. It shows how variation in optimalities of prospects are a function of (a) Person's autonomy, which may be enhanced, maintained, or lessened; (b) obstacles in the way of self-determined plans, which may be enhanced, maintained, or lessened; (c) opportunities to pursue plans, which may be enhanced, maintained, or constrained; and (d) results of enacted plans, which may be more, same, or less that expected. In other words, each self-determination episode is a function of an initial state of autonomy, social circumstance, and benefits that constitute conditions that affect Person's decision to choose and to act to satisfy subsequent unmet needs.

Equal Opportunity Theory

The equal opportunity principle is consistent with this conception of freedom and opportunity as *interacting* components of a changing condition of optimality prospects for self-determination. The *Brown* decision also recognized this interaction effect between capacity and opportunity. In that ruling, the Court found that the social circumstances of segregation affected African American students' capacity to develop their abilities to participate freely in the modern world:

> "Segregation of white and colored children in public schools has a detrimental effect on the colored children. The impact is greater when it has the sanction of law; for the policy of separating the races is usually interpreted as denoting the inferiority of the Negro group. A sense of inferiority affects the motivation of a child to learn. Segregation with the sanction of law, therefore, has a tendency to retard the educational and mental development of Negro children and to deprive them of some of the benefits they would receive in a racially integrated school system." (quoted in Adler, 1987, pp. 257-258)

The Court also indicated this deficit would have the effect of diminishing their prospects for success later in life because success in school was necessary for self-determined pursuits in adulthood:

> "Today, education is perhaps the most important function of state and local governments. Compulsory school attendance laws and the great expenditures for education both demonstrate our recognition of the importance of education to our democratic society. It is required in the performance of our most basic public responsibilities, even service in the armed forces. It is the very foundation of good citizenship. Today it is the principal instrument in awakening the child to cultural values, in preparing him for later professional training, and in helping him to adjust normally to his environment. In these days, it is doubtful that any child may reasonably expect to succeed in life if he is denied the opportunity of an education. Such an opportunity, where the state has undertaken to provide it, is a right which must be made available to all on equal terms." (quoted in Adler, 1987, pp. 257-258)

The theory behind this ruling can be stated as follows:

1. Everyone has a right to self-determination in adulthood.
2. Educational opportunity is a necessary condition for self-determination in adulthood.
3. Therefore, everyone has a right to an equal educational opportunity.

And application of this theory to the problem of school segregation might go as follows:

1. Segregated education is not equal educational opportunity because it causes segregated children to feel inferior, and this decreases their motivation and capacity to learn and to benefit from their education.
2. Children who lack motivation and capacity to learn and benefit from their education have diminished prospects for self-determination in adulthood.
3. Diminished prospects for self-determination in adulthood for some individuals is a denial of their right to self-determination.
4. Therefore, segregated education is unjust because it denies the right to self-determination in adulthood for those whose educational experiences are segregated.

Subsequent social policies to redress this injustice focused on building student *capacities* to benefit from instruction through compensatory education programs (Elementary and Secondary Education Act of 1965) and by reconstituting *social circumstances* of schooling via court mandated school desegregation programs. This is the significance of the equal opportunity principle. It offers guidance in redressing disadvantage resulting from personal capacity and social circumstance. The theory of person underlying this conception postulates variability in capacity for autonomous thought and action affecting and being affected by variability in social circumstance. The result of this interaction can be constrained opportunity that diminishes the self or expanded opportunity that empowers the self.

This is what Table 2.1 illustrates when freedom as power and freedom as right are understood as interdependent, and this is where the two theories of justice are insensitive. Rawls's conception of the person overlooks the importance of capacity building for greater expressions of self-determination, whereas Nozick's conception of person overlooks the importance of balancing expressions of self-determination with obligations and moral responsibilities for respecting the rights of others to have comparable opportunities for self-determination.

Equal opportunity theory generalizes the reasoning behind the equal educational opportunity principle. It also reflects important features of Rawls's theory of justice as fairness and Nozick's theory of justice as entitlement. On justice as entitlement, equal opportunity assumes individuals to be morally responsible for their actions and morally deserving of the results produced by those actions. On justice as fairness, it claims that unregulated accumulation of the social consequences due to the differential success of individual effort inevitably yields disadvantages for less well situated individuals and groups and that this is morally arbitrary. Equal opportunity theory accommodates these strong features of the theories by acknowledging the source of inequality—*variation in capacity* to self-determine that functions according to individual needs, interests, and abilities and *variation in optimalities of opportunity* to self-determine that functions according to accumulated social consequences from differential results of individually-determined acts.

The theory rests on the assumption that the penultimate value for regulating human conduct in social affairs is the *right* to self-determination. From this presumptive assertion, it argues that different individuals in the exercise of this basic right produce for themselves and for others inequality of prospects for self-determination by advancing their ends more quickly or more slowly and more effectively or less effectively than others. The resulting differential progress affects expectations for what can be accomplished on subsequent self-determination episodes, the options available on those occasions, and the time and behavior necessary to commit to those endeavors. As this differentiating of prospects unfolds, inequalities develop between individuals and groups. For Person who has a shorter distance to travel, less time and energy are necessary to reach goals, which leaves surplus resources for other pursuits. This gives Person more favorable subsequent opportunity and increases optimalities once again for those future prospects. For Other who has a greater distance to travel, more time and energy are necessary and less surplus is available for new opportunity and additional pursuit. Success in the original endeavor may be all that is possible. As Person and Other work through their respective pursuits, they experience markedly different trajectories in the optimality of their prospects. Person cumulates advantage and favorable opportunity, whereas Other loses advantage and favorable opportunity. These experiences calibrate in real differences in prospects for self-determination.

This is the problem that comes with claiming self-determination as a basic right. It inevitably incurs a moral obligation for equal protection. Given the empirical fact of some individuals and groups always suffering unequal prospects for self-determination, there will be a need for redress under this obligation. It follows that social intervention to equalize prospects among individuals is morally justified to restore rights to self-determination placed in jeopardy by the declining optimalities of opportunity experienced by some individuals. In other words, the implication of the right to self-determination is that each of us is entitled to experience *favorable* personal and environmental conditions for choosing and enacting choice in pursuit of our self-determined needs and interests. To experience unfavorable conditions compared to what is possible from less constraining governmental action or compared to conditions others experience in their pursuits is an abridgment of this right.

For Person who experiences optimal matches between environmental and personal conditions, autonomous thought and action are likely and successful outcomes from those thoughts and actions are probable. But for Other who does not experience optimal matches, autonomous thought and action are less likely and successful results impossible. When experiences such as these are repeated, substantial differences in prospects for self-determination develop because Person's success adds to his capacity to self-determine, increases his sense of self-mastery, and improves his optimalities of subsequent opportunity. At the same time, Other's repeated failure enervates her capacity to self-determine, diminishes her sense of self-mastery, and decreases her subsequent optimalities of opportunity. At some distant end state, prospects for self-determination become so disproportionate that Other's right to self-determination is effectively abridged. Not only does she feel helpless about her capacity to manage her personal resources, but she also sees more obstacles than opportunity for future prospects for getting what she needs and wants in life.

This is the dialectic of freedom as power and freedom as right. Initial prospects for self-determination, however distributed in a population of actors to define an originally fair condition, eventually evolve toward unequal prospects, thereby threatening the right to self-determine for some. Equal opportunity theory accounts for this dialectic by postulating the two conditions responsible for evolution toward inequality—lack of capacity and lack of opportunity. On the one hand, individuals vary in their *capacities* to choose and act on their own needs and interests effectively and efficiently, and on the other hand, they vary in *opportunities* they have to accommodate those needs, interests, and abilities. It is the interaction between capacity and opportunity—between conditions of autonomy and liberty—that affects their prospects for self-determination.

So self-determination as conceived here is liberty for autonomous thought and action, and guaranteeing it to all persons leads to its own abrogation. Ensuring the right to self-determination at any point in time sets in motion social processes that differentiate prospects for self-determination among different actors pursuing different aims in their lives. For actors who are fortunate to find optimal matches between autonomy and liberty, self-determination increases in strength and outcome, and for those who must engage their pursuits during suboptimal matches, it wanes toward extinction.

At best, therefore, the right to self-determination is a transient assurance in the absence of intermittent regulation to prevent its erosion for some and enhancement for others.

Equal opportunity theory postulates two regulatory interventions to equalize prospects and thereby to restore to baseline, at least temporarily, the rights of those suffering from declines in self-determination. These interventions correspond to the two conditions responsible for creating unequal prospects in the first place—differential development in autonomy and liberty over time. The first intervention builds individual capacity to self-determine by increasing autonomy, which is the ability to make choices and take actions consistent with one's needs, interests, and abilities. The second reconstitutes social opportunity by decreasing obstacles (negative freedom) and increasing options (positive freedom) to produce more favorable matches between autonomous action and social circumstance. In combination, the interventions increase the chances of those with fewer prospects to engage in opportunities for self-determination. The propositions of the theory summarize this argument for rectifying inequalities of capacity and opportunity.

EQUAL OPPORTUNITY THEORY

1. All individuals have the right to self-determination.
2. All societies have some individuals who lack the capacity to self-determine.
3. All societies generate unequal opportunities to self-determine.
4. Consequently, some individuals do not exercise the right to self-determine because they lack capacity and opportunity to do so.
5. Therefore, all societies should optimize prospects for self-determination among these least advantaged members by increasing their capacity and improving their opportunity for self-determination.

Equal opportunity theory implies two ends. One is to promote *equal distributions* of self-determination prospects among all members of society and the other is to *optimize prospects* for self-determination for all members of society, including those who are least advantaged. Toward the first end, the theory makes a claim for fairness by arguing from the assumption that all persons have a right to self-determination to draw the conclusion that prospects for self-determination should be equally distributed among all individuals and groups in society. In this sense, equal prospects mean equal probabilities for autonomous thought and action in response to opportunities to satisfy personal needs and interests. Toward the second end, the theory claims that the right to self-determination also includes the right to *optimal* chances to pursue one's own goals. Person is entitled to be, on average, as autonomously engaged and personally fulfilled as Other. Although Person and Other may have substantially different types of engagement and success, they deserve optimal *prospects* for thinking, acting, and succeeding autonomously. According to equal opportunity theory, then, the right to self-determination for all individuals and groups translates into *equally optimal prospects* for autonomous engagement and success. It means that one individual or group should not have substantially greater or lesser chances of being engaged and experiencing fulfillment through autonomous thought and action than another. All deserve the same chance, on average, of experiencing self-determination and the success or failure it produces.

To redress problems of unequal prospects naturally resulting from unregulated individually pursued ends, equal opportunity theory recommends optimizing prospects by finding just-right matches between social circumstances and individual capacity so that individuals are optimally challenged in their own way. This approach to social redress is consistent with Jefferson's conception of the pursuit of happiness as a basic human right in that in his conception of happiness individuals have the right of pursuit in the moral sense rather than in the psychological sense. They have the right to be fully engaged in self-defining and self-developing projects that produce personal fulfillment and satisfaction over the long term. This was his intent in the Declaration of Independence, which includes the *pursuit* rather than the *experience* of happiness. The purpose of government was to ensure the former, which is consistent with equalizing prospects through optimally challenging opportunity, as contrasted with ensuring everyone happiness from every pursuit (Adler, 1987, p. 54). Equalizing rewards for different pursuits is not relevant to social redress because rewards are different for different pursuits. All that can be equalized is prospects for engagement and success, which means Person will, on average, have the same chances of pursuing and succeeding in his plans as Other will have in pursuing and succeeding in hers. Over the long term, both have the same chances of pursuing and experiencing happiness because both pursue and experience happiness as a function of personally defined means and ends.

A Fair Chance

Now we can consider how equal opportunity theory and theories of justice relate to expectations for a fair chance. There are two meanings of a fair chance: the first and perhaps most fundamental being the chance of getting what we want in life. Given our individual capacities, interests, and needs, what are our chances of fulfillment? If they are good, we are satisfied with our attempts at securing the good in life. If they are not, we may think we are being treated unfairly in a cosmic sense, claiming some divine force gave us less than we deserve. We may give up the struggle because it is not worth the risk, the effort, and the frustration likely to result from probable failure; or we may resign ourselves to the luck of the draw and learn to live with our less than optimal circumstances by trying harder, becoming more clever in the use of our resources, or becoming more innovative in how we adapt to suboptimal circumstance. The fair chance in this sense has to do with *specific circumstances* affecting our individual prospects for attaining what we decide is good for our life.

A second meaning of the fair chance, and one not completely independent of the first, is how our chance for success compares with others. When other people have a substantially better chance of getting what they want in life, we consider our chance as being unfair in this comparative sense. Even though both probabilities are exceedingly good (or poor), the fact of unequal prospects makes the comparison condition unfair as well. If my chance of getting an A in a class is 85% but everyone else has a 95% chance for the same grade, I judge my prospects to be unfair. Even though the absolute chance for succeeding (the first meaning) is little affected by the 10% difference, I still regard the condition unfair.

These meanings of fair chance are also implied in Nozick's theory of justice as entitlement and Rawls's theory of justice as fairness. Nozick's entitlement theory, for example, does not consider interpersonal comparisons to be legitimate in judging fairness. That one person has a better chance of succeeding than another does not trouble Nozick's moral perspective because *all success* is a function of individual talent and effort. Hence, judgments about fair chances occur only to the extent that Person is *free of physical and social obstacles* that prevent him from fully using his capacity to secure the good in his life (first meaning of fairness). When there is a minimum of interference, Person's prospects are fair. They become unjust in a moral sense when others get in the way by violating rules of acquisition and transfer of goods, for example.

Rawls's theory assumes the other meaning of fair chances. Interpersonal comparisons on all dimensions defining the freedom condition—individual capacity, social and political opportunities and constraints, and social and economic outcomes of individual and group action—are legitimate grounds for judging fairness. Consequently, discrepancies between individuals and groups on any factor can justify social redress. If individual capacity, background, and social position are deficient in a comparative sense, then transfer of resources is justified to equalize conditions (Rawls, 1991):

> Thus the [difference] principle holds that in order to treat all persons equally, to provide genuine equality of opportunity, society must give more attention to those with fewer native assets and to those born into the less favorable social positions. The idea is to redress the bias of contingencies in the direction of equality. In pursuit of this principle greater resources might be spent on the education of the less rather than the more intelligent, at least over a certain time of life, say the earlier years of school. (pp. 100-101)

Equal opportunity theory is sensitive to both meanings of fairness, emphasizing as it does (a) the *individualization* of fair prospects in the achievement of personal ends (first meaning of fair chances) and (b) the *equal distribution* of prospects for individually defined pursuits across all actors (second meaning of fair chances). Equal opportunity theory has elements of Nozick's justice as entitlement by claiming individuals are entitled to their successes and responsible for their failures; and it has elements of Rawls's theory of a well-ordered society being responsible by ensuring all individuals an equal chance for fulfilling their needs in accordance with their abilities. It accomplishes this by claiming that everyone deserves a fair chance at finding a match between what they are able to do, what they want to do, and what the social environment allows and values that they do.

Table 2.2 compares these three conceptions of fairness according to their recommended interventions during different phases of a self-determination episode (column 1), during an initial condition of self-determination before Person has specific needs for autonomous thought and action (column 2), during a condition when Person has identified an unmet need to satisfy through autonomous thought and action (column 3), and then after Person has made a decision, taken action, and obtained results (column 4). Column 5 shows the locus of intervention (by row) suggested by the three conceptions of fairness—Nozick's entitlement, equal opportunity theory's equal prospects, and Rawls's justice as fairness. Nozick's area for legitimate intervention is the elimination of obstacles—"freedom from *Y*" in row 2—which constitutes his conception of the minimal state.

Rawls's area for legitimate intervention includes all areas—Person's autonomy (row 1), freedom from Y (row 2), freedom for Z (row 3), and results of self-determined action (row 4). Equal opportunity theory's area for legitimate intervention is intermediate between Nozick and Rawls. It includes Person's autonomy (row 1), freedom from Y (row 2), and freedom for Z (row 3).

The equal opportunity approach appears better than those recommended by Nozick and Rawls because it focuses on the causes of unequal prospects for self-determination—suboptimal matches between capacity for autonomous thoughts and actions and the social conditions of constraint and opportunity associated with those thoughts and actions. Simply protecting Person from obstacles to autonomous action does not address this matching of capacity and opportunity (Nozick's area of legitimate intervention), nor does equalizing results of Others' actions in social redress procedures (the difference principle) to reduce gross social and economic inequalities among different groups (Rawls's areas of legitimate intervention). The only areas of intervention that can promote more frequent self-determined thought and action are those that optimize matches between capacity and opportunity. This is the implication of equal opportunity theory's Proposition 5 that "All societies should optimize prospects for self-determination among these least advantaged members by increasing their capacity and improving their opportunity to self-determine." When social policies of redress build capacity and reconstitute opportunity toward more favorable matches, Person is more likely to think and act autonomously to attain what she needs and wants. She is more likely to solve problems to overcome obstacles in the way of her goals, and she is more likely to seek out and expand existing opportunity to advance toward her goals. In other words, she is more likely to self-determine. To the extent all persons are more likely to self-determine, including those from less well situated groups, prospects for self-determination move toward equality, which is the ideal specified in the theory that "All persons have the right to self-determination."

Indeed, this has been the direction of compensatory policies emanating from the equal opportunity principle over the past four decades. Court decisions and legislative mandates in the 1960s and 1970s focused on building student capacity for learning through Head Start for disadvantaged youth and through individualized educational planning and instruction for students with disabilities. At the same time, they attempted to restructure social opportunity by requiring capacity building to take place in desegregated

Table 2.2 Comparison of Theories on the Legitimate Interventions for Enhancing Prospects for Self-Determination

Column 1 Components of Self-Determination	Column 2 Initial State Capacity to Self-Determine	Column 3 Opportunity to Self-Determine	Column 4 End State Capacity to Self-Determine	Column 5 Areas of Legitimate Intervention
Row 1: Autonomy of X	Initial state of mental and physical abilities to choose and enact choice to satisfy needs and interests in life	Awareness of an unmet goal and presence of a plan for producing gain to meet that goal	End state of mental and physical abilities to choose and enact choice to satisfy needs and interests in life	Legitimate intervention on rows 1-3 according to the equal opportunity theory of equal prospects / Legitimate intervention on rows 1-4 according to Rawls's justice as fairness
Row 2: Freedom from Y	Initial state of obstacles of social status and cultural competence that prevent choices and actions to satisfy needs and interests in life	Presence of social status and cultural competence circumstances that prevent specific choices and actions from producing expected gain toward an unmet goal in life	End state of obstacles of social status and cultural competence that prevent choices and actions to satisfy needs and interests in life	Legitimate intervention on row 2 according to Nozick's justice as entitlement
Row 3: Freedom for Z	Initial state of opportunities of social status and cultural competence that allow choices and actions to satisfy own needs and interests in life	Presence of social status and cultural competence opportunities that allow specific choices and actions to produce expected gain toward an unmet goal in life	End state of opportunities of social status and cultural competence that allow choices and actions to satisfy own needs and interests in life	
Row 4: Results A-W	Initial state of experience in producing gain toward satisfying needs and interests in life	Results of specific choices and actions to produce an expected gain toward an unmet goal in life	End state of experience in producing gain toward satisfying needs and interests in life	

schools for African American students and in least restrictive environments (mainstreaming) for students with disabilities.

But the importance of matching capacity and opportunity did not show up in federal policy until school-to-work programs of the 1990s sought to increase correspondence between learning in school and work opportunity in the community so students could adjust more successfully to adult life. For the first time, the connection between learning what to do and demonstrating how to apply it for personal gain reflected this dynamic between capacity building and opportunity restructuring for students failing to enter adulthood with a fair chance at determining their own future on a footing equal to their peers. This capacity-opportunity nexus reflects what is necessary for the right of self-determination to be experienced by all persons, including those least well situated in society.

Equal opportunity theory and Rawls's theory of justice agree that the four groups identified earlier—African Americans, people with disabilities, non-college-bound students, and poor people—deserve social redress in some form, which contrasts implications of Nozick's theory denying mandatory redress of any kind for any group. Nevertheless, the approaches implied by the two theories are different. Equal opportunity theory recommends improvements in capacity and opportunity according to individual needs, interests, and abilities, which means treating members of less well situated groups as individuals whose capacities and opportunities must match if they are to engage in self-determined thought and action. This contrasts Rawls's conception of individuals sharing economic needs to be remedied through income transfers irrespective of their level of capacity and opportunity to self-determine. According to the theory of self underlying equal opportunity theory, this approach would depress rather than enhance prospects for self-determination, and as a consequence, jeopardize the basis for self-respect, a point we will return to in the next chapter. Only through interventions that optimize the match between Person and his or her circumstance will prospects for self-determination improve.

Notes

1. Part I, Article 1, and item 1 of the *International Covenant on Civil and Political Rights,* approved by the General Assembly of the United Nations in 1966, specified that " 'All peoples have the right to self-determination. By virtue of that right they freely determine their political status and freely pursue their economic, social and cultural development' " (quoted in Humana, 1992, p. 385).

2. Rothman (1993) is quoting from Robert N. Bellah et al. (1985). *Habits of the Heart: Individualism and Commitment in American Life* (p. 33). New York: Harper & Row.

3. " 'The application of the principles set forth in the *Brown* decision to the education of handicapped children became a legal theory in more than 30 separately filed case throughout the United States. Two of these cases culminated in landmark decisions in 1971 and 1972. In *Pennsylvania Association for Retarded Children* (PARC) *v. Pennsylvania* and *Mills v. Board of Education,* district courts approved consent decrees that enjoined states from denying education to mentally retarded and handicapped children without due process. The *Mills* consent decree went so far as to set out an elaborate framework for what that due process would entail. Both of these cases were based on constitutional theories of equal protection and due process under the fourteenth amendment and were the impetus for similar cases in a large number of other states' " (quoted in Rothstein, 1990, p. 2).

4. See, for example, the William T. Grant Foundation Commission on Work, Family and Citizenship (1988), *The Forgotten Half: Non-College Youth in America, An Interim Report on the School-to-Work Transition.* The decidedly unequal educational opportunities for the two groups became evident in comparisons of federal aid to students and schools for college graduates that averaged $15,200 per year and only $1,460 for young people who do not go to college.

Congressional initiatives to reduce this inequity are likely to be in the form of a school-to-work transition support through apprenticeships, community-based training, and employer incentives to assist noncollege youth establish careers for themselves in occupational areas that fit their needs, interests, and abilities.

5. The current plan to limit AFDC benefits to 2 years over a person's lifetime coupled with provisions for job training, child care, and strengthened child support enforcement assumes welfare mothers will respond to "tougher" contingencies defining eligibility. It is this new view that places welfare mothers in a different category from those whose entitlements emanate from their minority membership, disabling condition, or noncollege career aspirations. Some argue that the behavior of people who are poor is largely a cause of their poverty and that society's responsibility in the matter is its failure to enforce and encourage social obligations such as marriage and work, whereas others contradict such a view by claiming that centuries of poor relief have been based on the similar assumption that the behavior of the poor is to blame for their poverty. The Piven and Mead references are from Coughlin (1994, pp. A6-A7).

6. Rawls (1991) says,

> Let us assume, to fix ideas, that a society is more or less a self-sufficient association of person who in their relations to one another recognize certain rules of conduct as binding and who for the most part act in accordance with them. Suppose further that these rules specify a system of cooperation designed to advance the good of those taking part in it. Then, although a society is a cooperative venture for mutual advantage, it is typically marked by a conflict as well as by an identity of interests. There is an identity of interests since social cooperation makes possible a better life for all than any would have if each were to live solely by his own efforts. (p. 4)

Excerpts are reprinted by permission of the publisher from *A Theory of Justice* by John Rawls, Cambridge, Mass: The Belknap Press of Harvard University Press, Copyright © 1971 by the President and Fellows of Harvard College.

7. "But because there is no effort to preserve an equality, or similarity, of social conditions, except insofar as this is necessary to preserve the requisite background institutions, the initial distribution of assets for any period of time is strongly influenced by natural and social contingencies. The existing distributions of income and wealth, say, is the cumulative

effect of prior distributions of natural assets—that is, natural talents and abilities—as these have been developed or left unrealized, and their use favored or disfavored over time by social circumstances and chance contingencies such as accident and good fortune. Intuitively, the most obvious injustice of the system of natural liberty is that it permits distributive shares to be improperly influenced by these factors so arbitrary from a moral point of view" (Rawls, 1991, p. 72).

8. Reprinted by permission of BasicBooks, a division of HarperCollins Publishers, Inc.

9. Nozick (1974) distinguishes between entitlement and desert (p. 225).

10. The longer version is as follows: "From each according to what he chooses to do, to each according to what he makes for himself (perhaps with the contracted aid of others) and what others choose to do for him and choose to give him of what they've been give previously (under this maxim) and haven't yet expended or transferred" (Nozick, 1974, p. 160).

11. Weinreb (1987) provides a full account of the nature of this contradiction.

12. Rawls (1991) says,

> On several occasions I have mentioned that perhaps the most important primary good is that of self-respect. We must make sure that the conception of goodness as rationality explains why this should be so. We may define self-respect (or self-esteem) as having two aspects. First of all . . . it includes a person's sense of his own value, his secure conviction that his conception of his good, his plan of life, is worth carrying out. And second, self-respect implies a confidence in one's ability, so far as it is within one's power, to fulfill one's intentions. When we feel that our plans are of little value, we cannot pursue them with pleasure or take delight in their execution. Nor plagued by failure and self-doubt can we continue in our endeavors. It is clear then why self-respect is a primary good. Without it nothing may seem worth doing, or if some things have value for us, we lack the will to strive for them. All desire and activity becomes empty and vain, and we sink into apathy and cynicism. Therefore the parties in the original position would wish to avoid at almost any cost the social conditions that undermine self-respect. The fact that justice as fairness gives more support to self-esteem than other principles is a strong reason for them to adopt it. (p. 440)

13. See Gray (1991) for a discussion of different conceptions of freedom and how they manifest variations of MacCallum's (1967) formula.

14. Sen (1992) makes a similar distinction between freedom and the consequences of freedom that he calls achievement (see pp. 31-38).

Justice as Fairness

Judgments about fairness in social life depend on how membership in the group affects life prospects for its members, as well as how the work of its members is rewarded. When Person believes she has a fair chance of getting what she needs and wants in life by being a member of the group, she believes membership in the group to be worthwhile, and when Person is satisfied with the rewards she earns for her contribution to the cooperative endeavor, Person believes she is being treated fairly (see Beauchamp, 1980, for a discussion). Both judgments of fairness result from calculations about the advantage gained from different social relationships. They result from judgments about whether one would be better off in an absolute sense by joining another group or in a relative sense by getting a better return for contribution to the cooperative enterprise than what others get for their contribution. How Person answers these questions will affect her conclusion about justice through fairness.

The first question connects with the larger issue of how the group routinely distributes benefits and burdens of cooperation. Given that all such endeavors incur costs and gains that attach to group functions alone, there arises a need for rules for distributing those burdens and benefits fairly. According to John Rawls, there is a need to construct a just cooperative enterprise so rules governing allocation of rewards for individual contributions will occur within a socially just institutional background for all members of the group, as Allen Buchanan (1980) explains in the following:

> By the basic structure of a society Rawls means the entire set of major social, political, legal and economic institutions. As examples of some of the major institutions of our society, Rawls lists the Constitution, private ownership of the means of production, competitive markets, and the monogamous family. The function of the basic structure of society is to distribute the burdens and benefits of social cooperation among the members of society. The benefits of social cooperation include wealth and income, food and shelter, authority and power, rights and liberties. The burdens of social cooperation include various liabilities, duties, and obligations, including for example, the obligation to pay taxes. (p. 7)

The second question of fairness connects with the larger issue of how to justify differential opportunity and reward among group members so they believe they get what they deserve. According to Robert Nozick's theory of allocative justice, this question is settled when individuals receive social and nonsocial benefits according to the effort and merit of individual contribution. Individuals are entitled only to what they can get through their own means in accordance with principles of acquisition and transfer. Dissatisfaction with differential opportunity and outcomes made evident through interpersonal comparisons is justified, therefore, only to the extent that those who gain greater advantages do not do so through their own effort and ability. It follows that governments violate these rules of entitlement when they tax working people to provide income and support for nonworking people.

Rawls's and Nozick's responses to these different conceptions of fairness have conflicting implications for deciding what is fair and what is not. On the one hand, there is Rawls's focus on what burdens and benefits are to be shared by virtue of being a member of the group, and on the other hand, there are Nozick's rules for deciding what constitutes reasonable return for individual talent and effort. Depending on which set of rules applies, a different conclusion about fairness results. By arguing all benefit and burden in social life come from cooperation, as Rawls does, fairness favors collective intervention to promote social justice. On the other hand, by arguing all benefit and burden experienced in life come from individually driven projects of economic exchange, as Nozick does, fairness demands allocative justice.

The implication of this analysis is that judgments about what is fair depend on theories of the self and of the social group; these, in turn, relate directly to the two questions of fairness—one comparing prospects for self-determination among different individuals participating in the same circumstance of cooperation and the other involving a comparison of prospects for self-determination across different groups. Some examples are when Person believes she is being treated unfairly because Other receives more for the same contribution or when Other believes the group to be unjust because he cannot be his own person and pursue his own plans in life in that group.

Both perceptions of injustice reflect the larger question of balance between individual and group interest. When the boundary separating the rights of the individual and demands of the group drifts too far in one direction or the other, fairness is threatened. When the balance shifts toward collective control, individuals judge the system to be unfair compared to what is possible from another group, and when the balance shifts toward greater freedom of the individual, people are likely to judge their situation to be unfair in comparison with others. Rawls and Nozick focus on one or the other of these questions. Nozick's argument for minimal government is a reaction to the tendency of intrusive government to diminish opportunities for individuals to pursue their own ends, whereas Rawls's argument of greater government is a reaction to the tendency of unregulated freedom to differentiate opportunities and outcomes to the advantage of some and the disadvantage of others. The problem is that both are valid assessments of how we decide what is fair and what is not. For centuries the struggle has been to constrain the oppression of government, and in recent times the struggle has been to constrain the oppression of the majority.

The theories of justice offered by Nozick and Rawls address only one of the two fairness questions—Nozick's theory focusing on personal capacity and Rawls's theory on social circumstance. Nozick justifies the acquisitive success of individuals by defining an expanded self as constituting everything. As Weinreb (1987) describes the Nozick self, it is "the unlimited extension of desert, 'mine' meaning simply anything I can get and keep" (p. 240). Rawls justifies social redress on behalf of the less fortunate by offering a conception of a diminished self bereft of all natural assets and responsibilities. For Rawls, the self is deserving of nothing because all characteristics are environmentally determined from a moral point of view. According to Weinreb (1987), this means that "all that a person is and has being at the disposal of the community for the equal benefit of all" (pp. 239-240). Nozick's justice as entitlement is based on a theory of the expanded self and Rawls's justice as fairness is based on a theory of the expanded group. Nozick offers no theory of the group to regulate the hegemony of striving individuals, and Rawls offers no theory of the individual to balance the oppression of group regulation.

Equal opportunity theory addresses these inadequacies by basing its optimal prospects principle on *a theory of the group* that explains how social conditions evolve toward the advantage of some and the disadvantage of others and, as a consequence, justify constraints on personal freedom to ensure optimal prospects for self-determination for all. The optimal prospects principle is also consistent with *a theory of the self,* which explains why collective intervention on behalf of the less well situated—as suggested by Rawls's difference principle—will actually undermine the basis of self-respect necessary to achieve optimal prospects for self-determination among members of those groups.

By addressing questions of social and allocative justice, equal opportunity theory embraces both conceptions of fairness. Individuals experience optimal prospects for self-determination in an absolute sense by comparing their chances of getting what they want in life through various associations for collective advantage and then by choosing that social arrangement that optimizes their chances of fulfilling their own ends in life. When they compare opportunities for membership in different groups or forms of government, individuals judge their prospects for self-determination to be fair to the extent they can get what they want in life by joining that group.

On the other hand, when individuals compare themselves with others to determine what is fair, they do so with respect to specific circumstance and probable outcome. When Person's circumstance of capacity and opportunity is equal to Other's for a given pursuit, Person expects her chances for success to be equal, too. But, this is an extremely unlikely comparison in that circumstances of capacity, opportunity, and pursuit are nearly always unequal. Individuals have different needs, interests, and abilities, and they pursue different ends. So interpersonal comparisons on incomparable particulars only confuse conclusions about fairness. What is comparable between individuals, however, is their prospects or chances for getting what they want that is also consistent with their ability. This is how the second meaning of fairness is coherent. Person should be as successful or unsuccessful and as fulfilled or unfulfilled in pursuit of her self-determined life as Other is in his individual pursuit, even though the particulars of both pursuits are different. In this sense interpersonal comparisons can yield judgments of fairness.

This chapter and the next show how policies derived from theories by Rawls and Nozick emphasize different concepts of fairness and, as a consequence, leave unanswered one or the other of the fairness questions. We will see that Rawls's theory of justice is based on a *theory of social justice* derived from the observation that unregulated freedom of the few leads to cumulative loss of the many. The appeal of Rawls's approach is its attention to this unequalizing effect and its diagnosis of the morally arbitrary nature of social process that accumulates advantage and disadvantage depending on where in the social structure one happens to begin life. Rawls's focus on the underlying social structure has appeal because it calls into question the moral basis for allowing this tendency of social process to distribute prospects for self-determination unequally among a population of actors. At the same time, however, the difference principle he recommends fails to produce the desired result because it is based on an inadequate theory of self, and as a consequence, is insensitive to its effects in undermining self-respect, which is based on personal autonomy and the experience of self-determination.

In Chapter 4, Nozick's theory is shown to be a mirror image of Rawls's theory, focusing as it does on fairness through allocative justice rather than on fairness through social justice. Although Nozick's theory justifies the power to self-determine, whereas Rawls's theory does not, it does not acknowledge the harm created when that power is left unregulated for long periods of time. Consequently, his theory has no basis for anticipating the harm of accumulated gain and loss that affects prospects for self-determination for all members of society.

It seems that whereas Rawls's theory is appealing because it is based on a robust theory of social forces creating advantage and disadvantage, it is also problematic because it lacks a theory of self to guide applications of the difference principle in the enhancement of personal autonomy and self-determination. At the same time Nozick's theory is appealing for reasons that Rawls's theory is not because it bases its justification for property entitlement on a theory of the self that assumes that the greater the capacity and opportunity for an expansive autonomy of Person, the better. But this focus also runs into trouble in that it neglects the side effects of acquisitive individual pursuits that create disadvantage for persons losing out in the initial competition for advantage.

The two theories are appealing and troubling at the same time. Rawls's theory is troubling because the difference principle will actually reduce prospects for self-determination among the least well situated who are to benefit from gain produced by those better situated. The principle increases the sense of being a victim by those being helped at the same time it increases the sense of being superior among those providing the help. Nozick's theory is also troubling because it allows those with advantage to ignore those at a disadvantage even though these people have fewer resources with which to overcome greater obstacles than those better situated in life. Consequently, when the less fortunate persons fail to overcome their overwhelming difficulties, the rule of entitlement claims they are entitled to suffer.

Bases of Self-Respect

People who are fortunate enough to thrive by Nozick's entitlement principles enjoy the psychological and social bases for self-respect. They are self-determining by experience and by right, and this yields an integrity of principle and action that is necessary for self-respect. It leads to positive valuations and validations by self and others. Unfortunately not everyone emerges from Nozick's just society with this experiential base for self-respect. These individuals constitute that group of least well situated persons Rawls's theory of justice is designed to assist. For people who are least well situated in society, self-respect is continually at risk in that respecting one's self presumes confidence in one's capacity to satisfy those important needs and wants in life. It presumes respect for one's capacity to pursue opportunity leading to desirable ends, and it presumes understanding what ends are worth pursuing because they make life worth living.

Rawls's theory favors people who have been left out of the mainstream of life—people who gain little respect from others because of their lack of experience and proficiency in leading the self-determined life. Better situated individuals withhold respect because they believe these individuals lack capacity to improve their own prospects for becoming more than what they have been in the past. Their dependence on others—which defines their status as "least advantaged"—reinforces these beliefs. People withhold respect for anyone who cannot solve problems on their own. This, after all, is a common basis for evaluating a person's worth. Consequently, people who cannot manage their own affairs lose respect on the larger moral ideal of living the principle-governed life, as well. Lacking integrity of thought, action, and purpose in securing the primary goods everyone values, they incur pity rather than respect.

This has been the experience of people of color and people with disabilities for centuries. Both groups have been denied the self-determination experience and on this basis have been unable to build the personal and social bases for self-respect that come with full engagement in the self-determined pursuit. They have been denied the status of autonomous beings worthy of respect that is commonly associated with independent thought and action in the principle-governed life. Rawls's (1971, p. 62) theory of justice addresses this problem by identifying the principles of a just society that will dispense these primary goods in life—liberty and opportunity, income and wealth, and the bases of self-respect. Rawls regards self-respect as the most important of these goods to be distributed equally:

> On several occasions, I have mentioned that perhaps the most important primary good is that of self-respect. We must make sure that the conception of goodness as rationality explains why this should be so. We may define self-respect (or self-esteem) as having two aspects. First of all, as we noted earlier, . . . it includes a person's sense of his own value, his secure conviction that his conception of his good, his plan of life, is worth carrying out. And second, self-respect implies a confidence in one's ability, so far as it is within one's power, to fulfill one's intentions. When we feel that our plans are of little value, we cannot pursue them with pleasure or take delight in their execution. Nor plagued by failure and self-doubt can we continue in our endeavors. It is clear then why self-respect is a primary good. Without it nothing may seem worth doing, or if some things have value for us, we lack the will to strive for them. (p. 440)

Rawls believes the well-ordered society would guarantee everyone the bases of self-respect, and he predicts that rational participants in the construction of that just society would reject any principle undermining the equal distribution of this primary good because then all

> desire and activity becomes empty and vain, and we sink into apathy and cynicism. Therefore the parties in the original position would wish to

avoid at almost any cost the social conditions that undermine self-respect. The fact that justice as fairness gives more support to self-esteem than other principles is a strong reason for them to adopt it. (p. 440)

In Rawls's well-ordered society, self-respect—along with liberty, opportunity, income, and wealth—should be distributed equally among all members of society unless an unequal distribution of those goods is to everyone's advantage. So if the most favored individuals in society increase their share of primary goods, then the least advantaged members should gain shares of these primary goods as well, although they may not gain in the same amount or proportion. But at a minimum, they must be better off than if the most favored individuals did not improve their share at all. To demonstrate how this works, Rawls would regulate economic gain among the most advantaged members of society to ensure that the least advantaged members of society would gain economically as well. This means the productive, self-determined gain of the former would be yoked in a contingent relationship with the nonproductive, nondetermined pursuits of the latter group. For social justice to obtain, then, the success of the most advantaged in society would compensate for the nonsuccess of the least advantaged in society.

The problem with this application of the difference principle is that it would actually undermine the very basis of self-respect the principle was intended to enhance. Consider, for example, what it means for individuals to receive economic benefit based entirely on the success of other people's pursuits. What happens to Person's self-respect when she receives shares of the primary good in life because she is among the least successful in society? Being dependent on the success of another person's pursuit is destructive to one's own sense of self-determination, and it destroys both the psychological and social basis for self-respect. For each benefit received, Person would be reminded again of her status as being among the least successful in society and that receipt of benefit was based on a social recognition of her *incapacity* to secure gain as an individual—through her own self-determined pursuit. This social validation of her status as a nondetermined person would reinforce this debilitating conception of herself as being helpless and impotent in the social world. Being labeled as "faring less well than others" constitutes public confirmation of what is missing in one's life, which is belief in oneself and in the capacity to secure goods in life through one's own self-determined pursuits.

But according to Rawls's application of the difference principle, eligibility for receiving shares of the primary goods in life depends on categories officially defining one's incapacity to self-determine—or in his words "to fare less well" than others:

> "The least advantaged are defined very roughly, as the overlap between those who are least favored by each of the three main kinds of contingencies. Thus this group includes persons whose family and class origins are more disadvantaged than others, whose endowments have permitted them to fare less well, and whose fortune and luck have been relatively less favorable, all . . . with the relevant measures based on social primary goods."[1] (quoted in Beauchamp, 1980, p. 155)

So Person's benefits increase to the extent her family background, social position, and personal endowments "permit [her] to fare less well," while at the same time the benefits of Other would be taxed to support Person to the extent that his family background, social position, and personal endowments permit him to fare better. The social comparisons demanded by the difference principle would only exacerbate Person's sensitivity to the very condition Rawls claims is morally arbitrary—that variation in capacity produces variation in social advantage. The difference principle would invite invidious social comparisons that would undermine the self-respect of those benefiting from contingent redistribution of economic benefit, and at the same time it would enhance a sense of superiority among those whose success makes redistributed economic benefit possible.

Rawls's theory of justice overlooks this side effect because it assumes the basis of self-respect can be detached from the experience of self-determination and reattached instead to the right to self-determination—to "the status of equal citizenship for all." It assumes that the right to equal citizenship will translate automatically into a public affirmation of mutual respect. So when the theory separates the construction of the just society into two parts—one ensuring maximum *rights* to equal liberty for all and the other permitting unequal *experiences of liberty* only to the extent that those unequal distributions of primary goods benefit everyone—it allows Rawls to claim that mutual respect *will naturally result* because it is attached to the first priority—which is equal rights for all. By guaranteeing the right to self-determination as the primary rule for ordering the just society, Rawls (1971) establishes what he considers to be a social guarantee for mutual respect—a public affirmation based on his belief that mutual respect depends on equality of civil rights:

> Having chosen a conception of justice that seeks to eliminate the significance of relative economic and social advantages as supports for men's

self-confidence, it is essential that the priority of liberty be firmly maintained. So for this reason too the parties are led to adopt a serial ordering
of the two principles.

In a well-ordered society then, self-respect is secured by the public
affirmation of the status of equal citizenship for all; the distribution of
material means is left to take care of itself in accordance with the idea of
pure procedural justice. Of course, doing this assumes the requisite
background institutions that narrow the range of inequalities so that
excusable envy does not arise. (p. 545)

There can be no guarantee for self-respect, however, because it is based
on the *experience* not the *right* to self-determination. It is perhaps true that
the right provides the occasion for the experience and that the experience
in turn provides the occasion for feelings of personal and social respect. But
it is not true that this causal sequence always plays out we as might hope. It is
equally likely the right to self-determination becomes another unfulfilled
expectation for people in least advantaged positions in life because they lack
both capacity and opportunity to express themselves as they would like.
The right to vote—guaranteed to all—does not mean those in greatest need
of political representation will act on this right by selecting representatives
who will help improve their prospects for pursuing the good life.

Although Rawls's theory orders principles of a just society so self-
respect will attach to equal liberty for all as the first priority, he also
recognizes the difficulties in shifting the basis of respect from the right to
the experience of self-respect. He recognizes for example that an obstacle
to mutual respect results from its attachment to the experience of self-
determination as exhibited by an individual's "institutional position" and
"income share" in the social structure (Rawls, 1971):

Now it is quite possible that this idea cannot be carried through completely. To some extent men's sense of their own worth may hinge on their
institutional position and their income share. If, however, the account of
social envy and jealousy is sound, then with the appropriate background
arrangements, these inclinations should not be excessive, at least not when
the priority of liberty is effectively upheld. But theoretically we can if
necessary include self-respect in the primary goods, the index of which
defines expectations. Then in application of the difference principle, this
index can allow for the effects of excusable envy . . . the expectations of
the less advantaged are lower the more severe these effects. Whether some
adjustment for self-respect has to be made is best decided from the
standpoint of the legislative stage where the parties have more information
about social circumstances and the principle of political determination

applies. Admittedly this problem is an unwelcome complication. Since simplicity is itself desirable in the public conception of justice, the conditions that elicit excusable envy should if possible be avoided. I have mentioned this point not to settle it, but only to note that when necessary the expectations of the less advantaged can be understood so as to include the primary good of self-esteem. (pp. 535-536)

Unfortunately this "unwelcome complication" posed by the problem of excusable envy goes to the heart of what causes differential advantage and unequal prospects for self-determination. Person is justifiably envious of those whose experience of self-determination is greater and more fulfilling than hers. She is envious because she lacks comparable levels of confidence, competence, and personal efficacy due to *specific experiences* that tell Person she lacks what it takes to be effectively self-determining in securing what she needs and wants in life. This experience and feeling translate into complaints about social and allocative justice. One believes the social order favors those with personal, social, and economic advantage, and in time one comes to believe one has no chance of gaining control over one's life or of receiving the respect one wants and believes is deserved. This leads to personal and social alienation as one comes to reflect both the cause and effect of "excusable envy." Rawls (1971) describes this in the following:

> Now I assume that the main psychological root of the liability to envy is a lack of self-confidence in our own worth combined with a sense of impotence. Our way of life is without zest and we feel powerless to alter it or to acquire the means of doing what we still want to do. By contrast, someone sure of the worth of his plan of life and his ability to carry it out is not given to rancor nor is he jealous of his good fortune. Even if he could, he has no desire to level down the advantages of others at some expense to himself. This hypothesis implies that the least favored tend to be more envious of the better situation of the more favored the less secure their self-respect and the greater their feeling that they cannot improve their prospects . . .
>
> There are three conditions, I assure, that encourage hostile outbreaks of envy. The first of these is the psychological condition we have just noted: persons lack a sure confidence in their own value and in their ability to do anything worthwhile. Second (and one of two social conditions), many occasions arise when this psychological condition is experienced as painful and humiliating. The discrepancy between oneself and others is made visible by the social structure and type of life of one's society. The less fortunate are therefore often forcibly reminded of their situation, sometimes leading them to an even lower estimation of themselves and

their mode of living. And third, they see their social position as allowing no constructive alternative to opposing the favored circumstances of the more advantaged. To alleviate their feelings of anguish and inferiority, they believe they have no choice but to impose a loss on those better placed even at some cost to themselves, unless of course they are to relapse into resignation and apathy. (p. 536)

Rawls claims the difference principle will solve this problem because it will shift the basis of the just society from valuing economic gain for some to valuing equal liberty for all:

> In the public forum each person is treated with the respect due to a sovereign equal; and everyone has the same basic rights that would be acknowledged in an initial situation regarded as fair. The members of the community have a common sense of justice and they are bound by ties of civic friendship. . . . We can add that the greater advantages of some are in return for compensating benefits for the less favored; and no one supposes that those who have a larger share are more deserving from a moral point of view. . . . For all these reasons the less fortunate have no cause to consider themselves inferior and the public principles generally accepted underwrite their self-assurance. The disparities between themselves and others, whether absolute or relative, should be easier for them to accept than in other forms of polity. (p. 536)

Unfortunately the facts of social life dispute these wishful assertions. Claiming there is no basis for feeling inferior to others does little to assuage the feeling of inferiority after experiencing the effect of the difference principle. To begin with, the process of labeling people as disadvantaged so they can receive shares of income according to the difference principle may reduce *economic distance* between the least and the most advantaged, but it is unlikely to reduce social status difference between groups. In fact, the difference principle is likely to increase social difference, which in turn will undermine the purpose of Rawls's theory of justice. The problem with Rawls's institutional structure is that it is based on the assumption that all primary goods—income and wealth, freedom and opportunity, and the bases of self-respect—are interconnected in ways that permit their distribution according to weighted indexes to be tracked as so many commodity transfers. This assumption is ill founded, as Allen Buchanan (1980) has pointed out:

> Granted that maximizing the prospects of the representative worst off man requires maximizing the weighted sum of prospects of the entire list of

these goods—not just maximizing prospects of income or wealth—there is no reason to assume, as this strategy would have us do, that increasing the income prospects of the representative worst off man will maximize his prospects of the whole range of social primary goods. Moreover, Rawls does nothing to support this assumption.

It is important to sort out several versions of the needed assumption about the connection between increases in income prospects and increases in prospects of other primary goods such as self-respect and authority. Consider first the assumption that in our society at the present time, and for a period extending indefinitely into the future, the overall prospects of the worst off, including especially their prospects of self-respect, can be maximized simply by supplementing their wages through the use of tax revenues. It is not simply that Rawls fails to marshal any empirical evidence to show that this can be done, though this is bad enough. There is the more serious problem that there is a good deal of empirical evidence against the assumption that income and self-respect (and authority) arc correlated in this simple fashion even in our society at the present time . . .

It is wishful thinking to suppose that Rawls' simple and rather conservative institutional model for the satisfaction of the Difference Principle will come to grips with the awesome problem of adequately raising the representative worst off man's prospects for self-respect or meaningful work. To assume that these problems can be solved simply by redistributing income through conventional taxation measures is to make the same sort of error for which Marx took the French socialist of his day to task. It is to assume that problems which intimately involve persons' productive relations can be solved by purely distributive measures in the narrow sense. (pp. 37-38)

Rawls claims a social order based on equal distribution of rights to self-determination (through the first principle) and redistribution of the social and economic inequalities resulting from unequal power to self-determine (through the second principle) will enhance prospects for self-determination among the least advantaged. But this assumes, as Buchanan noted, "that problems which intimately involve persons' *productive* [power] relations can be solved by purely *distributive* measures in the narrow sense." It assumes a guarantee of rights and gains due to one's membership in society will yield equal experiences of self-determination and self-respect. This guarantee is ill founded for the reasons Buchanan suggested. The experience of self-determination and the feeling of self-respect do not result from *guaranteed* distributions of opportunities and gains. They come from individual pursuits that connect personal action with social opportunity. They come from interaction between the right to self-determine and the power to express that right through engagement of social opportunity.

Theory of Self-Regulation

Rawls's theory of justice argues for a society structured so right prevails over might in the expression of freedom. His lexical ordering of institutional principles governing the just society reflects this priority, with the first principle proclaiming equal citizenship and self-respect for all and the second principle regulating the personal, social, and economic resources accumulated by the most favored in society. By emphasizing right over power in the expression of liberty for all, he recommends the difference principle to prevent the power of the advantaged from accumulating gain without also ensuring collateral gain for the disadvantaged. This is what is attractive about his theory. It guarantees gain for everyone, regardless of their personal capacity or social opportunity. It guarantees fair shares in the productive output of the group by virtue of membership in the group. It appeals to our sense of social justice—that the structure of society should be guided by principles of fairness for all. Everyone benefits from the cooperative enterprise that ensures equal citizenship and equal respect. Everyone shares in the success of the group because the fate of the most advantaged is yoked to the fate of the least advantaged.

EXCUSABLE ENVY

But we should also try to understand what the theory does not guarantee. It does not guarantee to the powerless that they will change their status when it comes to determining their own future. This is because the experience evoked by the difference principle is an experience of helplessness, and that experience maintains the status quo. Consequently, those already powerful will become even more powerful, whereas those who are powerless will become more powerless. Moreover, this accelerated differentiation of personal and social power will further erode the personal and social bases of self-respect. In short, Rawls's theory of justice will exacerbate rather than ameliorate the problem of inequality by increasing invidious social comparisons that undermine the bases for self-respect. This returns to Rawls's (1971) excusable envy problem and his diagnosis of its basis:

> The psychological root of the liability to envy is a lack of self-confidence in our own worth combined with a sense of impotence. Our way of life is without zest and we feel powerless to alter it or to acquire the means of doing what we still want to do. By contrast, someone sure of the worth of

his plan of life and his ability to carry it out is not given to rancor nor is
he jealous of his good fortune. Even if he could, he has no desire to level
down the advantages of others at some expense to himself. (p. 535)

People feeling powerless in the determination of their own ends in life
will be dissatisfied when they compare themselves with the powerful who
are in control of their lives. So the problem of excusable envy continues
unabated unless the psychological cause of declining self-respect is treated
directly. Unfortunately, Rawls's theory of justice offers no solution to this
problem because justice as fairness is not based on a theory of self that can
account for the psychological mechanisms responsible for variation in
self-esteem and self-respect. It offers no explanation for how the *capacity*
to self-determinate interacts with the *opportunity* to self-determine to
produce the *experience of self-determination,* which is the basis for self-
respect.

Engagement of just-right opportunity in pursuit of desired ends in life
is what creates valuation of self. No amount of public affirmation on equal
rights and equal respect can replace this means of personal and social
fulfillment. Guarantees of equality of right have little effect when the
psychological basis of self-respect has eroded. Moreover, when the experience of declining personal efficacy affects the social basis for respect,
constitutional or legislative guarantees of equal rights matter little, either.
This is because the experience of helplessness is psychological first and
social second. Rawls acknowledges as much in his explanation for the
causes of excusable envy:

The first of these is the psychological condition . . . persons lack a sure
confidence in their own value and in their ability to do anything worthwhile. Second . . . many occasions arise when this psychological condition
is experienced as painful and humiliating. The discrepancy between
oneself and others is made visible by the social structure and style of life
of one's society. The less fortunate are therefore often forcibly reminded
of their situation, sometimes leading them to an even lower estimation of
themselves and their mode of living. (p. 535)

SELF-REGULATION

Equal opportunity theory is based on a psychological theory that
accounts for how the sense of self waxes and wanes in accordance with
variation in capacity and opportunity to self-regulate in search for desirable

ends in life. This theory of self-regulation explains how all individuals adjust to environmental change to adapt to circumstances that define their opportunities in life. It provides a basis for understanding how the power and right interact to produce the experience of self-determination. According to the theory, the power to self-determine is equivalent to the capacity to regulate one's resources to satisfy one's needs and interests, whereas the right to self-determine is equivalent to a guaranteed opportunity to self-regulate in accordance with those needs and interests.

In other words, the terminology of self-regulation explaining how people adjust to change equates power and right with capacity and opportunity. Power is the capacity to self-determine and right is the guaranteed opportunity to express (or not to express) choice and action with respect to the content of the right. So the power to vote is the capacity to consider candidates and then decide which one offers the best prospect for gain, whereas the right to vote is the guaranteed opportunity to go to the voting booth and vote. Self-regulation theory explains how individuals adjust to these variations in environmental circumstance. Consequently, it accounts for how change in personal and social circumstance leads to adjustment through *self*-determined thought and action and it also accounts for how change in circumstance yields adjustments through *other*-determined thought and action.

The theory explains why some combinations of capacity and opportunity produce self-determination and how this baseline experience sets the occasion for higher expectations, increased sense of self-respect, and higher levels of confidence. The theory explains how enhancements of personal autonomy contribute to higher levels of personal capacity for self-directed thought and action and how these factors, in turn, optimize subsequent opportunities for engagement and success. The theory describes how this pattern of experience creates a cycle of cumulative advantage that empowers individuals to broaden their prospects for optimizing opportunity, which further enhances their sense of self-esteem and self-respect. In short, it explains how variations in the sense of self are both cause and consequence of the self-directed life.

Self-regulation theory also explains how variation in personal and social circumstance generates patterns of self-regulation that are other-determined and that yield experiences that are as debilitating and degrading as those characterized as self-determined are empowering and emancipating. The sense of enslavement, loss of personal autonomy, destruction of self-respect that results from other-determined patterns of personal and social adjustment are a consequence of the same process that creates more fulfilling forms of adjustment to environmental circumstance. What differentiates other-determined from self-determined pursuits in life is that people engaged in the former regulate their problem solving to meet other people's needs, interests, and goals. When this condition persists, people in this situation develop the feeling they live in a world beyond their control. This leads to a loss of faith in their power to act and creates beliefs that no matter what they do they cannot change their status in life. Lacking both power and opportunity to improve their own prospects for self-determination, they resign themselves to reacting day-to-day according to whatever the external world demands. Long-term goals and life-fulfilling plans are impossible because all time and effort are consumed by reactionary adjustment to life's exigencies.

These grossly different patterns of adjustment to life's circumstance are distinguishable to the extent individuals are free from obstacles to act on behalf of their own needs and interests and to the extent they are free for pursuit of opportunity that promises gain toward their own ends in life. People who are self-determining have optimal proportions of power to overcome the constraints of daily survival and optimal shares of public rights permitting them to express whatever power they have accumulated to expand the perimeters of their being. Taken together the power and the right of self-determination are those necessary and sufficient conditions for emancipating the spirit of human existence in hope of changing one's status and improving one's future over a lifetime. Power and right are what give direction in life; they are what make humans morally accountable for that sense of autonomy they hold in common.

PROBLEM SOLVING TO MEET A GOAL

Self-regulation theory claims that interaction between the power and the right to self-determine functions according to the same principles that explain other forms of adjustment to environmental circumstance—including those yielding less self-determined outcomes. The core of the explanation for adjustment in general is the theory that all processes of self-regulation commence with *problem solving to meet a goal*. All organisms attempt to improve their adjustments to environmental circumstance by reducing discrepancies between present and desired capacities to get what they need and want from their environments. Given their present capacities are inadequate to secure a desired outcome, they search the environment for opportunities that will generate the capacity (means) to produce the desired outcome. The three-step process common to all adjustment comes down to three questions: (a) What is the discrepancy between actual and desired capacity (means) for securing a desirable end? (b) What opportunities are most likely to provide the means (capacity) to secure the desirable end? (c) Did the opportunity pursued improve one's means (capacity) to secure the desirable end?

All adjustment—human and nonhuman—involves these steps. But in human adaptation, the process accelerates differentiation of prospects for self-determination among individuals and groups. This differentiation is due to variation in the intergenerational accumulation and transfer of knowledge and skills, and to differential association among individuals exchanging assets to expand capacity and optimize opportunity. Consequently, the repetition of goal-directed problem-solving episodes over long periods of time tends to accumulate gain and loss to produce end-state conditions reflecting a net maintenance, depletion, or enhancement of an individual's capacity to self-determine. Those who are fortunate to experience enhancements of capacity will have the power to exercise their rights and consequently, will attempt to optimize environmental circumstance to get what they need and want in life. They will feel empowered because they feel they have control over life's circumstances. They experience *freedom from* and *freedom for* because they have sufficient capacity and opportunity to enhance their capacity and this frees them *from obstacles* due to limited capacity and increases their *freedom to* pursue new opportunity. It motivates them to engage the environment to become more than what they are so they get more than they have.

All of these variations in adjustment outcomes depend on *interaction* between capacity and opportunity—interaction between the power and right of individuals to adjust to life in a sociopolitical world. The causal pattern explaining the interactions leading to goal attainment is similar to John Dewey's explanation for human problem solving, which he formulated with these three questions: " 'What is the problem? What are the alternatives? Which alternative is best?' " (quoted in Simon, 1960, p. 3). It is also similar to Allen Newell and Herbert Simon's computer simulation of human problem solving, which has three steps: (a) Find the discrepancy between the goal state and the current state, (b) find an operator to reduce the discrepancy, and (c) apply an operator and evaluate its effects on the discrepancy. The following description of that simulation illustrates the recursive dynamic involved in problem solving to meet a goal (Newell & Simon, 1972):

A problem is defined for GPS [General Problem Solver] by giving it a starting situation and a goal situation (or a test for determining whether the goal has been reached), together with a set of operators that may be used, separately or severally, to transform the starting situation into the goal situation by a sequence of successive applications. Means-ends analysis is the technique used by GPS to decide which operator to apply next:

1. It compares current situation with goal situation to detect one or more differences between them.
2. It retrieves from memory an operator that is associated with a difference it has found (i.e., an operator that has the usual effect of reducing differences of this kind.)
3. It applies the operator or, if it is not applicable in the current situation, sets up the new goal of creating the conditions that will make it applicable. (p. 36)

Figure 3.1 shows how this causal sequence explains capacity-opportunity interactions during human problem solving to meet a goal. The process begins when Person compares her present capacity for getting what she needs and wants with the capacity that is necessary to secure those ends. This comparison between *actual* and *expected* capacity alerts her to a discrepancy condition indicating that she lacks capacity (resources) to get what she wants. The discrepancy, in turn, motivates Person to pursue opportunity to enhance her present capacity so she can fulfill what is missing in her life. In the language of Newell and Simon's General Problem Solver, Person's goal is to make her actual capacity equal her expected capacity, as indicated in the figure. So Person searches for an opportunity (Opportunity 1) to optimize circumstances so she can get what she needs to change her capacity from the actual to the expected condition. After producing gain from opportunity 1, she evaluates by comparing actual with expected capacity and discovers her actual capacity is still lacking, so Person pursues opportunity 2, and gets the same result. Then Person considers a third attempt. But this time Person considers discontinuing her search because the enterprise is becoming costly. It is drawing down existing resources and, hence, weakening present capacity.

Engaging opportunity to optimize circumstance is risky in that it requires an *exchange* of personal resources for hoped-for gain in capacity from the environment. Person must search the environment and then engage its circumstances, hoping the costs incurred in the search and engagement will be less than the gain in enhanced capacity that results. Person hopes

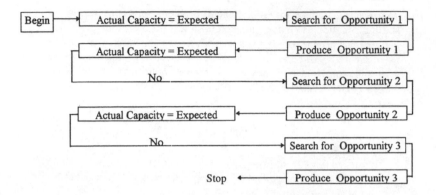

Figure 3.1. Example of Enhancing Capacity Through Opportunity

to find an exchange rate that produces a net advantage by enhancing her capacity. The investment in time, effort, and other resources, temporarily at least, decreases Person's existing capacity. This investment is made in anticipation that a successful pursuit will more than compensate that initial cost. But there is no guarantee of success. Pursuing opportunity always means risking existing capital and weakening current capacity. Person could end up with less capacity than what she had before she commenced the pursuit. This is why Person decided to forego her pursuit in Figure 3.1. She wanted to avoid weakening her capacity further.

Should Person decide to continue the pursuit, it might lead to a point where she is incapable of securing other ends in life due to debilitated capacity. Now Person is motivated to *maintain* her capacity by securing access to resources she had come to depend on in the past, whereas in the first example, Person's motivation was to *enhance* her capacity by securing control over new resources to satisfy new needs and interests in life. So although the source of the discrepancy condition may be different as it is in these two situations, the effect is the same—to motivate Person to solve problems to meet goals. The adjustment process and outcome are the same, as well—to gain control over the means of producing gain. Control guarantees capacity for self-determined pursuits.

Self-regulation theory describes this process of gaining control over the means of producing gain. Although the process eventually comes down to problem solving to meet a goal, it always begins with an attempt to secure access to a valued resource with existing capacity. If this succeeds, no problem solving is necessary and no new pattern of self-regulation likely.

Person acts as she always has, conducting exchanges with the environment as before to secure access to those resources she uses routinely to satisfy her needs in life. It is only when past exchanges fail to secure access to these goods or when Person needs or wants something different that she adjusts her transactions with the environment. Even then, the adjustment may be minor, as in reallocating resources in a different way or exchanging surplus assets for a different resource that will satisfy a new need or interest. But occasionally the adjustment is substantial, requiring that Person *increase her capacity* because she has insufficient assets to secure what she wants. All of these adjustments, nevertheless, come down to the same discrepancy condition motivating problem solving to gain access to a new resource.

THE EXPERIENCE OF SELF-DETERMINATION

According to self-regulation theory then, all individuals vary in their capacity and opportunity to self-determine. Some have substantial capacity and frequent opportunity, others have ample capacity but few opportunities, others lack capacity but have frequent opportunities, and still others lack both capacity and opportunity. Such variation in circumstance is not necessarily permanent, however, depending as it does on the resource being sought and the end in life being pursued. Consequently, the experience of control comes and goes according to the mean and the end defining the pursuit. What Person wants in life affects her experience of self-determination because her capacity and opportunity determine success and failure in getting what she wants. If Person wants substantially more than her capacity and opportunity allow, she may become frustrated and feel impotent because her goal is unrealistic. Person experiences a situation that many experience from time to time and she is likely to do as they have done: adjust expectations to eliminate the source of frustration and disappointment. She will reset her expectations to match her capacity.

This is the *first step* in self-regulation. It is adjusting to life's circumstances by determining what ends are achievable and what ends are not. By ignoring those that are unattainable, we eliminate the discrepancy condition that prompts us to commence problem solving to meet a goal. With disappearance of the discrepancy goes any interest in pursuing opportunity to change what we are, who we want to become, or what we need to achieve a new status in life. We become "realistic" in that we have adjusted expectations to what we perceive to be our current capacity and present opportunity.

So the first step in self-regulation is deciding whether to seek out and engage new opportunity for gain. More often than not, we decide to abort; we decide to adjust expectations downward so they match our existing capacity and circumstance. We avoid risk of failure and its anticipated cost to our existing capacity. But this risk of failure weighs especially heavily on people who must adjust to life's circumstances with limited capacity and constrained opportunity. The cost of failure is proportionately greater because these individuals lack surplus resources needed to carry on satisfactorily if they fail. Life would be too costly to endure should they lose access to the resources they have depended on in the past to maintain what they have in life.

The experience of self-determination depends on decisions to search for opportunity to secure access to resources currently lacking in one's life. Decisions that avoid new opportunity constrain one's access to valued resources and reduce one's capacity for satisfying unmet needs in life. They create a cycle of declining prospects for self-determination. Lowered expectations decrease motivation to search, lack of motivation to search decreases the frequency of engagement in new opportunity, lack of engagement of new opportunity decreases the chances of enhancing capacity, and limitations in capacity for satisfying unmet needs create feelings of powerlessness over life's circumstances. This lack of control over life translates into an experience of other-determination. The external world, not Person, is controlling her life.

The opposite occurs when expectations increase to create discrepancies between actual and needed capacity causing Person to seek out and engage new opportunity, use its results to enhance capacity, and then use enhanced capacity to fulfill what is missing in life. Now the operable cycle is change and expansion rather than stasis and contraction. Enhanced capacity gives rise to higher expectations, which motivates new searches, new engagements, more success, and additional capacity. This enhancement of capacity allows Person to improve her ability to search for new opportunity, to engage it successfully, and then to enhance her capacity so she can optimize ever more challenging opportunity. It allows her to become successively more powerful in all of her pursuits.

People who enjoy this experience of self-determination have three conditions favoring their adjustment to life's circumstance: (a) They know how to regulate the use of existing resources to secure control over the additional means necessary to satisfy unmet needs and interests in life; (b) they are free from constraints created by a lack of personal, social, economic, or technical resources necessary to engage new opportunity for gain; and (c) they are free to pursue new opportunity in that options are available for them to decide how best to use their capacity to optimize their circumstance. People *become* self-determining when they have sufficient power and right—capacity and opportunity—to change their environment to enhance their capacity for living the life they want.

THE JUST-RIGHT EXCHANGE

These exchanges with the environment are most likely when individuals find *just-right matches* between their capacity and their opportunity. Under these conditions of optimal prospects, individuals are, according to MacCallum's definition of freedom, autonomous persons free from Y to pursue Z (cited in Gray, 1991). They are free to regulate their resources on their own by choosing the means of getting what they need and want from a set of reasonably favorable opportunities or options that empower them to satisfy unmet needs.

Optimal prospects are just-right matches between capacity and opportunity when they encourage individuals to think and act independently of others to decide what is important in life, to set goals that specify what they want to pursue to satisfy unmet needs, and then to regulate problem solving toward those ends. This is the meaning of self-regulated problem solving to meet a goal. It comes down to (a) finding the match between capacity and opportunity that is necessary to commence goal pursuit, (b) developing a strategy for optimizing opportunity for gain, (c) acting on that strategy to optimize opportunity to produce expected gain, and then (d) adjusting to results by repeating the cycle until goal attainment or goal abandonment.

Individuals vary in capacity to self-regulate to the extent they can solve these types of problems. First, they vary to the extent they are able to search environments for opportunity to produce the gain needed to reduce the discrepancy between actual and expected capacity. Success depends on Person's assessment of her needs and interests, what is best for her over the long term, and what resources she has at her disposal to pursue opportunities that will satisfy unmet needs. Success also depends on Person's beliefs about the causal factors operating in the environment and how to use this understanding to identify new opportunity for gain. Person must be able to estimate the resources she will expend to operate on these causal factors to optimize her circumstance. Can she afford the possibility of failure in her attempt to produce expected gain? Will she produce the opportunity that produces the greatest gain at the lowest cost? In the best of all searches, Person will find that just-right match that satisfies the risk-benefit ratio she believes to be a good prospect for gain.

A second way individuals vary in capacity to self-regulate is in their ability to convert opportunities into a net resource gain for themselves—the extent to which they know how to optimize circumstances for gain production. In this second set of problem solving activities, Person must decide what strategies to employ, what resources to allocate, when to deploy them, and how. Here, Person develops a plan that she believes will optimize circumstances for the greatest gain at the lowest cost. Person constructs an optimizing strategy that is consistent with her estimate of the opportunity's cost-benefit ratio and probability of success. This is Person's estimate of the *optimality of that opportunity*. She infers this optimality from an assessment of her prospects of converting the circumstances of that opportunity into net resource gain for herself.

The third way individuals vary in capacity to self-regulate is in their ability to act on their plans to optimize opportunity. As Person strives to overcome obstacles to converting existing circumstance to favorable opportunity, she gathers information on the results of her actions to identify what to change to improve the situation with new action. Person's capacity to overcome obstacles that threaten to increase costs, reduce gain, and reduce prospects for success depends on accurate and reliable information about what she is doing, what gain she is producing, and how production results compare with expectations for gain. By gathering feedback and adjusting subsequent problem solving repeatedly over time and over many self-regulation episodes, Person increases capacity incrementally. This, in turn, optimizes Person's opportunity incrementally.

In sum, the self-regulated problem solver is motivated and focused. Such a person is motivated when she experiences a discrepancy between actual capacity to produce what she needs and wants in life and the capacity necessary to attain those ends. She exhibits this motivation by focusing her thoughts and actions on reducing the discrepancy by engaging in three types of problem solving: (a) one type that finds opportunities (circumstances) to be optimized through use of existing resources, (b) a second type of problem solving that produces a strategy for optimizing that set of circumstances, and (c) a third type of problem solving that acts on those circumstances by producing gain, evaluating results, and then adjusting subsequent problem solving.

Individuals with capacities to solve these problems effectively and efficiently optimize their adjustments and maximize their gain. They reduce discrepancies between what they have and what they need to satisfy their ends in life within the limits defined by their circumstances. In other words, they do the best they can with what they have available to them.

THE OPTIMAL ADJUSTMENT

Self-regulation theory explains how we optimize adjustment to maximize gain during exchange with the environment. Its four propositions describe conditions that affect how we set expectations for gain (the expectation proposition), how we select opportunities for producing gain (the choice proposition), how we act on those choices (the response proposition), and how the gain we produce affects the optimalities of subsequent expectations, choices, and actions (the gain proposition). These are described by Mithaug (1993) in the following:

1. *The expectation proposition:* The closer to optimal the past gain toward goal attainment and the smaller the discrepancy between the actual state and goal state, the closer to optimal the expectation for gain.
2. *The choice proposition:* The closer to optimal the past gain toward goal attainment and the more salient the differences between options, the closer to optimal the choice.
3. *The response proposition:* The closer to optimal the past gain, expectations, and choices, then the closer to optimal the distribution of responses between task completion to meet the goal and feedback about goal state-actual state discrepancies, options, task performance, and gain.
4. *The gain proposition:* The closer to optimal the past gain, expectations, choices, and responses, then the closer to maximum the gain toward goal attainment. (p. 59)

The expectation proposition states that experience in producing gain and the size of the discrepancy between current and expected capacity affect our ability to set optimal expectations for gain (the highest expectations possible from available opportunity), as the following illustrates[2] (Mithaug, 1993):

Experience in producing gain toward goal attainment increases Person's capacity to judge what is possible under the circumstances (options). The size of the discrepancy affects Person's judgments, too. For example, the smaller the discrepancy, the more likely Person will find a gain (solution) that will either eliminate the difference or maximize its reduction. Conversely, as discrepancies between goal states and actual states increase, the probability of finding completely effective solutions decreases. Large discrepancy reductions frequently require multiple solutions with varying reduction effects. This makes it difficult to identify the option that produces the greatest incremental gain toward goal attainment. (p. 58)

The choice proposition states that optimal choice making depends on previous choice making. It also identifies salience between opportunities as being important for choosers. When one opportunity is clearly superior to others, chances are good the chooser will notice the difference and pursue the better option. The proposition also alerts us to the problem of ambiguity between options that makes it difficult to identify the optimal selection (Mithaug, 1993):

The choice proposition specifies conditions under which Person chooses the operation that produces the greatest gain at the lowest cost. Again, there are two factors that influence optimal choosing. The first is experience or past gain toward the goal: the closer to optimal the past gain, the more likely Person will select the best operation to produce expected gain. The second factor is the difficulty of identifying important differences between options. The proposition states that the more salient the difference between options, then the more likely Person will choose optimally. During less than ideal choice circumstances in which differences are subtle and options are many, discriminations are difficult and time consuming (costly). They reduce the likelihood of choosing optimally. (pp. 58-59)

The response proposition specifies conditions affecting the effectiveness and efficiency of action to produce gain. Again, past gain, expectations for gain, and choices are influential. When individuals have little experience with a pending pursuit, when their expectations for gain are unrealistic, and when they choose opportunities that demand more skill and greater resources than they have at their disposal, then they must expend so much time and energy gathering information and learning what to do that the cost of their pursuit increases and the gain that results decreases. This is different for experts who set expectations for gain that are consistent with the resources available to them. They know how to identify opportunity most likely to produce the gain they need. They also know how to perform tasks required to optimize that opportunity. Consequently, they spend little time and effort learning what to do. They simply engage the opportunity to produce the gain it promises. Experts are effective and efficient (Mithaug, 1993):

The response proposition specifies the conditions under which Person maximizes responses to produce gain and minimizes responses that seek feedback. . . . Improvements in any of these conditions [of past gain optimalities, expectation optimalities, or choice optimalities] indicate the regulator's greater experience and understanding of what causes what. This leads to more effective and efficient distribution of responses. Person spends less time and effort monitoring performance accuracy, goal state-actual state discrepancies, options, and results and more time and effort performing the operations necessary to produce gain toward goal attainment. (pp. 59-60)

The gain proposition explains what happens when expectations, choices, and responses are optimal: Then gain toward goal attainment maximizes. Under these conditions, gain equals expectations, expectations are as high as possible under the circumstances, choices are the best of the options available, and actions are as efficient and effective as possible. Error responses minimize and effective responses maximize. The result is optimal adjustment and maximum gain (Mithaug, 1993):

> The gain proposition describes the effects of adjustment optimalities on gain toward the goal. The proposition states that as past gains, expectations, choices, and responses approach maximum optimalities, gain toward reducing the discrepancy between the actual state and goal state maximizes, too. The upper limit—maximum gain—occurs when (1) past gain equals expected gain, (2) expectations for gain equal the maximum possible from the options available, (3) choices produce the greatest gain at the lowest cost, and (4) resource allocations maximize responding to produce gain and minimize feedback seeking on goal states, choices, performances, and gains . . .
>
> In summary, self-regulation theory states that we maximize progress toward goals when (1) past gains match expectations, (2) present expectations are the maximum possible, (3) choices are the best possible, and (4) follow-through on choice is as effective and efficient as possible. Under these conditions, regulation is optimal and return from the environment is maximal. (pp. 60-61)

An important implication of self-regulation theory is its explanation for the *cumulative* effect resulting from interaction among past gain, expectations for gain, choices, and actions. Change in one optimality factor produces change in the others to create cycles of optimal and suboptimal adjustment resulting in accumulations of positive or negative experiences of self-determination—with one pattern yielding feelings of optimism, empowerment, and confidence and another creating feelings of hopelessness, impotence, and despair. The sense of helplessness and hopelessness occurs when repetitions of self-regulated problem solving lead to successive experiences of suboptimal adjustment. The cycle begins when one suboptimal adjustment produces less gain than expected that affects the next self-regulation episode by producing a suboptimal expectation for producing gain that reduces motivation to search for an optimal opportunity that yields a suboptimal choice that generates less gain than would be possible with a better selection. The cycle continues to spiral downward when the actor's actions on the suboptimal opportunity are also suboptimal, reducing gain production to negatively affect the next self-regulation episode by reducing expectations and motivation even further. The result is decreased motivation, infrequent search for new opportunity, reduced engagement of new opportunity, declining gain in resource production, and constrained capacity to self-determine. Left on its own, the negative cycle of self-regulation creates a basis for the sense of helplessness and feeling of despair that characterizes people whose prospects for self-determination have deteriorated.

These cycles of suboptimal adjustment occur when self-regulated problem solving is repeatedly unsuccessful over time—when interaction among the optimality factors of past gain, expectations, choices, and actions work together to accelerate the creation of increasingly suboptimal adjustments. Left on its own, a negative cycle leaves the regulator with little motivation, capacity, or opportunity to direct problem solving toward the capacity building necessary to secure resources that will satisfy one's needs in life. It leaves the regulator bereft of the *experience* of self-determination that is necessary to exercise the *right* to self-determination. The only problems people in this condition can solve are those they are forced to solve to maintain their subsistent adjustment to life's circumstance.

Self-regulation cycles can also lead to opposite end-state patterns of adjustment, for example, when they generate experiences of self-determination and empowerment that build self-esteem and self-respect. During these cycles of interaction among the four optimality factors, feelings of momentum develop because everything goes just as expected. Person sets expectations that are just right, chooses the best option from those available, acts on that option with her best performance, and produces results she expects. Moreover, the positive experience of one self-regulation episode affects the next, enabling Person to repeat the cycle, each time being encouraged to repeat the previous success by setting slightly higher expectations that provide the just-right challenge to motivate her to enhance her capacity further. She feels empowered and perfectly matched with the opportunity she engages. Mihali Csikszentmihalyi (1990) calls this optimal experience "flow":

> The optimal state of inner experience is one in which there is *order in consciousness*. This happens when psychic energy—or attention—is invested in realistic goals, and when skills match the opportunities for action. The pursuit of a goal brings order in awareness because a person must concentrate attention on the task at hand and momentarily forget everything else. These periods of struggling to overcome challenges are what people find to be the most enjoyable times of their lives . . . A person who has achieved control over psychic energy and has invested it in consciously chosen goals cannot help but grow into a more complex being. By stretching skills, by reaching toward higher challenges, such a person becomes an increasingly extraordinary individual. (p. 6)

Central to flow is the sense of power that comes with ordering one's consciousness toward expectations, choices, and performances that produce exactly what one expects and wants from an optimal challenge. It is the same experience Gilbert Brim (1992) describes in the search for those "just manageable difficulties":

> When we win, the response is to increase the degree of difficulty. We set a shorter timetable for the next endeavor, raising expectations of how much we can achieve, even broadening out and adding new goals. We will try to get there earlier or faster, and to get more or better . . .
>
> Winning raises our hopes; losing lowers them. As Tocqueville wrote about democracy in the United States when it was a new nation, social movements are not caused by failure and frustration but spring from rising strength. And so it is today. Recently at Howard University, the leading primarily black university in the United States, students escalated a demonstration after achieving their goal of forcing the resignation of the Republican Party chairman, Lee Atwater, from the college's board of trustees. The protesters went on to disrupt classes and demand assurances of financial aid and improved campus housing. It is when inequality declines that aspirations rise and rebellions occur. T. George Harris, former editor of *Psychology Today,* spoke of this to me as "the snake of hope"; prison riots, he notes, start when the food is getting better, not worse.
>
> There are broad implications here for what happens to people when they are successful at work. Once you get good at a particular job, it no longer takes most of your ability to do it well. So you set your sights higher and push on to more demanding work . . .
>
> But here's the hitch. People can become psychologically trapped by their own success as they race to keep up with the rising expectations bred

by each new achievement. With each success, they raise their level of difficulty, climbing up a ladder of subgoals, moving faster, raising aspirations, and at some point reaching the limit of their capacity. (pp. 31-32)

The experience generated during self-regulation is a function of repeated interaction between capacity and opportunity over time. Consequently, as capacity waxes and wanes, optimalities of opportunity wax and wane; and as optimalities of opportunity increase and decrease, capacities to regulate effectively and efficiently change to create difference experiences. Some of these experiences are empowering, some are discouraging, and some are neither. When capacity and opportunity interact to produce repeated patterns of optimal adjustment and maximum gain, however, individuals have ceased searching for new opportunity for gain because their routines are sufficient to produce the ends they expect to achieve in this domain in life. The same occurs when capacity and opportunity interact to produce repeated patterns of suboptimal adjustment and minimum gain. These persons have also ceased searching for new opportunity because their routines are sufficient to produce the ends they expect to reach in that domain in life. In both of those domains in life, capacity-opportunity interactions stabilize to maintain an accepted and expected exchange with the environment.

This is what persons who are most and least advantaged in society have in common. They are equally motivated to keep what they have. Those at the top have maximized the acquisition of new resources so they regulate their problem solving to maintain access to resources already under their control. Those at the bottom have reached the limits of what they can afford to lose so they regulate their problem solving to maintain access to resources they must have to survive. Psychologically, the motivation of the two groups is similar, although the basis of that motivation is different. People at the top have surplus capacity to prevent the worry of losing what they have, whereas those at the bottom have marginal capacity that creates worry and undermines the basis of their self-confidence and self-respect.

Redress Through the Difference Principle

This is the social problem Rawls's theory of justice intended to solve. A society founded on principles of justice compensates those least advantaged in society for their failure to acquire what they need and want in life by giving them resources they are unable to acquire through their own self-directed effort. It accomplishes this by yoking resource gain produced by the most advantaged to entitlement gain for those least advantaged. Few will argue against a principle such as this that guarantees every member of society a level of security in health, income, and well-being that ensures freedom from oppression due to egregious social and material circumstances of life. In fact, societies routinely claim their moral worth on the basis of the protection they provide against harsh conditions that make life intolerable. Reports of living standards in different countries of the world reflect this interest in baseline conditions of collective support. So when individuals are seen as living substantially below the standard expected for all, we feel obliged to help raise them from these unfortunate circumstances. We feel a collective responsibility to reduce the distance between where they are and where everyone else is.

From this perspective of social justice, one can argue for a minimum level of collective support due all people, regardless of who they are, what they do, or how valuable their contribution is to the common good. Simply being human and a member of the group is sufficient to receive the social support necessary to live a decent and secure life. This is social justice. Rawls claims, and I agree, this assurance should include liberty and self-respect in that these conditions are necessary means for leading a decent life. Individuals least well situated in society deserve as much liberty and self-respect as individuals more favorably situated in that absent either of these experiences life is meaningless. It does not qualify as decent. So the goal of the just society in general and justice as fairness in particular is to ensure that all members of society receive that baseline of support needed to lead a life filled with liberty and self-respect.

The implication of this analysis for our understanding of the effects of capacity-opportunity interactions is that these two ends—economic support and self-respect—cannot be achieved by the same means. Although the difference principle can perhaps guarantee a minimum level of economic support for those least well situated in society, it cannot maximize liberty and self-respect for all. At best, the principle can reduce the economic distance separating individuals in the upper and lower strata of society. But altering the economic distance separating these groups will not enhance their experience of self-determination nor will it alter their feelings of self-respect. For people in least favorable circumstances, feelings of helplessness and hopelessness will persist with or without the difference principle. In fact, application of the principle may exacerbate the condition, for reasons described earlier. Economic gain or loss relative to what others produce will have an adverse effect on the experience of self-determination and the sense of self-respect in that receiving resource gain by means of other people's self-determined acts does not create the sense of control necessary to experience self-determination. David Myers (1992) explains this in the following manner:

> A similar loss of control can exacerbate the stress of poverty. The small effect of money on well-being comes less from enabling us to have what we want than to do what we want—to feel empowered, in control of our lives. Matthew Dumont, a community psychiatrist in Chelsea, which has Massachusetts' lowest-per-person income, reflects on the powerlessness of its distress-prone people:
> "What is poverty? It soon became evident to me that what is pathogenic about it is not merely the lack of money. The amount of money, the buying power, commanded by a welfare recipient in Chelsea would have been like a king's ransom to any member of a thriving hunter-gatherer tribe in the Kalahari. Yet the life of the welfare recipient appears terribly impoverished in contrast to that of the tribe member. A closer observation of life in Chelsea resolves the paradox. Chelsea residents possess material things unknown to the hunter but, despite this [meager] purchasing power, *they experience little control over the circumstances of their lives.* The efforts of the Kalahari hunters, on the other hand, had a direct effect on the shape of their lives and the possibilities of their existence."
> Increasing people's control can noticeably improve their health and morale. One study by Yale psychologist Judith Rodin encouraged nursing home patients to exert more control—to make choices about their environment and to influence policy. As a result, 93 percent became more alert, active, and happy. Similar results have been observed after allowing prisoners to move chairs and control the room lights and TV, and after enabling workers to participate in decision making [italics added]. (pp. 114-115)

Applications of the difference principle do not give impoverished individuals a sense of control over their lives. In fact, it is based on an entirely different rationale—a belief that one person's lack of capacity for self-determined pursuits is the basis for receiving resources from another person who has that capacity. Unfortunately, this rationale is another reminder for those lacking capacity that they do not control what is most important in life.

The difference principle is also insensitive to those conditions of economic difference that no longer demand reduction. What happens, for example, when the difference principle reduces the economic distance separating persons in the lowest and highest strata of society to a point where those in the lowest strata are able to lead a decent life on their own? Does the difference principle cease its difference reductions? Apparently not, because, according to the logic of differences, there will always be stratification of opportunity and outcome separating one group from another. No matter how small the difference separating groups, a discrepancy will remain and the difference principle be applied.

This points to the basic problem with the principle: It is insensitive to its effects on prospects for self-determination. Because its task is splitting differences, as Allen Buchanan (1980) explains in the following:

> The task is never-ending because the representative worst off man, like the Gospel's poor, will always be with us; there will always be a minimum share.... By requiring too much of the socio-economic arrangements, the Difference Principle would require too much of us. To accept a principle which requires that the minimum be continuously raised, no matter what the cost and no matter how high the minimum already is, would be to view society as a monolithic machine straining after an ever-receding production goal. (pp. 34-35)

The basis of these difficulties with Rawls's approach to social redress is a misconception about the nature of the autonomous self, opportunities that encourage expressions of that autonomy, and the consequences emanating from those expressions. Simply stated, the difference principle is indifferent to the causal connections among these three factors because Rawls treats the autonomous self as being independent of opportunity and of the consequences its engagement produces. Moreover, his approach is insensitive to the experience of self-determination created by the interplay between capacity for autonomous thought and action, opportunity for that autonomous thought and action, and outcomes of those autonomous acts. Consequently, he fails to account for how the process of redistribution—via use of the difference principle—will affect the self and its capacity to pursue opportunity for self-determination. In other words, Rawls overlooks the effect of control on the feeling of empowerment that comes when Person has the capacity to use resources to reach desirable ends in life. He also overlooks that without control and absent feelings of empowerment there can be no pursuit of opportunity, and without pursuit of new opportunity, there can be no enhanced capacity.

In the final analysis, then, *control comes from capacity*. People lacking in capacity lack control over their lives, lack motivation to grow and to learn, and feel helpless to act. By contrast, people who grow in capacity feel motivated to act and find ways to succeed. Success increases power to control, stimulates action for gain, and improves capacity for control. Either way the cycle unfolds, capacity to control varies as a consequence, and this variation affects prospects for self-determination.

Capacity and Opportunity

What then is the collective responsibility when it comes to guaranteeing a decent life to all members of the socially just society? If the difference principle is insensitive to prospects for self-determination of least advantaged members, what principle of fairness is responsive? The answer to this question rests with what we understand to be the primary obstacle to self-determination among people who are least advantaged in society— lack of control over the means necessary for the self-determined life. This understanding shifts the emphasis of social redress from distributing outcomes of self-determined pursuits to building capacity for self-determined pursuits. A redress principle that accomplishes this will increase that sense of power necessary for the experience of self-determination that is the basis for self-esteem and self-respect.

Basic to this understanding is acknowledging that the expression of self-determination is dynamic, not static, and that factors contributing to its variation are themselves variable. This means that the experience of self-determination will change within and between individuals over time. Some individuals will be more self-determining in one situation than in another and at one point in their lives more than at another. Groups of individuals will experience variations of self-determination throughout their history as well, experiencing modest control in their lives during some periods and optimal control in others.

Recognizing this is important to understanding that the right and the power to self-determine affect the experience of self-determination as well. So by focusing initially on the experience of self-determination, we can identify those psychological and social factors that affect its variation. This accomplished, we can turn to the relationship between the power and the right to self-determination and how this dynamic affects the experience of self-determination. Chapter 3 describes the effects of various sources of power on the experience of self-determination among different groups, and Chapter 4 describes how variation in the *interaction* between the power

Table 3.1 Typology of Capacity-Opportunity States

	Substantial Opportunity	*Limited Opportunity*
Substantial capacity	Person 1: Maximum control	Person 2: Moderate control
Limited capacity	Person 3: Moderate control	Person 4: Minimum control

and the right to self-determination also affects the experience of self-determination for different groups in society.

The remainder of this chapter describes how personal capacity (power) interacts with social opportunity (right) to alter subsequent capacity and opportunity to self-determination that in turn, creates different experiences of self-determination. These patterns become evident when we take snapshots of various states of self-determination to illustrate different patterns of the self-determined pursuit. The typology for capacity-opportunity variations in Table 3.1 illustrates four such patterns. It distinguishes actors according to their capacity—substantial or limited—and according to their opportunity—substantial or limited. In the first cell, Person 1 experiences maximum control over her environment because in those areas that are most important, Person 1 has substantial capacity and opportunity to get what she needs and wants. In fact, Person 1 has a surplus capacity to pursue new opportunity and has abundant opportunity from which to select options promising to incur low costs, yield high gain, and promise high probability for success. Person 1's prospects for engaging new opportunity are optimal.

Prospects change as we move to the other cells. In cell 2, where Person 2 has substantial capacity but limited opportunity, there are fewer opportunities to produce high gain at low costs with reasonable chance of success. Consequently, Person 2 must reach more deeply into his reserves to convert new opportunity into additional resources. Person 2's prospects are less favorable than Person 1's because he risks depleting his capacity should his pursuit fail to produce the gain he needs. Person 2's limited opportunities increase the chance of failure. A comparable level of risk holds for Person 3 in cell 3 but for different reasons. Person 3's diminished prospects are due to limited capacity rather than limited opportunity. Nevertheless, the consequences for self-determined action are similar to Person 2's because risk also increases and this translates into less favorable prospects for engagement. Person 3's costs increase because of fewer resources to invest in converting new opportunity to resource gain, and this increases risk of failure.

Prospects are lowest in cell 4 in which Person 4 lacks both capacity and opportunity. This is the worst of all possible conditions in that Person 4 has no chance of changing his situation. With limited capacity and limited opportunity, any action undertaken to gain control over additional resources is too risky to consider. Only a desperate person, one who has nothing to lose and everything to gain, is likely to pursue new opportunity. Typically, people in this situation are too impoverished to act effectively any way, which guarantees failure should they pursue new opportunity. Add to this the fear of losing control over resources they still have at their disposal and there is a sufficient deterrent to maintain them in this condition of psychological, social, and economic paralysis.

The typology Table 3.1 suggests is that as levels of capacity and opportunity change individuals move from one experience of self-determination to another because an increase or decrease in capacity or opportunity triggers a new pattern of adjustment and a different experience of self-determination. Moreover, an accumulation of experiences in any of the four conditions is likely to affect a person's long-term sense of control and experience of self-determination corresponding to the experience identified in each cell. People in cell 1 experience maximum control over life's circumstances, those in cells 2 and 3 alternate between gain and loss experience and moderate control over their circumstances, whereas those in cell 4 experience minimum control over their lives.

The following propositions summarize these predicted relationships between capacity, opportunity, and experience of self-determination.

> The greater the capacity and opportunity to determine one's ends in life, the more frequent the experience of self-determination and the greater the sense of control over one's life.
>
> The more frequent the experience of self-determination and the greater the sense of control over one's life, the greater the capacity and opportunity to self-determine one's ends in life.

To extend the analysis, we can also say that one's personal, social, economic, and technical circumstances in life affect the capacity to self-determine. These circumstances affect one's capacity to secure access to those resources necessary to achieve individually defined ends in life that are personally satisfying. Whereas one combination of these circumstances may allow Person to interact with opportunity to produce the gain she needs to get what she wants in life, another combination may constrain Person from interacting with the environment at all. For every individual then, there is a set of circumstances that promotes interaction between capacity and opportunity. For every individual, there are circumstances that make prospects for self-determination optimal. Moreover, under these circumstances, Person is most likely to use her existing capacity to pursue new opportunity. When this occurs and the pursuit of gain is successful, an experience of self-determination results and Person feels empowered. She experiences an enhanced sense of control and is encouraged to engage new opportunity again.

The experience of self-determination motivates individuals to act on new opportunity. This experience is most likely when conditions of capacity and opportunity are just right, because just-right combinations of capacity and opportunity tell Person that her prospects are good for translating opportunity into gain. With repeated success in self-determined pursuits, Person comes to believe in herself, in her capacity to get what she needs and wants in life, and in her right to pursue ends that give her life meaning and significance.[2] In other words, accumulated gain through self-determined pursuit increases self-esteem—the primary good Rawls claims should be guaranteed by the just society.

Understanding this connection between experiences of self-determination and feelings of self-esteem reveals the error in claiming social policy can intervene in people's lives to create the experience of self-determination and generate feelings of self-esteem. Experience and feelings are not distributable commodities to be governed by social policies of the just society. They are *consequences* of individual thought and action. Self-esteem, self-efficacy, and self-respect emanate from the experience of self-determination. Consequently they depend on actions to enhance one's capacity to access previously unavailable resources. So if there is no action to enhance capacity, to stimulate personal growth, and to promote new learning, then there can be no experience of self-determination, and there can be no feeling of esteem, efficacy, or respect.

On the other hand, when there is self-determined action and when there is the experience of benefit through an enhanced self, then the derivative feelings of self-esteem, self-efficacy, and self-respect create a sense of personal power and moral legitimacy that motivates pursuit of new opportunity. Then experiences of self-determination and feelings of self-confidence can combine to motivate new levels of self-determined action, gain, and

experience, as suggested by Person 1 in Table 3.1. Under these circumstances, a cycle of accumulated advantage is likely because each increment
in self-esteem and self-determination experience accumulates to build
confidence in one's capacity to think and act effectively in adjusting to
life's challenging opportunity. Nathaniel Branden[3] (1994) describes these
cumulative effects as follows:

> To trust one's mind and to know that one is worthy of happiness is the
> essence of self-esteem.
>
> The power of this conviction about oneself lies in the fact that it is
> more than a judgment or a feeling. It is a motivator. It inspires behavior.
>
> In turn, it is directly affected by how we act. Causation flows in both
> directions. There is a continuous feedback loop between our actions in the
> world and our self-esteem. The level of our self-esteem influences how
> we act, and how we act influences the level of our self-esteem.
>
> If I trust my mind and judgment, I am more likely to operate as a
> thinking being. Exercising my ability to think, bringing appropriate aware-
> ness to my activities, my life works better. This reinforces trust in my
> mind. If I distrust my mind, I am more likely to be mentally passive, to
> bring less awareness than I need to my activities, and less persistence in
> the face of difficulties. When my actions lead to disappointing or painful
> results, I feel justified in distrusting my mind.
>
> With high self-esteem, I am more likely to persist in the face of
> difficulties. With low self-esteem, I am more likely to give up or go
> through the motions of trying without really giving my best. . . . If I
> persevere, the likelihood is that I will succeed more often than I fail. If I
> don't, the likelihood is that I will fail more often than I succeed. Either
> way, my view of myself will be reinforced.
>
> If I respect myself and require that others deal with me respectfully,
> I send out signals and behave in ways that increase the likelihood that
> others will respond appropriately. When they do, I am reinforced and
> confirmed in my initial belief. If I lack self-respect and consequently
> accept discourtesy, abuse, or exploitation from others as natural, I uncon-
> sciously transmit this, and some people will treat me at my self-estimate.
> When this happens, and I submit to it, my self-respect deteriorates still
> more.
>
> The value of self-esteem lies not merely in the fact that it allows us
> to *feel* better but that it allows us to *live* better—to respond to challenges
> and opportunities more resourcefully and more appropriately [italics
> added]. (pp. 4-5)

As this analysis suggests, Person's capacity has two components—an
experience component that acts on and reacts to a *resource* component.
Person moves from one capacity state to another as experience and re-

sources interact to expand or contract Person's control over circumstances that affect what she needs and wants in life. The experience component of this capacity determines how Person will manage her resources. More precisely, it determines how Person will construct means-ends causal chains to get what she needs and wants in life. The rules Person uses to create these causal sequences constitute her beliefs about her capacity and how it interacts with environmental circumstance to promote or constrain her prospects for getting what she needs and wants. The information Person collects about specific environmental circumstances that will yield what Person expects from actions she proposes constitutes her knowledge about her opportunities. The actions Person takes in converting an existing circumstance into an optimal circumstance constitute her ability to act effectively and efficiently. And the emotions evoked while thinking, planning, and acting constitute Person's feelings about her position in the environment.

The resource component of Person's capacity includes the personal, social, economic, and technical resources Person uses to change her environment. Persons' personal resources include the time and behavior that she uses to make environmental circumstances more favorable for gain production; her social resources include the time and behavior of other people that Person uses to optimize environmental opportunity; Person's economic resources are those generalized resources that she uses to gain control over resources that Person does not have but needs to alter the environment; and Person's technical resources are the techniques and procedures that Person can use to solve specific types of problems while optimizing environmental circumstance.

In combination, these experiences and resources constitute Person's capacity to self-determine. Consequently, an increase or decrease in either will produce a commensurate change in Person's prospects for self-determination. Therefore, Person can increase her capacity to self-determine by enhancing her experience that can occur by changing her beliefs about the causal forces operating in the environment, by improving her knowledge about opportunities presented by these environmental circumstances, by increasing her ability to act effectively, and by building feelings of self-esteem, self-efficacy, and self respect. These four areas of experience constitute the broad spectrum of self-improvement domains that contribute to Person's capacity to self-determine over time. But they are not the only means of enhancing capacity.

Person can also enhance her capacity by augmenting resources. This can be accomplished by increasing the personal, social, economic, and technical resources Person has at her disposal to secure what she needs and wants in life. Person can increase personal resources by arranging time and behavior so that she has more of each—so that there is a surplus to invest in new opportunity for resource gain, for example. For it is *surplus resources* that Person needs to expand her capacity through investments in the conversion of suboptimal opportunity into optimal opportunity. The same is true for social resources. Person can increase her capacity by getting others to use their time and behavior to satisfy her needs. She can do this by exchanging resources with them—giving others time and behavior to help them reach their goals in return for their time and behavior to help her pursue her goals. If Person negotiates these exchanges to her advantage, she can maximize gain and minimize cost that yield a net gain in time and behavior that will enhance her capacity.

A third way of enhancing resources is through economic gain. Rather than exchanging directly with others, Person engages opportunities in the marketplace to secure liquid assets she can then use to secure other resources that are lacking. Again, Person strives to maximize gain and minimize costs during those exchanges so that a net gain in resource will enhance her capacity. Finding a job that requires fewer hours for the same pay as the present job nets a resource gain because it frees time and behavior to pursue other opportunities.

A fourth way of enhancing resource capacity is to gain access to those technical methods and materials that solve specific types of problems effectively and efficiently. People with access to these resources gain time and increase success because the methods they use produce reliable and accurate results. Use of a calculator is a time saver and produces more accurate results, as is use of a personal computer, which solves problems more quickly and effectively than any individual or group can accomplish working at full capacity. People with access to technical resources such as these increase their capacity in that it allows them to spend time and material resource on problems that do not have proven ways of being resolved.

In sum, Person's capacity to self-determine depends on the experience she has in managing the resources that are under her control. She will succeed in enhancing her capacity to the extent her experience and resources interact to yield optimal adjustments and maximum gains. In that when Person's adjustment is optimal and prospects are good, she will have sufficient resources available to pursue new opportunity and succeed. Moreover, the experience resulting from these transactions affect how she

Table 3.2 Types of Experience-Resource Interactions Affecting Person's Capacity to Self-Determine

	Resources			
Experience	*Personal*	*Social*	*Economic*	*Technical*
Beliefs	1	2	3	4
Knowledge	5	6	7	8
Ability	9	10	11	12
Feelings	13	14	15	16

will use the resources she has in the future. Accordingly, we can expect that the more successful the experience in a past exchange, the more likely the effective and efficient use of resources in the next transaction; the more effective and efficient the use of resources in the next transaction, the more likely the optimal adjustment and maximum gain.

Table 3.2 classifies these interactions between experience and resources by locating the areas (cells) where they affect the level of an individual's capacity to self-determine. As indicated in the table, experience (column 1) affects Person's management of her resources by influencing (a) Persons's *beliefs* about how the world works and how she can use personal, social, economic, and technical resources to produce the changes she wants in that world (row 1); (b) Person's *knowledge* about the resources she will need to change a particular set of environmental circumstances to get what she needs and wants (row 2); (c) Person's *ability* to translate what she knows about her resources and environmental circumstance to make those circumstances more favorable for producing the gain she seeks (row 3); and (d) Person's *feelings* of self-esteem, self-efficacy, and self-respect that result from her efforts to control environmental circumstances in pursuit of her own ends (row 4). Each cell in the table represents an interaction between one of these experiences and one of these resources.

From this, we can see how pursuit outcomes that fall short of expectations could alter our experience by changing our beliefs about the causal factors operating in the environment, by changing our knowledge about opportunities for using our resources to get what we need and want from that environment, by changing our ability to perform essential tasks in the conversion of existing circumstance to favorable opportunity, and by changing our feelings of confidence and esteem about our transactions with the environment. For example, when results frequently fall short of expectations, we may begin to believe the world and our place in it is much different than what we once thought. We may think that perhaps what we have to offer in exchange for what we want is not valuable and consequently, there is little we can do to get what we want. We may conclude that we simply lack the resources and opportunities to adjust well. Negative results can also affect the availability of resources that we have to alter subsequent pursuits, for example, by reducing the time and behavior available for new pursuits, by reducing the time and behavior available from other people to help us in those pursuits, by reducing the financial assets available for investing in opportunity, or by demanding use of technical resources that are expensive for us to acquire and use.

Taken together, Person's capacity for self-determination will change in some measure after each transaction with the environment. If that capacity should become more constrained as a function of a previous pursuit, Person's prospects for subsequent pursuits would become less optimal. Moreover, if Person should fail repeatedly to meet expectations for gain in subsequent pursuits, her resources for engaging new opportunity would decline accordingly, and her beliefs, knowledge, abilities, and self-perceptions would adjust to match this decline. But by the end of the decline, these adjustments in experiences and resources would stabilize in that Person's expectations and results would finally match. At that point, Person would have lowered her expectations to match her accomplishments.

We can also analyze this interaction between capacity and opportunity as exchange between what individuals have to invest or give to the environment and what a resulting change in environmental circumstance would give in return (which is what the actor hopes to gain). From this perspective, exchanges netting greater gain than loss expand Person's capacity, whereas exchanges netting greater loss than gain deplete her capacity. So when Person compares her experiences and resources before and after an environmental exchange, she concludes whether it was an empowering or debilitating experience. When exchange outcomes are frequently empowering, Person accumulates gain and feels good about her prospects for future engagement. Her enhanced capacity allows her to pursue new opportunities more successfully. When outcomes are frequently debilitating, she feels frustrated and ineffective in that after each transaction she has even fewer resources for subsequent investment. This constrains Person's capacity, reduces the number of opportunities she can

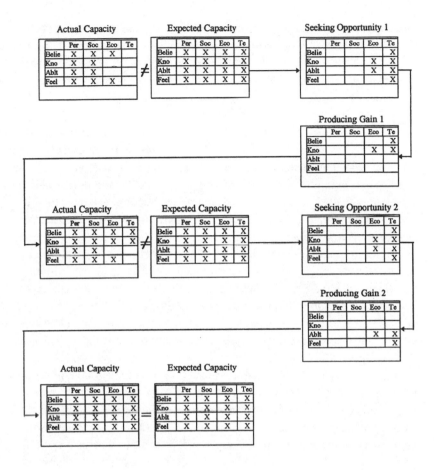

Figure 3.2. Self-Regulated Problem Solving to Meet a Goal

engage in, and decreases her chances of success. Person's prospects for self-determination have declined.

Figure 3.2 illustrates the mechanics of this process of enhancing capacity through engagement of new opportunity. It begins when Person recognizes that she does not have the capacity to get what she needs and wants in life—when she recognizes that actual capacity does not equal the capacity necessary to reach those ends in life. The figure illustrates these deficiencies with six empty cells. Person pursues Opportunity 1, which promises to provide the gain she needs to convert present capacity into an expected capacity (the capacity she needs). After engaging that opportunity, she produces a net gain in capacity but still lacks sufficient resources to get what she wants (three cells remain empty). So Person pursues Opportunity 2, which has the same prospects for gain as Opportunity 1. This time Person succeeds and fulfills her capacity to pursue the end she has in mind.

This illustrates how self-regulated problem solving to meet a goal—which is the mechanism that produces variation in the experience of self-determination—can also be construed as interaction between Person and her environment. Here, instead of focusing on Person as a problem solver, the analysis focuses on *net change* in Person's capacity to self-regulate following a transaction with the environment because each exchange constitutes an attempt to gain control over a resource that is important for securing a particular end in life. It is also an occasion for gain or loss in net capacity to engage subsequent environmental opportunity. The figure illustrates one of these episodes. When many exchanges occur over extended periods and when the same individuals experience success, then patterns of positive experience and resource gain accumulate that differentially favor prospects for self-determination for the successful over the less successful.

The primary cause of these differential prospects for self-determination is the *interaction effect* that occurs between capacity and opportunity. It works in the following manner. When there is change in an individual's capacity or a change in an environmental opportunity, a *discrepancy* between expected and actual capacity develops and this discrepancy motivates pursuit and engagement of new opportunity. Following the pursuit of opportunity, a *second discrepancy* may develop as well. This one occurs between the expected gain and the gain actually resulting from the pursuit. This discrepancy motivates additional adjustment that commences yet another cycle of pursuit. These two discrepancy conditions feed on each other to motivate repeated pursuit that accelerates change in prospects for self-determination. The process continues until expectations match outcomes and actual capacity equals needed capacity. It is in these relatively stable periods of equilibrium that (a) Person has the resources she needs to gain access to goods and ends she desires *and* (b) she knows what actions to take to produce the expected results.

The implication of this explanation is that if the primary justification for instituting the just society is to ensure equal distributions of self-esteem and self-respect among all members of the collective, then institutions in the just society must consider the effects of these capacity-opportunity interactions on the experience of self-determination. For as we have seen, self-esteem and self-respect are not external commodities to be redistributed in the same way income or wealth might be redistributed. Self-esteem and self-respect are part of Person's capacity—more specifically they are part of Person's experience. Person's resources are also part of her capacity. Consequently, they too are unavailable for confiscation and redistribution by the state. Person's experiences and resources define how she deals with the external world to get what she needs and wants. They define who she is as a self-determining person.

What is excluded from Person's capacity is, of course, opportunity. Person does not have a claim on opportunity; it is not a part of Person's capacity. Opportunity is merely the occasion for the expression of her capacity. It is a more or less favorable occasion in life during which Person can use her experiences and resources to alter an environmental circumstance to get what she needs and wants in life. By acting in her own interests during those moments in space and circumstance, Person can make her prospects more favorable for gaining access to what she needs in life.

On these points, as we saw in Chapter 1, equal opportunity theory departs from both Rawls's and Nozick's conceptions of what constitutes Person. Rawls diminishes the conception of Person to a rational entity that is morally disconnected from experience, resource, and opportunity that makes each of these goods available for redistribution according to principles of the just state. Nozick expands the conception of Person to include experience, resources, and opportunity, leaving nothing for redistribution by the state. Equal opportunity theory strikes a midpoint by claiming *opportunity alone* is external to Person, even though the judgment of its favorableness for gain production—its optimality—is Person's.

Given this conception of self as composed of experience *and* resources, fairness is not to be found by changing the self, for example, by equalizing experiences or resources in some respect. Because doing this violates what constitutes a person—what identifies an individual as having unique experience and accomplishment worthy of respect. Person's capacities to self-determine depend on her experiences, resources, and how she uses them to become what she values most. Given all persons are who they are *because* of accumulated experience and acquired resources over a lifetime, there can be no external manipulation of those self-defining components without violating one's sense of autonomy. This would be, as Nozick asserts, a denial of the right to liberty that even Rawls argues is the first principle of the just society. Nozick, therefore, is right when he argues that Person is what Person gets on her own or through her legitimate exchange with others. Equal opportunity theory, as Nozick's entitlement theory, argues for a conception of the self that includes experiences and resources or properties acquired in accordance with fair principles of acquisition and transfer. But unlike Nozick's theory, equal opportunity theory does not include opportunity among those properties defining Person's capacity. The reason, as we shall see in the next chapter, is that opportunity ownership accumulates advantage to the disadvantage of others, which produces egregious harm to others. It deprives others of their right to self-determination.

Notes

1. Beauchamp is citing from Rawls, (1977), "A Kantian Conception of Equality," *Cambridge Review, 95.*
2. Reprinted with permission of Greenwood Publishing Group, Inc. Westport, CT. Copyright © 1993.
3. From *The Six Pillars of Self-Esteem* by Nathaniel Branden. Copyright © 1994 by Nathaniel Branden. Used by permission of Bantam Books, a division of Bantam Doubleday Dell Publishing Group, Inc.
Branden (1994) defines self-esteem as (a) confidence in our ability to think, confidence in our ability to cope with the basic challenges of life, and (b) confidence in our right to be successful and happy, the feeling of being worthy, deserving, entitled to assert our needs and wants, achieve our values, and enjoy the fruits of our efforts (p. 4).

Freedom as Power

In an attempt to understand the discrepancy between the right to self-determination and the experience of self-determination, I have considered three explanations. The first explanation was John Rawls's theory of social justice that argues that membership in the human group is sufficient to entitle everyone to the right and the experience of self-determination. All members of the group deserve a fair chance to pursue personally desirable ends in life regardless of their individual circumstances, status in the group, or ability to contribute to group goals. Being human and a member are sufficient to entitle everyone to the personal, social, economic, and technical resources necessary for a decent life. The group has a moral obligation to provide these essentials for everyone on an equal basis. Fairness in social life occurs when societies regulate social relationships toward this end. The two conditions best suited for this regulation ensure maximum liberty for all by permitting social and economic inequalities only to the extent that they benefit everyone.

Rawls offers the difference principle to produce this condition of justice. He claims it will reduce the economic and social distance separating the rich and powerful from the poor and powerless by yoking the success of the most advantaged with the failure of the least advantaged. Chapter 2 challenged this prediction. Although the difference principle may be effective in increasing economic gain for the poor, it is likely to have the opposite effect on their freedom and self-respect. For these goods, which Rawls regards as primary, the difference principle will actually reduce the experience of self-determination and undermine the basis for self-respect. People receiving redress through the difference principle may be better off economically, but they will feel less powerful and less confident socially and psychologically. They will feel more dependent on the group and less effective on their own. Moreover, they will feel envious of those on whom they must depend for collateral gain through the yoked contingency. They may even come to believe that if they had the same resources and opportunities as the most advantaged, they too could become powerful benefactors rather than powerless beneficiaries. In sum, excusable envy will increase in direct proportion to the need for social redress administered through the difference principle.

Problems of allocative justice do not resolve themselves simply because they emanate from a social structure functioning according to the difference principle, as Rawls claims. The reason for this as explained in the previous chapter is that people who lack control over their lives are unhappy when they compare themselves with others who have that power and control. No amount of income transfer will satisfy this sense of injustice that comes from knowing that for some members in the society controlling access to the good in life is much easier and much more probable. Dissatisfaction does not come solely because some members of society have greater material wealth, are more successful, and are perceived to be more deserving. It also comes about because some members of society have a better chance of leading their life the way they want.

This is the basis for the excusable envy that does not disappear through applications of Rawls's difference principle. Recall David Myers's (1992, pp. 114-115) analysis of the effects of income on the sense of control: "The small effect of money on well-being comes less from enabling us to have what we want than to do what we want—*to feel empowered, in control of our lives*" [italics added]. The issue is not, as Rawls implies, the amount of social and economic goods one receives through transfers resulting from applications of the difference principle. The issue is what access to those goods does to one's sense of control over the means that are necessary for leading the decent life. Rawls's theory of social justice does not solve this problem of allocative justice. The least advantaged in life experience excusable envy even though their economic prospects are slightly better than they would have been without those benefits. This is because their relative control over life continues to be diminished compared to control others experience in life. People with less control in their life are less powerful in an absolute sense, too. Consequently, they continue to feel impoverished, powerless, and hopeless. In Rawls's (1971) own words, they

> lack a sure confidence in their own value and in their ability to do anything worthwhile . . . [and] many occasions arise when this psychological condition is experienced as painful and humiliating. The discrepancy between oneself and others is made visible by the social structure and style of life of one's society. The less fortunate are therefore often forcibly reminded of their situation, sometimes leading them to an even lower estimation of themselves and their mode of living. . . . they see their social position as allowing no constructive alternative to opposing the favored circumstances of the more advantaged. (p. 535)

The second explanation for the discrepancy between the right and the experience of self-determination was Nozick's theory of entitlement that claims that Person is entitled to whatever she can acquire through her own means or through legitimate exchange with others. This theory affords no occasion for collective intervention on behalf of those least advantaged in life in that only individuals can decide whether to assist others in need. According to justice as entitlement, there is no moral obligation to help others in that individuals get what they deserve through their own enterprise; they deserve what they acquire according to their capacity to self-determine.

This conception of the just society views social life as composed of a multitude of exchanges among individuals pursuing ends in life that correspond to their various levels of personal capacity. Moreover, individuals are responsible for these differences in capacity, opportunity, and outcome, and they exhibit this responsibility by exchanging resources with others as they attempt to expand their capacity to get what they need and want in life. Finally, no external agency such as the state can interfere with these fair exchanges because this would violate Person's autonomy and right to self-determination. That people have different capacities, opportunities, and outcomes is a fact that has no bearing on fairness. Accordingly, justice is from each as they choose, to each as they are chosen:

> From each according to what he chooses to do, to each according to what
> he makes for himself (perhaps with the contracted aid of others) and what
> others choose to do for him and choose to give him of what they've been
> given previously (under this maxim) and haven't yet expended or trans-
> ferred. (Nozick, 1974, p. 160)

Resolving the discrepancy between the right and the experience of
self-determination, therefore, depends on individual not collective action.
Rights do not come from above, gracing and entitling every member of society
based on some universal, normative principle. Rights are earned and once
earned are appropriated by the person who has earned them. Rights emanate
from specific transactions initiated and consummated between individuals
voluntarily entering into transactions whereby Person gives a portion of her
resources to Other in exchange for a portion of Other's resources given to
Person. Legitimacy in exchange occurs when Person agrees to respect Other's
claims in one area of opportunity in return for Other's agreement to respect
Person's claims in another area of opportunity.

The result divides resource opportunities into entitlements and responsibilities, with Person's entitlement to opportunity X depending on Other's
responsibility for permitting Person access to opportunity X, and Other's
entitlement to opportunity Y depending on Person's responsibility for
allowing Other access to opportunity Y. In other words, Person and Other
agree to respect each other's rights with regard to the distribution of
opportunities for access to various resources. What is fair is what is agreed
on in the distribution of opportunities for accessing different resources.
What ends up in Person's possession is justly hers because it was obtained
through a fair exchange with Other in accordance with Nozick's principles
of acquisition and transfer. Similarly, what ends up in Other's possession
is fairly his for the same reason. No opportunity can be distributed any
other way. To do so would be to violate a past agreement justly arrived at
through negotiations between free and equal actors.

The implication of this line of reasoning is that there can be no
discrepancy between the right and the experience of self-determination in
that what is right is what has been determined to be a right through past
acts of self-determination. Rights are entitled opportunities derived from
fair exchanges between individuals acting in accordance with Nozick's
principles of acquisition and transfer. Consequently, what becomes Person's right depends on what she is capable of securing through a negotiation with Other, and what is negotiated with Other depends on Person's
capacity and opportunity for self-determination. If Person lacks capacity

and opportunity to determine her own future by negotiating a new opportunity with Other, then she will not be able to secure that new opportunity. Consequently, Other will be under no obligation to respect that expected opportunity, and Person will never be able to claim it as her right. Given that Person lacks the right of access to a resource opportunity in question and given that she lacks the capacity to pursue that right through an exchange with Other, Person can never claim a discrepancy between the right and the experience of self-determination. She lacks both the right and the experience of self-determination, which obviates her claim to resolve a discrepancy.

The conclusion to be drawn from this analysis is that Person will have only those opportunities or rights she can control with her existing capacity—through use experiences and existing resources. She can have only what she can get, and what she cannot get, she cannot have. Person's rights are only those opportunities she can get others to acknowledge and respect due to her own power in exchange. Similarly, Person's obligations to Other are what she must acknowledge and respect due to Other's claims, which are a function of his power in exchange. So if Person is less powerful than Other in their exchange relationship, Person's rights and responsibilities will reflect this power imbalance—giving Person relatively fewer entitlements and more responsibilities and Other more entitlements and fewer responsibilities. But because the match between the experience and right of self-determination is complete with respect to Person and Other, there is no discrepancy. There may be *imbalance in power* and in the distribution of what they agree to, but both rights and experiences will match on either side of the equation.

If the distribution of freedom through self-determination is explained using Nozick's theory, one is forced to conclude there can never be a discrepancy between the right and the experience. Person's power matches her rights in that her power produces those rights through exchange with others. Person owns her capacities and opportunities in that she has secured them through the marketplace of social exchange. Moreover, they define what Person is as well—the sum of her experiences, resources, and opportunities or rights. Opportunities are as much a part of Person's identity as are experiences and personal, social, economic, and technical resources. All opportunities and resources are appropriated through social exchange:

> The major objection to speaking of everyone's having a right to various
> things such as equality of opportunity, life, and so on, and enforcing this

right, is that these "rights" require a substructure of things and materials and actions; and other people may have rights and entitlements over these. No one has a right to something whose realization requires certain uses of things and activities that other people have rights and entitlements over. Other people's rights and entitlements to particular things (that pencil, their body, and so on) and how they choose to exercise these rights and entitlements fix the external environment of any given individual and the means that will be available to him. If his goal requires the use of means which others have rights over, he must enlist their voluntary cooperation. Even to exercise his right to determine how something he owns is to be used may require other means he must acquire a right to, for example, food to keep him alive; he must put together, with the cooperation of others, a feasible package. (Nozick, 1974, p. 238)

The logic of entitlement theory preempts any consideration of social redress on the basis of discrepancies between rights and experiences of self-determination. This is because the first conclusion to be drawn from the theory concerning redress is that what one has is what one has earned. What one has earned is what one deserves in a moral and practical sense. Those who have accumulated gain through exchange are meritorious morally and practically because they have proved their worth through the marketplace of social and economic exchange. They have demonstrated their capacity to get what they need and want in life through exchange of resources with others. The same logic applies to those with less capacity and fewer opportunities and rights. They have proved themselves to be less capable in the marketplace of social exchange due to the relatively fewer entitlements and greater responsibilities they have accumulated through interaction with others. Justice is satisfied in both cases. The less fortunate earn a limited set of rights and an expanded set of obligations commensurate with their capacity, and the more fortunate earn an enhanced set of rights and a limited set of obligations commensurate with their capacity.

The social redress recommended by this approach, to the extent there is any, is voluntary assistance through exchange between individuals who are unequal in power and resource. Even so, both parties benefit from the redress in that it is still an exchange. In this exchange, however, the more powerful benefit by receiving gratitude and deference from the less powerful who receive temporary economic relief. The problem with this mode of redress is that it, too, promotes rather than reduces the basis for excusable envy and decreases rather than increases the basis of self-respect. Although less coercive than Rawls's difference principle that forces the more advantaged to give a portion of their gain to the less advantaged, the voluntary transaction has the same effect of reinforcing feelings of helplessness and impoverishment among its beneficiaries. Receiving charity does little to improve prospects for self-determination.

The third explanation for the discrepancy between the right and the experience of self-determination was proposed by equal opportunity theory, which claims the source of the problem to be a lack of capacity and lack of opportunity to self-determine. The theory argues that all societies have persons who lack capacity to self-determine, that all societies generate unequal opportunities to self-determine, and as a consequence, all societies have individuals who lack both capacity and opportunity to self-determine. Societies claiming a universal right to self-determination, therefore, should reduce the discrepancy between the right and the experience by optimizing prospects for self-determination among the least advantaged members of society. Finally, this optimization of prospects can be accomplished by enhancing capacities and improving opportunities to self-determine among those lacking the experience of self-determination.

Although this perspective shares the basic premise of Rawls and Nozick that all persons have a right to choose their own plans for leading the good life, it departs from that common premise by distinguishing between individual capacity and environmental opportunity and then by claiming that lack of self-determination is due to interaction between that capacity and opportunity. This contrasts Rawls's perspective that affixes responsibility for failure of the least advantaged with the collective alone and Nozick's perspective that affixes responsibility for failure with the individual alone. The basis for these different views rests with their definitions of what constitutes the individual. Whereas Rawls defines the individual as what is left after one's experiences and resources are deemed morally arbitrary in determining what one has and what one deserves in life and whereas Nozick defines the individual as being all of what Rawls excludes, including experiences, resources, and opportunities, equal opportunity theory defines Person as including only experiences and resources. It excludes opportunities that define those environmental circumstances from which Person infers her prospects to be favorable or unfavorable on a continuum identified by the phrase *optimalities of opportunity*. According to this view, opportunities are circumstances in time and space where Person can use her experience and resources to gain new experience and to acquire new resources. But these opportunities or circumstances are not Person's in any moral sense. They are simply present or not in an empirical sense.

This perspective is supported by a theory of the self that describes the psychological conditions determining the likelihood individuals will pursue opportunity and, as a consequence, gain experience and resource for subsequent self-determined pursuits. The theory explains how various inferences regarding the favorability of a specific environmental circumstance—its optimality of opportunity—affects the likelihood of a self-determined pursuit. For example, we learned from self-regulation theory that an individual's experience, expectations for future gain, choices, and performance affect one's gain toward important ends in one's life. When all four conditions are optimal, gain toward a given end is maximum, and the experience of self-determination is sufficiently empowering to propel another pursuit and to add another episode of self-determination to the experiential baseline. We also know that when all four conditions are suboptimal, gain toward desirable ends in life is unlikely, as is the experience of self-determination. This causes prospects for engaging subsequent pursuits to decline as well. So by examining Person's experiences, we can gain insight regarding her capacity to self-determine. When Person manages her resources effectively and efficiently, she optimizes adjustments and maximizes gain. In other words, Person does the best she can with the opportunities that are available to her. Person uses experience optimally by expecting and getting as much as is possible, given the environmental circumstance defining her opportunities.

But even when Person adjusts optimally to her circumstances, even when she does everything possible to lead the self-determined life, opportunities can function to constrain her capacity and to diminish her sense of power by limiting the results. When these engagements with suboptimal opportunity occur repeatedly by demanding more experience and greater resources than she has, Person's capacity to pursue her own ends diminishes. In this case, interaction between her capacity and opportunity causes her to believe less in herself, it causes her to underestimate what she can get from the external world, and it encourages her to settle for short-term gain rather than long-term fulfillment. This pattern of interaction between capacity and opportunity discourages Person from doing her very best in that the odds of success are the very worst. Over time, these unfavorable prospects slowly but inexorably reduce Person's capacity to adjust optimally to any opportunity. At some end point, Person is no longer able to think and to act effectively and efficiently to get what she wants because she lacks both capacity and opportunity. She is unable to enhance her capacity or to improve her opportunity on her own, and improvement of one or both of these is necessary for the experience of self-determination.

The explanation for the state of impoverishment is the same as for the state of empowerment. Both were described in Table 3.1, with the empowerment state leading to accumulated gain and favorable opportunity (cell 1), an intermediate state (cells 2 and 3) leading to a mixture of gain and loss resulting in a moderately favorable opportunity, and a state of impoverishment (cell 4) leading to cumulated loss and unfavorable opportunity. The empowerment pattern maximized opportunity control, the intermediate state yielded moderate opportunity control, and the impoverished state minimized opportunity control. The classification captured important differences in the experience of self-determination for those persons who have optimal capacity and favorable opportunity (cell 1) and for those who have suboptimal capacity and unfavorable opportunity (cell 4). Individuals in the optimal condition can predict and control opportunity for gain and those in the suboptimal situation cannot. Moreover, the former can maintain access to the goods they desire, whereas the latter lose access to those goods they deem necessary for decent living.

This analysis holds as well when the context for gaining control over opportunity is the marketplace of social exchange—the context Nozick prefers when arguing for allocative justice through application of entitlement principles. Here individuals and the resources they control constitute mutually advantageous opportunities, given that Person and Other can agree on how much of Person's resources should go to Other and how much of Other's resources should go to Person. The basis for determining what will be agreed on is how much Person needs of the resource Other controls and how much Other needs of the resource Person controls. In other words, the exchange will reflect the power imbalance created when Person or Other has an alternative for obtaining the valued good. For example, if Person has more alternatives for obtaining the good she wants than Other has, then Person has an advantage and can offer less for the good Other has to offer than what Other can offer Person for the good she has to offer. Although Person and Other may still agree to exchange resources, the resulting transaction will reflect the power imbalance by costing Person less and Other more.

Exchanges are inequitable when the capacities and opportunities of the actors are different. When one actor has greater opportunity control than another or when one actor has greater capacity than another, then the resulting power imbalance will give the better situated actor easier access to resources held by the less well situated actor. Although this condition is unlikely to be socially constraining for either actor when their exchanges

with each other are intermittent and transitory, it becomes socially significant when these same actors are connected frequently in that way. Then
accumulated advantage favors the better situated and accumulated disadvantage penalizes the less well situated. The net effect is a change in
prospects for self-determination that differentiates the control each experiences over the means necessary for producing desirable ends in life.

Individuals with the greatest capacity and most favorable opportunity
experience accelerated increases in their control over the means of producing what they want in life, individuals with only moderate capacity and
moderately favorable opportunity experience a gradual increase in their
control over the means of gain production, and individuals with the least
capacity and least favorable opportunity experience an exponential decrease in their control over the means of productive gain. Eventually,
however, all three groups experience a stable ratio—an equilibrium—of
cost-gain exchanges with their social environment representing a consistent level of control over the means necessary for producing what they need
and want in life. At this point, one predicts that those in the most favorable
positions will experience high prospects for self-determination, those in
moderately favorable positions will experience moderate prospects for
self-determination, and those in the least favorable positions will experience low prospects for self-determination.

Figure 4.1 illustrates these predictions for the experience of self-
determination for the four capacity-opportunity types described in Table 3.1.
Figure 4.1 shows that for any given pursuit, individuals appear to have equal
prospects for self-determination because during the initial stage of pursuit they
are equally ignorant about what they must do to get what they want. Each actor
explores the environment, considers options, develops plans to pursue the best
prospects, takes action, and then adjusts to results. This pattern changes,
however, when each actor repeats this searching, choosing, acting, and adjusting to improve prospects for self-determination.

Figure 4.1 illustrates these repeated episodes of self-regulated problem
solving to reach self-determined ends in life. During the early stages of these
pursuits, there is little evidence of change in prospects for self-determination,
as indicated by the common line of progress showing comparable prospect
levels for all actors. Only after many episodes is it evident that some individuals have improved their chances of getting what they want, as indicated by the
new trajectories for the different groups. For the first group, the change in
prospects indicates an accelerated increase in control over the means of
productive gain; for the second and third groups, the change reflects an

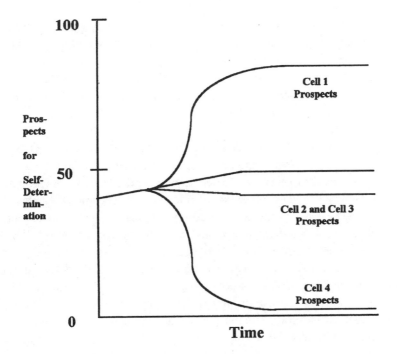

Figure 4.1. Four Trajectories for Prospects for Self-Determination

incremental change in control over the means for productive gain; and for the fourth group, the change indicates an exponential decline in control over the means necessary for producing desired gain.

The factors responsible for these different trajectories are indicated by the cell prospects attached to each. Cell 1 prospects (from Table 3.1) indicate that a condition of substantial capacity and optimal opportunity is responsible for the accelerated prospects trajectory. Cell 2 and 3 prospects, attached to the middle groups, indicate conditions of substantial capacity and suboptimal opportunity and limited capacity and optimal opportunity are responsible for incremental increase and decrease prospects trajectories. Cell 4 prospects, attached to the last group, indicate a condition of limited capacity and suboptimal opportunity is responsible for the declining prospects trajectory.

Figure 4.1 also shows the four trajectories stabilizing at different prospect levels. At this phase of adjustment, the actors are no longer building their capacity to optimize new opportunity for new gain. Instead, they are using their existing capacity to maintain control over their existing opportunities for gain. Consequently, the actors in each of the conditions are similarly motivated to maintain what they have. So they regulate their problem solving toward maintaining control over those means (circumstances or opportunities) on which they depend for getting what they need and want in life.

There are several implications to be drawn from this analysis. One is that prospects for self-determination are not attached solely to individual talent or ability. Prospects for self-determination are as much a function of what is being pursued as they are a function of who is engaging the pursuit. Person may have good prospects for one type of pursuit, a moderate chance of succeeding at another pursuit, and an unlikely chance of fulfilling expectations in a third pursuit. At the same time, Other may have poor prospects for a pursuit that is a good prospect for Person and a good chance of success for a pursuit that is a poor prospect for Person. It is also possible for the distribution of prospects among actors to change substantially over time so that when averaged for many actors and for many different pursuits, prospects are more or less comparable for those actors. On some days, months, or over years, Person achieves everything she pursues and on other days, months, and years, Person gets nothing she needs and wants to reach her ends in life. Over her lifetime, Person's prospects for finding fulfillment are comparable to Other's prospects over his lifetime.

According to this scenario, experiencing cell 1 prospects is no more guaranteed over the long-term than experiencing cell 4 prospects. In fact, over a lifetime of pursuing desirable ends in life, Person and Other experience all possible capacity-opportunity conditions and, as a consequence, experience all possible prospects for fulfillment. Sometimes, they feel the high of empowerment when their capacity and opportunity work together to accumulate advantage, occasionally they experience boredom from incremental change when their prospects promise intermittent gain or loss, and other times they experience depression from the failure that comes when nothing goes right and there is little hope of improving the situation. Nevertheless, these different experiences are on average not much different from the experience of others. There are "highs" and "lows" in life for everyone, but on average, prospects are sufficiently promising to encourage all persons to strive to improve their capacity and opportunity—to be self-determining.

Over the long-term, then, Figure 4.1 indicates what can happen to any representative member of society on any given period and for any given pursuit. That representative person can find himself or herself on any one of four trajectories—one leading to accelerated gain, another leading to incremental gain, another leading to incremental loss, and a fourth leading to an accelerated loss. In this sense, there is no question of fairness because on a different day or for a different pursuit, Person may find herself on a different trajectory, one more promising than the previous one, one equally promising, or one less promising. Whatever the next opportunity, it is as reasonable for Person to expect to be as successful in her pursuits as Other will be in his. This is because everyone in society experiences similar prospects for succeeding at their pursuits. Consequently, no one feels unfairly treated by life, by society, or by those with whom they exchange in gaining access to new opportunity.

A question of fairness does arise, however, when the same individuals consistently experience the same prospects regardless of the pursuits they attempt and when the prospect trajectory these individuals experience is substantially different from the trajectory others experience. According to equal opportunity theory, this is most likely when deficiencies in capacity combine with suboptimalities of opportunity. This condition makes it difficult for Person to chart a direction in life that is consistent with her needs and interests. Her capacity and opportunity for the self-directed life are simply insufficient. Moreover, if left to its own evolutionary drift, this condition becomes so egregiously unfavorable for Person's pursuits that it matters little what pursuit she engages. The probability of Person gaining control over the means necessary to secure her ends in life is too low to prompt her to attempt to optimize any new opportunity. Consequently, she works to avoid loss rather than to pursue gain.

In addition to feeling she is treated unfairly by society, which is a problem of social justice, Person also feels that she is treated unfairly compared with others, which is a problem of allocative justice. This comparative sense of injustice becomes especially acute as Person's prospects for success become progressively more hopeless, causing her to wonder why those with greater capacity and more favorable opportunity are able to experience more favorable opportunity for their pursuits, whereas she, with comparatively less capacity, must struggle with less favorable opportunity. What basis of fair return for reasonable contribution justifies this inequity?

Person feels the excusable envy Rawls predicts for all people in her circumstance. Gross difference in accumulated gain for individuals striving under the same rules of justice violates the notion of fairness according to the idea of differential rewards for differential contributions. This sense of fairness is violated when differences in prospects and outcomes become so great among a population of actors that their causal connection with talent and effort contradict what is reasonably attributed to individuals acting on their own. Then, justifiable envy is inevitable. Allocative justice has failed and ideologies of might making right justify freedom as power.

This is Nozick's theory of entitlement. All advantage and disadvantage, whether acquired through accelerated accumulation or incremental production, are attached to individuals and their acts. Consequently, they need no correction through collective redress. What individuals have they are entitled to keep. Even though gain and advantage accumulated at an exponential rate are beyond what can be produced by any individual acting alone, those results are, according to entitlement theory, rightfully attached to the person in control of the means for their production. This is the logic of freedom as power.

Equal opportunity theory claims individuals deserve gain accumulation in a moral sense to the extent that gain can be reasonably attributed to their talent and ability. The theory also claims individuals are entitled to accelerated gain accumulation in a practical sense to the extent that entitlement does no harm to others, for example, by impeding others from producing similar accumulations. So in this sense, the theory agrees with Nozick's position that there is no moral basis for the fortuitous association between capacity and opportunity and the accelerated accumulations that result. This does not preclude individuals from being entitled, however. They simply are not deserving, in a moral sense, as Nozick (1974) explains:

> And if, correctly, we describe people as entitled to their natural assets even if it's not the case that they can be said to deserve them, then we have the following argument:
>
> 1. People are entitled to their natural assets.
> 2. If people are entitled to something, they are entitled to whatever flows from it (via specified types of processes).
> 3. People's holding flow from their natural assets.
>
> Therefore,
>
> 4. People are entitled to their holdings.
> 5. If people are entitled to something, then they ought to have it (and this overrides any presumption of equality there may be about holdings). (pp. 225-226)

These distinctions separate moral from practical judgments about who gets what. Equal opportunity theory argues that although all people deserve the right to self-determination in the moral sense, they do not experience equal capacity or opportunity to self-determine in a practical sense, and this leads to a problem of unequal rights to self-determination that then becomes a problem in the moral sense. To achieve fairness in liberty for all in the moral and practical sense, equal opportunity makes a moral claim for fair prospects for liberty for all and for correcting unequal capacity and opportunity when either or both create unfair prospects for liberty for some. The theory recognizes that in all societies there are some individuals who lack capacity to self-determine, in all societies there are social exchanges between individuals and groups that yield unequal opportunities to self-determine, and as a consequence, in all societies some individuals will lack both capacity and opportunity to self-determination. When this occurs, the unequal experience of self-determination that results for some undermines their right to self-determination, and this is an undeserving condition requiring collective redress.

Equal opportunity theory bases its claim for collective redress on a theory of the self that explains the effects of individual capacity on prospects for self-determination and on a theory of social selection that explains the effects of opportunity on an individual's capacity to self-determine. Self-regulation theory explains how individuals manage their resources to improve their prospects for getting what they want in life and social selection theory explains how optimalities of opportunity constrain or enhance individual capacity to succeed in various self-determined pursuits. In other words, the two processes—self-regulation and social selection—interact to accelerate the accumulation of gain or loss that, in turn, increases or decreases prospects for self-determination. So when freedom is defined as individual power (capacity) to self-determine and when differential accumulations of gain expand or contract the power base of different groups of individuals, then the distribution of freedom within that population of actors will correspond to those differential accumulations of gain or loss. The problem of fairness arises as a consequence of these changes in capacity and opportunity that evolve to produce a *harm effect* among those experiencing diminished capacity and suboptimal opportunity.

Equal opportunity theory recognizes this harm effect by noting that some of the disadvantages experienced by individuals are a function of accelerated loss that is disconnected from individual talent and effort and, as a consequence, is outside the domain of moral desert. Consequently, social redress is justified. On the other hand, when there is no harm because there is no differential long-term advantage or disadvantage due to accelerated gain or loss, then those benefiting from it are entitled to the gain, even though they were not meritorious in a moral sense in producing the effect; similarly, those suffering a temporary accelerated loss are not deserving of that hardship in any moral sense, either, although they are entitled to it because it flows from a particular opportunity they engaged. Individuals are entitled to benefit or suffer from accelerated gain or loss in Nozick's (1974) sense that "If people are entitled to something, they are entitled to *whatever* [italics added] flows from it (via specified types of processes)" (p. 225).

Neither accelerated gain nor accelerated loss, therefore, requires moral judgment or collective redress if it is occasional and randomly associated with individuals in their various pursuits. The moral question of fairness arises, however, when accelerated gain and loss consistently benefit one group and disadvantage another group. This condition provokes a moral claim of injustice because harm results to the extent it abrogates the right to self-determination for members of the group experiencing loss.

The Basis for Accelerated Gain

This argument for social redress comes down to an empirical claim that accelerated gain is responsible for producing inequality in social life. What follows is an explanation for how this phenomenon has functioned during different expressions of freedom as power throughout human history. In the first period to be described, freedom as power was expressed as the capacity of the human species to control the environment. This capacity became gradually more potent during a period 30,000 years ago when our ancestors were hunters and gatherers. Then, freedom as power was the least harmful in a social sense in that the relationships it produced were more egalitarian than at any other period.

During the following 10,000 years, however, the evolution of freedom as power yielded social organizations that produced gross differences in advantage among members of the human species. There were two reasons for this. First, the capacity (power) of humans to control the means for productive gain improved dramatically. Through improved use of social, economic, and technical resources, humans were able to generate more than they needed to survive. This created surplus time, behavior, and material resources that they used to improve their chances of success in subsequent pursuits. This investment of surplus resources to improve subsequent opportunity created a self-perpetuating cycle that accelerated advantage for the species. A second factor that contributed to the creation of inequality within the species was the adoption of sedentary modes of adjustment that came about as a result of the transition from hunting and gathering to the horticulture era, which gave rise to ecological positioning to control the means of producing gain. In that some positions in the physical and social environment yielded greater control over productive output than others, individuals occupying those positions improved their prospects for the good life. These individuals were better able to increase their capacity to optimize their opportunity to the extent they had access to the means needed for their ends from the positions they occupied. For example, some individuals took advantage of their social positions that controlled production by organizing other people's time and behavior, others took advantage of their economic positions that allowed them to dominate financial negotiations with others, and others took advantage of their positions as experts that permitted them to develop and monopolize use of the technological means of producing gain.

The consequence of these two factors—the *reinvestment factor* that accelerated gain for the human species in general and the *positioning factor* that reflected differential access to the means of producing gain among different members of the species in particular—was inequality of opportunity and outcome within the human group. Moreover, these two factors worked in tandem to create gross differences between the most and least advantaged in society. While those well positioned ecologically benefited from the accelerated increase in productivity due to improvements in human control over environmental opportunity, those less well situated ecologically experienced consistently less favorable prospects for pursuing and obtaining the good in life. This was a side effect of social evolution toward greater human capacity for environmental control. History is replete with examples of how this acceleration of gain production and differential positioning of individuals to control that production worked to the advantage of some and to the disadvantage of others. Every society since the hunting and gathering era has used its surplus gain from improved environmental control to construct social relationships benefiting those in positions of control over the means of productive gain for the group. Consequently, the resulting systems of social stratification have perpetuated advantage for those occupying those positions and perpetuated disadvantage for those denied access to those positions.

The argument to be made here is not that these systems were morally unjust—although we can argue they were—but that the social mechanism responsible for their creation is the same then as now. The causal chain jump-starting the cycle of accumulated advantage is the same, as well, beginning as it does with surplus resource to improve the circumstance for subsequent pursuit. When individuals and groups acquire a surplus, they can expand their capacity to improve their opportunity for additional gain. When this investment in new opportunity becomes self-perpetuating, it jump-starts the gain cycle to accelerate the accumulation of advantage. The converse implied is also true. Without surplus, there can be no investment and without investment in new opportunity, there can be no optimized opportunity. When humans adapted to environmental change with time and behavior to spare and then invested that surplus to make new opportunity more favorable, they accumulated advantage over other species. They operated on their environment in ways no other species had. Moreover, by investing their excess time and behavior to make inhospitable environments hospitable, they also learned to make suboptimal opportunities optimal by reducing their costs and maximizing their gain. This accelerated their advantage.

By the time hominids appeared, it was clear their adaptive problem solving to control the means of producing gain would be a selective advantage in that it was clear that tool use would be far more important in securing desired ends over the long-term than any comparable adaptive invention that had occurred before. By focusing on control over means rather than ends, humans had the capacity to gain incrementally toward distant ends. Their means-ends incremental problem solving connected one causal link with another to accumulate advantage and produce an acceleration effect, with each gain setting a new benchmark for subsequent problem solving and a subsequent increment in gain.

The advantage of this type of adaptive problem solving was greater efficiency and effectiveness—greater efficiency by solving problems more quickly than before and greater effectiveness by solving more difficult problems than before. The efficiency advantage came with the capacity for conceptual trial-and-error problem solving and the effectiveness advantage came with the capacity for means-ends planning linking together causal chains leading to distant outcomes. This permitted pursuit of long-term projects using human resources from many generations. Finally, the human capacity to communicate in the completion of increasingly complex tasks through a division of labor translated long-term, complex plans into practical, daily action distributed over time and space. Again, the net effect was a level of accumulated gain and adaptive success no other species has been able to duplicate. Only humans were able to adapt to environmental circumstance through mechanisms indirectly related to their genetic makeup because, in the final analysis, the specific solutions responsible for their survival were not hard-wired to their neural development. They were not inherited through transmission of genetic codes, either. The human advantage over other species was due to the species' capacity for considering more options (greater efficiency), developing better solutions (greater effectiveness), and remembering more solutions (accumulation of advantage) over generational time. This yielded the acceleration effect that differentiated humans from other species, making it the most powerful and most dominant adaptive organism on earth.

This acceleration of efficient and effective solution accumulation also differentiated prospects for adaptive success for those within the human group who varied in how well they regulated their problem solving to meet individual ends in life. Consequently, some individuals consistently maximize control over life's circumstances, whereas others maintained only the control necessary to survive. So even within the human family, the creation and use of solutions to life's problems were distributed unequally. As communities evolved toward greater differentiation in capacity and opportunity for individual adjustment, these differences also accelerated, leading one to conclude that perhaps there would always be substantial variation in capacity and opportunity to control the means of adjusting to life's circumstances.

Nevertheless, there was a substantial period when all members of the group enjoyed reasonably equal prospects for getting what they needed and wanted in life. With the exception perhaps of dividing labor on the basis of gender, for example, there was little differentiation in gain or advantage within the human family during this period of relative egalitarianism that lasted for the better part of the 40,000 years. Then, our distant ancestors survived in small bands as hunters and gatherers and were sufficiently effective in their mode of adaptation to secure the necessities for survival and still have time and energy to enjoy life, as Maryanski and Turner (1992) suggest in their description of the lifestyle of contemporary hunters and gatherers:

> Contrary to earlier opinions, most studied hunters and gatherers do not have to work hard to meet their nutritional requirements, even under what

appear to be extreme environmental conditions . . . men normally provide far less food with their labor than females, primarily because hunting is not always successful but also because men spend considerable time talking, gambling, and smoking when possible. Women and their off-spring are much more likely to secure the necessary food through their activities, but generally they too do not need to spend long hours in gathering fruits, nuts, berries, roots, and other edible foods. Hunters and gatherers generally live what has been called a "leisure-intensive" life-style. (p. 79)

These groups differentiated their adaptive success from other members of the hominid line by gaining control over the social, economic, and technological means of producing desired gain. They achieved this control by managing these resources in ways that created surplus for use in changing an unfavorable circumstance into an optimal opportunity. For the longest period, the increase in adaptive advantage resulting from this modest gain in efficiency was incremental and the line of progress was arithmetic not exponential. Consequently, there was no accelerated advantage or disadvantage between or within groups in that, on the one hand, there was little systematic investment of surplus resources toward improved control, and on the other hand, there were substantial physiological obstacles to commencing such reinvestments.

One of these physiological obstacles was the pace of evolutionary development in conceptual problem solving that was necessary before humans could engage in complex levels of cooperation toward common ends. To illustrate the time it took for this to occur, consider that our oldest ancestors *Homo habilis* lived 2.0 to 1.5 million years ago, *Homo erectus* lived 1.6 millions years ago, and *Homo sapiens* arrived just 100,000 years ago. Even when *Homo sapiens* finally arrived, he was still evolving the capacity to solve problems and to organize socially to maximize the benefit of cooperative endeavor. So there was evidence then suggesting how this evolutionary outcome would gradually work to the benefit of those with greater capacity to solve problems efficiently and then to communicate the best solutions to others in the group.

Maryanski and Turner (1992) describe the pattern of these develop-ments, arguing that the expanded neocortex of *Homo habilis* permitted him to manufacture crude stone choppers and scrapers, and that the increased brain size of *Homo erectus* was necessary for language and speech, for specialization in use of tools and fire, and for the development of social organization in practices such as hunting that involved "planning, calculating, and cooperating in stalking and trapping big game" (pp. 70-72). Because these were adaptive advantages for *Homo erectus* and not for *Homo habilis,* the former experienced more favorable prospects for survival and as a consequence populated areas from Africa to parts of Europe and Asia. In other words, *Homo erectus* developed specific social and technological adjustments to environmental circumstance that produced the adaptive efficiencies necessary to accumulate surplus gain (Maryanski & Turner, 1992)[1]:

> [*Homo erectus's*] increased reproductive fitness [was because it was a] fire-using, tool-making, game-hunting, and group-organizing hominid [that could] adjust and adapt to various habitats. At this phase of hominid evolution, such fitness was not the result of individual selection alone, but also the result of cultural selection operating on social groupings. Selection worked at the individual level to create more efficient tool-use and social organization by favoring those individuals with expanded neurological capacities, but once these capacities could be harnessed for symbolization and organization, the social network also became a crucial unit, or mediator, of selection processes. Those groupings that could best organize to hunt, gather, and reproduce would be most likely to survive. (p. 72)

Maryanski and Turner claim *Homo sapiens sapiens,* whose brain size was on average 1,300 cm greater than *Homo erectus,* developed similar adaptive advantages due to interaction between neurological capacity and cultural benefit, this time with selection working on groups of individuals because survival advantage attached to the gain produced through cooperation:

> Once the neocortex was developed to the point of organization in terms of symbolic codes, networks of individuals were selected for their increased capacity to organize in terms of cultural codes, causing the expansion of the neocortex at the individual level, a development that led to stable and flexible social groupings. By the time of *Homo sapiens sapiens,* we believe, selection was working disproportionately on collectivities; those populations that could use culture to organize in ways that created a set of stable bonds, a viable division of labor, and a capacity to learn and adjust organizational patterns to new and changing habitats could outcompete any hominids who were not so flexibly organized. . . . Moreover, once cultural codes could be used to organize populations, the diffusion of ideas about how best to organize became possible, enabling hominid populations to learn from one another. (p. 75)

So for the 40,000 years that our species, *Homo sapiens sapiens,* has been in existence, approximately 30,000 years were devoted to a nomadic mode of adaptation that did not favor differential accumulation of advantage or disadvantage according to one's position of access to the means of production. As Maryanski and Turner (1992) suggest, that period was perhaps the most egalitarian of any time in the history of our species:

> Turning to the stratifying dimension of societal organization, we can say that hunters and gatherers come close to being a fully egalitarian system. . . . There is no real inequality over material wealth, since all adults have access to the same resources. Of course, there is very little material wealth—bows, arrows, spears, pots, simple building supplies—to be accumulated, since all possessions must be carried to the next settlement site. Some individuals enjoy greater prestige because of their skill and talent, but this prestige does not give them either power or extra material wealth. And although a band may have a headman, he has no real power to compel individuals to do as he asks. Thus, there is very little in the way of unequal distribution of resources in hunting and gathering societies; and as a result, there are no categories or social classes based on varying shares of resources. (p. 85)

Of course, this all changed, as we shall see, when the human group settled down, increased its control over the environment, accumulated gain, and distributed advantage among members of the groups according to their positions of access to the means of production.

Cumulative Gain for the Advantaged

Nevertheless, it is worth being reminded that for the greater part of our history as a species, there was little class distinction, and as well, there was little warfare, at least for 30 of our 40,000 years (Maryanski & Turner, 1992). Consequently, those arguing that our genetic constitution predisposes us to acquisitiveness and aggression may want to rethink that claim in light of this distant past, because there is evidence that then there was greater equality and perhaps greater mutual respect than what we find even today. In fact, there is evidence that as far back as 45,000 years, Shanidar I, who had a disabling right shoulder and upper right arm bone, was, according to Scheerenberger (1983), favored and protected from harm by his tribe, which "found a productive place for him in their society" (p. 5). The following description illustrates his position:

[He was] an individual who lived to the relatively old age of forty years, a very old man for a Neanderthal—equivalent to a man of about eighty today. He was plagued by arthritis, which seems to have been a rather common ailment among Neanderthals—and no wonder, considering the kind of life they led. As a case of rehabilitation, Shanidar I was a prime example. Not only did he possess a disability from the day he was born, but he must have been blind in the left eye . . . examinations disclosed that the right arm, collarbone, and shoulder blade had never fully grown from birth. Furthermore, there was extensive bone scar tissue on the left side of his face. And as if this were not enough, there is evidence that the top right side of his skull had received some damage which had healed well before the time of death. In short, Shanidar I—or "Nandy," as we called him around the table—was at a distinct disadvantage in an environment where even men in the best of condition had a hard time. He could barely forage and fend for himself, and we must assume that he was accepted and supported by his people up to the day he died. Any manpower must have been an asset to this ancient little community, especially since it undoubtedly took group activity to hunt the gregarious beasts of the wild. That "Nandy" made himself useful around the hearth (two hearths were found very close to him) is evidenced by the unusual wear on his front teeth. It presumably indicates that in lieu of a right arm, he used his jaws for grasping, while manipulating with his good left arm and hand. The stone heap over his remains, and the mammal food remains, show that even in death his person was an object of some esteem, if not respect, born out of close association against a hostile outside. (Scheerenberger, quoted in Solecki, 1991, pp. 195-196)

Apparently, this finding was not unusual because evidence from ancient graves indicates many tribes of that period supported members who had various disabling conditions that must have imposed on the group from time to time (see Scheerenberger, 1983, pp. 5-6).

INDIVIDUAL RESOURCES

But something happened during the 10 millennia following the hunting and gathering era to produce vast differences in opportunity and outcome that fully differentiated life prospects among different members of the human group. What happened was a fundamental restructuring of how humans produced what they needed and wanted in life. This restructuring commenced with the transformation from the nomadic life of hunting and gathering to the sedentary life of planting and harvesting between 7000 B.C. and 3000 B.C. Following this period, social regulation increased to another level of efficiency through improved tool use that occurred between 3000 B.C. and A.D. 1800; following that, regulation increased to yet a third level of efficiency when machines replaced animals and humans to power even higher levels of productive gain.

Each era represented another step toward greater control over the means of producing gain. The horticultural era that introduced a sedentary division of labor increased food production by controlling the cultivation of plants and the domestication of animals, the agrarian era built on these efficiencies in social organization and improved productive yield further through the use of tools during food cultivation, and the industrial era increased production once again by replacing animal and human power with machine power to operate tools. Conceived broadly, each of these eras backed the locus of control from the intended production target, until energy itself became the principle means for achieving greater control over environmental circumstance. The process continues today as we seek to replace fossil fuels with solar, geothermal, and nuclear energy. This backward chaining to secure greater access and greater control over the means of production has substantially decreased the cost of adjustment. Consequently, as the expenditure of human time, energy, and behavior per unit of gain has declined exponentially, the productive output per unit of time has increased exponentially.

Another way of expressing this transformation is to track the number of inventions humans created over the millennia that increased their capacity to change suboptimal circumstance into optimal opportunity for gain. The earliest demonstrations of this came with the emergence of *Homo habilis* who demonstrated this proclivity to seek out the means or the tools necessary for reaching desired ends. *Homo erectus* showed the same capacity through use of hand axes, fire, and organized hunting, as did *Homo sapiens* who invented even more sophisticated tools and learned to cooperate in hunting and gathering to extend the realm of control as well. When the human species began differentiating itself from other species, therefore, it did so because of its capacity to optimize opportunity that depended on the cognitive ability to identify different means of producing gain. It was this capacity for optimizing circumstance—not the tools themselves—that gave us a selective advantage over other species.

Still, this focus on the means to desirable ends did not have the explosive-like acceleration effect in the earliest period of human evolution that it had in the modern world. Perhaps this is because the entire life of our species is measured in thousands of years rather than in decades or centuries. Consequently, the acceleration effect was not as evident in that

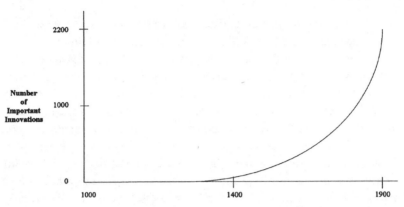

Figure 4.2. Number of Important Innovations From A.D. 1000 to 1900

prehistoric period. Nevertheless, a comparison of the rate of innovation during the Lower Paleolithic period with the rate during the Mesolithic period when modern humans were present shows increases of over 6,000%, whereas the rate of innovation from A.D. 1000 to A.D. 1900 increased about 1,000% (Lenski & Lenski, 1974, pp. 68, 132). Figure 4.2 shows this latter effect.

Even during the earliest period, the underlying cause of this acceleration was the same as it is now—the accumulation of innovative means for optimizing circumstances. The cultural base for creating new possibilities for means-ends solutions to problems posed by environmental circumstance expanded exponentially as each innovation added to a preceding innovation and as each new problem solver became available to make another addition to the ever expanding solution base. As human populations increased, therefore, so did the probability of their securing greater control over environmental circumstance. The resulting cycle of cumulative gain increasing control and increased control accumulating gain accelerated the process of problem solving and solution using. The result was an ever expanding warehouse of means-ends solutions available for transforming an ever expanding array of suboptimal circumstances. In other words, this storehouse of useful tools and materials for optimizing circumstance enhanced the human capacity to pursue ever more challenging opportunities. This, in turn, created the perception that humans had the potential of gaining whatever they desired and that their only competitors for advantage in a world of their own creation were other humans.

This experience with cumulative gain and accelerated advantage and disadvantage within and across individuals and groups is so different now from what our ancestors experienced it is difficult to understand how the fast-paced life of the present relates to patterns of adjustment in the distant past, and what factors produced the transformation that began a mere 10,000 years ago and led to where it is today. When we ask why our ancestors changed from nomadic life in the bush to sedentary life in the city, therefore, we are really asking what problems they faced back then, how they solved those problems, and how the solutions they chose produced the social stratification systems we experience today.

We know, for example, that during that prehistoric era the principle means of producing subsistence gain was hunting game and gathering food in different environments. When supplies declined in one territory, the tribe moved to another territory. During that period, tribe members controlled their food supply by following it. Their means of gain production was based primarily on the resources of the individual—the individual's time, skills, and effort. Consequently, their adaptive success was tied closely to each individual's capacity to use those resources optimally.

SOCIAL RESOURCES

During the horticultural era, this means of production changed. For the first time, cooperation was more important than individual enterprise and initiative. Large numbers of people had to coordinate their activities to plant seeds, protect crops, harvest yields, and distribute food. The significance of this transformation was that gain advantage went to those in positions of control over other people's time and behavior and it went, as well, to those who knew how to coordinate and to use those human resources effectively. This meant that an individual's capacity to manage other humans affected his value to the group. Consequently, those in control of social resources also ended up with greater capacity and better prospects for getting what they needed and wanted in life than those lacking that control. This shift in the distribution of power also affected prospects for freedom of other members in the new community. For some, it meant less freedom and more external control than ever before, as Maryanski and Turner (1992) explain in the following:

> If there was a "garden of Eden" in human history, hunting and gathering
> comes as close to it as was ever possible. . . . Obviously, wandering bands
> with few possessions and dependent on wild game and indigenous plants
> for food are not living in great luxury. But they had something that most
> humans have yet to recapture—equality (with respect to social, economic,
> and political rights), leisure, considerable freedom from sociocultural
> constraints, and relative insulation from the ravages of external war and
> internal conflict. (p. 93)

If we explain this transformation from the point of view of natural
selection, we would conclude that individuals and groups who switched from
nomadic to sedentary life survived, whereas those who did not perished. If we
explain it from the point of view of social selection, however, we would
conclude, as Maryanski and Turner (1992) have, that sedentary modes of
production increased in frequency, whereas nomadic modes declined:

> The adoption of "horticulture," or simple farming without the benefit of
> the plow and animal power, was not rapid. But once adopted, it tended to
> deplete resources in an area. For while the object of horticultural farming
> is to increase the energy yield on a plot of land, the early practitioners
> relied on the nutrients already present in the soil, and after a few years the
> soil was exhausted, requiring that garden plots be moved. Moreover,
> horticulturists typically hunt and kill most of the game in an area, espe-
> cially as the settled population grows. The result is that hunters and
> gatherers are often forced to leave those territories where horticulturists
> have settled, or give up and join them in farming to sustain themselves.
> Horticulture thus pushes aside the older hunting and gathering system;
> and so, as the number of horticulturists increased, there was a correspond-
> ing decrease in hunting and gathering. (pp. 91-92)

Social selection theory locates the cause of this transition to sedentary
life with the greater effectiveness and efficiency of farming. Consequently,
groups that adopted it benefited from the greater productivity it produced.
Nevertheless, this adoption had a cost. It required individuals to learn a
different way of life. Instead of hunting and gathering as their ancestors
had for 30 millennia, they had to learn to farm the land, to harvest and
distribute its products, to protect the land and surrounding community from
external threat, and to manage and coordinate the use of human and
material resources. They also had to learn how to participate in a complex
of social relationships that distributed access to resources according to
position in the social structure determined by one's membership in a

kinship group. They had to accept that differential access to resources would determine their capacity and opportunity for securing desirable ends in life. Finally, they had to accept a position in life according to their birth into a kinship that determined access to community resources according to its position in the social structure.

In other words, the cost of this transformation from nomadic to sedentary life was a structure of social positions that determined the opportunities and outcomes each individual and group would experience throughout life. This meant that individual initiative, talent, and effort would be less important in determining one's hope for the future than the system of social stratification that automatically placed individuals in the social structure according to their membership in a kinship group.[2] Maryanski and Turner (1992) describe this transformation in the following:

> One of the most dramatic transformations in the movement from hunting and gathering as a way of life to horticulture is the growth of stratification. . . . The unequal distribution of resources—material, political, and symbolic—increases slowly but steadily; and by the time a society is at an advanced horticultural stage, clear social classes are evident. Such classes revolve around political, religious, and military activities, kin affiliation (various kin groups often become ranked), craft specialties, trade and commerce, and unskilled work (ranging from free workers to slaves). Moreover, ethnic classes often exist as a result of war and conquest, although these are frequently co-extensive with a slave class. Thus, from moderate levels of inequality in simple horticultural societies, stratification becomes ever more elaborate and rigid as the population, the amount of economic surplus, the concentration of power, and the specialization of labor increase.
>
> With increases in size and complexity, the number of social categories multiply. In simple systems, one's kin affiliation (lineage and clan), age, and sex are the most relevant categories, but in more advanced systems, these distinctions are supplemented by ethnic, economic, religious, political, and class categories. *Each of these categories locates individuals in the social web, dictates the resources available to them, controls their perceptions and actions, and circumscribes how others respond to them* [italics added]. (p. 109)

ECONOMIC AND TECHNICAL RESOURCES

These systems of stratification produced selection effects in accordance with various divisions of work, power, and authority. They worked only as long as they ensured the survival and well-being of the group. Consequently, when gain production declined or when the need satisfaction of the group was threatened, kinship groups realigned themselves relative to control of a new means of producing gain toward community survival. Changes such as these occurred when horticultural societies evolved into agrarian societies and then again when agrarian societies transformed into industrial societies. During both periods of change, individuals and groups in positions of economic and technical control over the means of production for the community ascended to higher positions in the social structure. During the agrarian period when trade became important, individuals and groups who controlled economic transactions between communities benefited by improving their own positions within a new economic order, and during the industrial period when technical obstacles to producing desired products demanded resolution, individuals and groups who could create solutions to these problems improved their prospects for gain by improving their positions.

The underlying mechanism for change that stimulated these transformations was the *need-problem-solution* cycle that propelled even the earliest societies in directions that occasionally freed individuals from their fixed positions in the social structure to improve their prospects for self-determination. To the extent these individuals could solve the problems of production valued by the community, they could also improve their positions of control over production and, as a consequence, improve their prospects for getting what they wanted in life. In other words, the need problem-solution cycle altered in an inexorable way the community's optimalities of opportunity for producing gain. As this sociocultural force took on a life of its own, it stimulated sufficient change in environmental and social circumstances to improve prospects for some individuals who could then optimize those circumstances and reposition themselves relative to the means of producing gain. The following passage illustrates this sociocultural force at work in ancient Egypt:

> Improvements in irrigation and ploughing produced enough food to support non-food producers. By 3000 BC the political structure of Egyptian society was organized into water provinces connected by canals. Labor was divided between those who dug and maintained the irrigation systems and those who supervised and directed the diggers and maintainers.
> Meanwhile, the need-problem-solution cycle took on a life of its own as solutions for one set of problems generated problems that required another set of solutions. For example, the need to store surplus grain led to the development of permanent containers—fire-hardened clay pots; the

need to identify ownership of pots led to the development of writing on containers; and the need to coordinate an increasingly complex labor force of craftsmen (carpenters, potters, weavers, bakers, leather-workers) led to the development of a monetary system including taxation. This, in turn, required improved methods of counting, measuring, and calculating to build canals, record seasons, pay workers, and levy taxes.

The need-discovery cycle affected other areas of the social order as well. Agriculturally based communities with their surpluses were increasingly vulnerable to raids from outside because the producers—farmers, artisans, craftsmen, administrators, and tax collectors—were poor defenders. So they set aside a portion of their surplus to support a military force. But this created a new set of problems because warriors needed weapons, and the materials necessary for their construction came from copper deposits across the Red Sea in the Sinai. Fortunately, these neighboring communities also had unmet needs and were willing to trade minerals for foodstuffs. A barter system developed. (Mithaug, 1993, p. 20)

This mechanism of sociocultural evolution affected opportunities quite simply. For every solution created within the community, a new need emerged, and for every new need that developed and demanded satisfaction, there was an opportunity for someone to optimize circumstances by solving the problem preventing that need from being fulfilled. New needs and new problems created new access points for controlling the means of producing gain toward satisfying a need and solving a problem. These new access points constituted opportunities for some members of the community to improve their prospects. The pace of sociocultural change and adaptive problem solving to meet new goals and to satisfy new needs increased exponentially from there, as did the access points for resource control and productive gain. The result was increased complexities in the division of labor and increased surplus wealth and opportunity associated with that greater differentiation of labor. Whereas in hunting and gathering societies labor was divided by gender, now it was divided by function. It specialized according to the type of problem to be solved and the type of solution derived to solve it. The *means-ends causal links* composing each new solution translated into new occupational slots defining the human capacities that would be required to solve the problem organizationally and institutionally. These occupational slots or positions, in turn, constituted the means-ends causal links for controlling the means of producing new gain in a newly evolved social structure. Now, instead of searching for environmental niches in the physical environment, individuals searched for *resource-control points* (occupational positions) in the social environment.

In this respect, pursuing gain through civilized adaptation was more challenging than pursuing it through nomadic adaptation because civilized life demanded greater levels of control over personal, social, economic, and technical means of producing gain. Whereas in hunting and gathering, individuals secured most of what they needed and wanted on their own with only modest assistance from others, civilized life required highly regulated forms of cooperation. Whereas self-sufficient nomads survived in small bands with a minimum of constraints on individual freedom, autonomy, and self-interest,[3] individuals in the sedentary community surrendered substantial proportions of their personal time, energy, and behavior to supervision by others.

This was a new necessity of collective life because for it to succeed, the work of individuals had to be coordinated. Only through coordination would benefits outweigh costs. The new venture required everyone in the group to contribute a substantial share of their time, energy, and behavior to producing what everyone needed and wanted. Moreover, it required that time and behavior be coordinated so the divided activity would yield the desired output at the right time and at the right place. It also required exchange of resources within the divided activities so the output of a means-end link of one part could satisfy the needs of a means-end link of another part in a chain ending with a final product. Finally, it required continuous problem solving to remove obstacles emanating from a complex of interactions connecting individuals and their groups within and across social strata that constituted civilized life.

In sum, this new way of life became stable and predictable because of the social stratification of expectations, opportunities, and outcomes. The new system distributed opportunities according to the functions of different positions located throughout the social structure. Some of these opportunities were associated with completing the tasks that actually produced the gain everyone needed in the community; some opportunities were associated with supervising and managing the work of those who actually produced the gain the community needed, some opportunities were associated with resource exchange among groups located in various positions throughout the social structure, and some opportunities were associated with finding solutions to the technical obstacles that threatened the successful functions of the divided labor. But all of these opportunities were in one way or another associated with greater regulation of the community's social, economic, and technical resources. This meant that individuals who participated in this sedentary mode of adaptation would benefit from it personally to the extent they had the capacity to produce gain for themselves as a consequence of producing gain for the community. More-over, they would be able to accomplish these dual ends to the extent they could find a match between their capacity for gain production and the opportunity provided by the structure of their community.

But as we know from the history of civilized life, relatively few individuals and groups have been able to capitalize fully on their positions in the community to accomplish these dual ends in life. We know, for example, that those who were able to benefit themselves while serving in positions highly valued by the community were members of elite groups whose assets accumulated due to the positions they occupied that freed them from the exigencies of day-to-day survival so they could pursue control over additional social, economic, and technical resources. These groups ascended the ranks of the community's hierarchical structure by securing social control over the bureaucratic, political, military, and religious means of satisfying community needs, by dominating economic transactions through various methods of taxation backed by coercive power, and by gaining technical control over innovative means of producing gain for the community.

Cumulative Loss for the Disadvantaged

The chief beneficiaries of the sedentary mode of adaptation, therefore, were individuals well situated within a system of social stratification that defined each person's capacity and opportunity for pursuing the good in life. Those individuals were able to accumulate disproportionate shares of the community wealth by controlling the social, economic, and technical means of producing gain surplus. As a consequence of this concentration of control in the hands of the few, a class system developed that distributed opportunity and outcomes to favor those in positions of control. This created a self-perpetuating cycle of opportunity differentiation according to the distribution of power in the community that had the effect of accelerating the accumulation of resource gain for those initially advantaged by their position in the social structure. The practice of allocating positions according to membership in a kinship group maintained this cycle of accumulated advantage for thousands of years.

SOCIAL CONTROL

This was the price of sedentary adaptation. Opportunities and outcomes would be allocated according to positions in a social structure that divided labor to improve the efficiency of cooperative gain. Gone forever was the egalitarianism of hunting and gathering when social distinctions were based on gender, age, and personal resources. Gone also was the sense of freedom and self-sufficiency that came with knowing that one could survive by pursuing opportunity commensurate with one's effort and ability. Because with civilization came a complex of social opportunities intervening between a person's effort and its expression. These opportunities were differentially weighted, more favorable for some and less favorable for others.

Civilization locked individuals into different levels of interdependent choosing and acting that went beyond anything comparable in nomadic life. This new social interconnectedness constrained freedom and autonomy in new ways. These new constraints functioned differently for some than for others in that it differentiated opportunities for gain and loss according to position. For those most egregiously affected by their positions, this meant there would be little hope of ever expanding capacity or improving opportunity for the self-determined life. As a consequence, some people would spend their lives inhabiting the worst nooks and crannies of the new social cage defining the parameters of human adjustment through civilized opportunity and outcome.[4]

Worse yet, in looking back at this transformation in human adaptation, is knowing this condition would persist throughout history. It is knowing that differences in capacity and opportunity among individuals and groups would increase for thousands of years before there would be social upheavals of sufficient magnitude to change the balance of power in favor of those who were marginally positioned so that they too could have a chance to determine their own direction in life. Finally, it is disconcerting to know also that, even during these intermittent social upheavals giving temporary opportunity for the few ready to act on slightly more favorable circumstance, the same social processes creating inequality of capacity and opportunity in the past would function to create new patterns of unequal capacity and unequal opportunity in the future. Moreover, these new patterns of inequality would constitute yet another bifurcation in the distribution of power so that once again a powerful elite would secure control over the essential resources for producing gain in the new community—other people's time, energy, and behavior; other people's productive gain; and other people's technical inventiveness.

Throughout this history of change in the evolution of social power, there would always be those individuals who were bereft of any capacity or opportunity to self-determine. Lacking surplus in even their own time, energy, and behavior, these persons would become enslaved in the service of others—fulfilling dreams, building empires, and constructing monuments that testified to the majesty of those privileged few. Individuals with the least capacity and least opportunity in life would be sacrificed at the lowest cost for the greatest gain of the few and the powerful. And this would occur at the same time the new collective effort was creating greater gain for greater numbers of people than was ever possible through nomadic hunting and gathering. Compared with tribal life, this new life would mean survival of many more. This was because opportunities were more predictable and more profitable than ever before, even though they were unequally shared. Consequently, there would be an overall elevation of life's prospects for most members of the new community.

Of course, the principle for distributing opportunities would still be based on position in the hierarchy of advantage and opportunity: The higher the position in the hierarchy, the greater the share of material goods associated with that position. Its converse would also hold true: The greater the share of the goods accumulated by an individual, the greater the advance in the hierarchy of advantage and opportunity. This meant there would always be contrasting levels of capacity and opportunity, with a steady expansion of capacity and opportunity among those well positioned and a steady contracting of capacity and opportunity among the masses who were less well situated socially, economically, and technically. These groups would have few options for enhancing their capacity because their only resource for greater control over life's circumstance would be their own time, energy, and behavior. At the same time, members of elite groups would retain positions that permitted them to enhance their capacity and opportunity by using their time and behavior to control other people's behavior, to control the economic transactions of others, and to control the use of innovative solutions developed by others.

This evolution toward inequality of opportunity and outcome was evident early in the transition from nomadic to sedentary life, as Lenski and Lenski (1974) have noted. For example, slavery was present in only 10% of hunting and gathering societies and 14% of simple horticultural societies, but it was present in 83% of advanced horticultural societies. At the same time, only 2% of hunting and gathering societies had full-scale social stratification systems, whereas 17% of simple horticultural societies, 54% of advanced horticultural societies, and 71% of agrarian societies had well-developed class systems (see p. 107). Overall, the rate of social differentiation accelerated during the transition from hunting and gathering to farming. Lenski and Lenski[5] describe this trend as follows:

> Social inequality is generally rather limited [at first], though societies differ in this. Although extremes of wealth and political power are absent, substantial differences in prestige are not uncommon. Political and religious leaders unusually enjoy high status, but this depends far more on their achievements than on mere occupancy of the office. There are few sinecures in these societies. Other bases of status include military prowess (which is highly honored in nearly all societies), skill in oratory, age, lineage, and in some cases wealth in the form of wives, pigs, and ornaments. Each society has its own peculiar combination of these criteria.
>
> The more advanced the technology and economy in one of these groups, the greater social inequality tends to be. Societies that practice irrigation, own domesticated animals, or practice metallurgy for ornamental and ceremonial purposes are usually less egalitarian than groups that have not taken these steps. We can see this when we compare the villagers of eastern Brazil and the Amazon River basin with their more advanced neighbors to the north and west who, in pre-Spanish days, practiced irrigation and metallurgy (since they used gold, which is too soft for tools and weapons, they cannot be considered advanced horticulturists). Hereditary class differences were absent in the former groups but quite common in the latter, where a hereditary governing class of chiefs and nobles was set apart from the larger class of commoners. (p. 193)

The least advantaged members of the new societies were, as predicted, the poor, the enslaved, and the disabled. With the emergence of the earliest civilization, large numbers of individuals found themselves without the personal, social, economic, and technical means of optimizing opportunity. In many communities, the status of the least advantaged members of society was that of slaves—they who lacked any capacity to control any means of producing any gain toward any end in life. These people even lacked control over their own time and behavior. Slightly better off than slaves were poor people who could barely survive on their own. Although better off than slaves to the extent they owned their time, energy, and behavior, they had no social means of improving their position in the community hierarchy of opportunity, nor did they have the economic or technical means of securing the resources that would enable them to alter these circumstances. Their positions were so marginal many were forced to sell their children, their wives, and even themselves into slavery to pay debt incurred in transactions with those better positioned in the community.

ECONOMIC CONTROL

The effect of this ecological positioning in sedentary life was to favor those initially positioned to control the means of production in the new community, which allowed them to secure additional resources to enhance their control and, with repeated reinvestment of surplus gain, to optimize new opportunity for gain. This accelerated the advantage over others less well positioned, and it produced divergent trajectories of adjustment and gain over generational time that enhanced capacity and optimized prospects for some groups and constrained capacity and depressed prospects for others. Lenski and Lenski (1974) explain it as follows:

> Specifically, the development of the state and the growth of social inequality that followed the shift from horticulture to agriculture created a situation in which those who were engaged in the daily tasks of production were gradually reduced to the barest subsistence level, and held there, by their more powerful superiors. Thus these peasant producers lost the normal incentive for creativity; any benefits that might result from an invention or discovery would simply be appropriated by the governing class. (pp. 218-219)

This condition of unequal opportunity accelerated in the 19th century when economic resources became a principle means of producing gain. By then, peasants replaced slaves for being those most often victimized by unfortunate positioning in the social structure, as Lenski and Lenski's (1974) description of 19th-century Russia illustrates:

> Systems of slavery and serfdom have been common in agrarian societies, with large landholdings and large numbers of slaves or serfs normally going hand in hand. Thus it was only natural that a nineteenth-century Russian nobleman who owned 2 million acres of land also owned nearly 3,000,000 serfs. Rulers, understandably, had the largest holdings. Prior to the emancipation of the serfs in Russia, the czar owned 27.4 million of them.
>
> But even when the peasant owned his own land and was legally free, he usually found it difficult to make ends meet. A bad crop one year, and he had to borrow money at usurious rates, sometimes as high as 120 per cent a year. In any event, there were always taxes, and these usually fell more heavily on the peasant landowner than on his wealthier neighbor, either because of special exemptions granted the latter or simply because of his greater ability to evade such obligations. If a peasant did not own his land, he had to pay rent, which was always set high. In addition, he

was often subject to compulsory labor service, tithes, fines, and obligatory "gifts" to the governing class.

Because the number and variety of obligations were so great, it is difficult to determine just how large the total was, but in most societies it appears to have been not less than half the total value of the goods the peasants produced. The basic philosophy of the governing class seems to have been to tax the peasants to the limit of their ability to pay. This philosophy is illustrated by a story told of a leading Japanese official of the seventeenth century who, returning to one of his estates after an absence of ten years and finding the villagers in well-built houses instead of the hovels he remembered, explained, "These people are too comfortable. They must be more heavily taxed." (pp. 237-238)

The productive gain in this era of sedentary adaptation depended increasingly on the exchange of goods and services between societies and regions. This new adjustment in civilized life was a consequence of the growing economic connections among large population centers that had grown dependent on trade and commerce to meet the increasingly diverse needs of specialized productive activity. The problems created by this need produced new opportunities for entrepreneurial gain. Whereas in the past, position in the social structure of a given community was the primary determinant of opportunity, now economic position in commercial activity connecting different communities determined opportunity for gain. So as labor differentiated across regions—with one region producing goods, another mining resources needed for their production, and a third distributing those goods across regions—a need developed to connect these varied, interdependent resources and outputs. This need could not be satisfied by individuals located in positions within a given community. It could be met only by individuals in positions to connect the resource needs of one area with the resource outputs available from another area. This created new opportunity for traders, merchants, and businessmen whose positions made these connections and transactions possible. Their positions enabled them to facilitate the transport of resources and products from one location in the world to another, having the effect of increasing economic relationships among producers and consumers. It also had the effect of improving opportunities for those entrepreneurs who brokered these relationships.

The Economics of Slavery

By the second half of the 17th century commerce expanded from the Mediterranean to northern Europe where English, Dutch, Portuguese, and

Spanish traders dominated maritime activity due to their advantageous geographic locations near large bodies of water. At the same time those individuals least well positioned socially, economically, and technically suffered, especially if they happened to be the commodities being traded in this rapidly expanding maritime commerce, as J. M. Roberts (1993) explains in the following:

> In this economy an important and growing part was played by slaves. Most of them were black Africans, the first of whom to be brought to Europe were sold at Lisbon in 1444. In Europe itself, slavery had by then all but withered away (though Europeans were still being enslaved and sold into slavery by Arabs and Turks). Now it was to undergo a vast extension in other continents. Within two or three years over a thousand more blacks had been sold by the Portuguese, who soon set up a permanent slaving station in West Africa. Such figures show the rapid discovery of the profitability of the new traffic but gave little hint of the scale of what was to come. What was already clear was the brutality of the business (the Portuguese quickly noted that the seizure of children usually ensured the docile captivity of the parents) and the complicity of Africans in it; as the search for slaves went further inland, it became simpler to rely on local potentates, who would round up captives and barter them wholesale. (p. 443)

By 1460, the Portuguese were importing 700 to 800 slaves captured from Africa per year. Later in the 15th century, Spain joined in the trade as did Arab traders. England joined in the latter half of the 16th century, followed by France, Holland, and Denmark; finally, the American colonies began importing slaves, with the first arriving at Jamestown in 1619. In the latter half of the 17th century, slaves were used as domestics in the northern colonies, as agricultural laborers in the Middle Atlantic colonies, and to work plantations in the southern colonies. By the 19th century, slavery had become a prime means of economic gain throughout the United States, especially in the South, which depended on some 857,097 slaves to support the plantation system—a number that grew to 3,953,760 by 1860, 3 years before Lincoln issued the Emancipation Proclamation (Microsoft Encarta, 1993b).

Although slave trade was abolished in Great Britain in 1807, in the United States in 1808, and at the Congress of Vienna in 1814, where the other major powers adopted similar policies, the actual freeing of slaves in these countries took longer—with the French emancipating their slaves in 1848, the Americans and the Dutch doing the same in 1863, and Brazil abolishing its system of slavery in 1888. Moreover, it was not until the early part of the 20th century that the International Slavery Convention of the League of Nations articulated commitments to suppress and prohibit slave trade and slavery in all forms, and it was not until more than two decades later that the Universal Declaration of Human Rights, adopted by the United Nations in 1948, reaffirmed the right to self-determination of peoples of the world. Article 1 stated that "All human beings are born free and equal in dignity and rights; They are endowed with reason and conscience and should act toward one another in a spirit of brotherhood;" and Article 2 stated that "Everyone is entitled to all the rights and freedoms set forth in this Declaration, without distinction of any kind, such as race, colour, sex, language, religion, political or other opinion, national or social origin, property, birth or other status" (Humana, 1992, p. 382; also see Microsoft Encarta, 1993b).

The reason slavery persisted so long was that it was an efficient means of producing gain during the agricultural era. This was not the case in the prehistoric era when capturing and enslaving enemies was expensive. Then, slaves required food and had to be guarded, which increased costs relative to what they could contribute to gain production. It was more efficient to kill the enemy, take whatever possessions he had, and move on. This changed in the agrarian economy in that working fields was time-consuming and required human (and animal) labor that could be supervised inexpensively, especially when that labor was free (enslaved). So for the agrarian period (which began circa 5000 B.C. and extended well into the 19th century) slavery was a substantial economic means for productive gain. Its value peaked during a period of global commerce that began in the 16th century and extended through the 19th century. Milton Meltzer's (1993) *Slavery: A World History* describes the economics of slavery as follows:

> Where farming or herding had gone beyond this early stage, an agricultural people could produce far more than they needed, and this made the taking of slaves practical. Instead of killing a defeated enemy, the victor enslaved him. The loser kept his life and, in return, was made to work. Man had already learned how to tame animals. Now he found that his own kind like cattle, sheep, or dogs—could be domesticated, too.
>
> Slaves could be used to care for the flocks or to labor in the fields. They added to the captor's wealth and comfort. They provided food for him and they spared him from doing the hard and unpleasant tasks himself. Eventually, agriculture advanced to the point where it was profitable to use slaves in great numbers on the land.
>
> So enslaving an enemy rather than killing him became a means to harvest a man's labor, and the result was a new dimension added to a

society. For a new tool was acquired, the slave. Enslaving a man also increased the pleasure of the victor, for the defeated man was humiliated and punished for daring to fight in the first place. This means of humiliating foreign enemies eventually became a form of punishment used by rulers against people in the same cultural group who committed some wrong or injury. A man guilty of a crime might be rated unworthy of citizenship and be condemned to slavery.

As man became more "civilized," still other sources of slavery developed. A needy man could borrow money against the pledge of his labor. If he failed to pay his debt, his enslavement redeemed the loan. There were also free men too weak to survive alone in the community, who voluntarily chose the shelter of slavery rather than the hunger and risks of freedom. Exiles from another community might surrender their labor to prosperous men on the same terms.

The "children of Israel" found refuge in Egypt around the eighteenth century BC by offering their services in exchange for life. They were not the only Asiatic tribe to have done this. Terrible droughts often forced whole communities from their homeland. They were allowed to settle in valleys or oases in return for dues or services.

The accident of birth was another source of slaves. A child born to slave parents could be nothing but a slave himself.

As the desire for slave labor grew, there were always men eager to profit from it. Kidnapping and piracy became good business to meet a scarcity or satisfy a growing demand. The traffic in slaves became one of the earliest forms of commerce. Slaves were sent as commodities to wherever their muscle or skill, beauty or brains, would bring the highest price. (pp. 2-3)

While Europe pursued economic advantage through slave trade and while its merchants and traders benefited as a consequence, a growing middle class led a renaissance of entrepreneurial activity that began in the Mediterranean and spread throughout western Europe. New conceptions of human potential reflected a reversal in social status as economic power replaced social power to create a new means of gaining sociopolitical advantage. Characteristics of individuality, self-determination, and intelligence became ennobled, at least among those gaining access to these new means of success. The Renaissance surged with the belief and feeling that any human could chart a destiny that was independent of social circumstance.

The Economics of Disability

At the same time these newly positioned entrepreneurs were coming of age in an expression of artistic and economic activity, the suffering of the least advantaged members of society continued as before. In the circumstances created by the new economic order, there would be no place for those lacking position and lacking capacity to acquire resources on their own. This meant those least capable of securing a productive position in society would be left out, and being left out would become conspicuously out of place in an increasingly production-oriented civilization. With agricultural activity on the decline and commercial activity on the rise and with populations concentrated in cities, those left idle and with no place to go attracted negative attention that resulted in community policies that determined their fate.

This began as early as the 16th century when individuals deviating most conspicuously from the productive ideal were people with disabilities who found themselves in lunatic asylums in Europe by 1533. Even then, it was evident that separation, segregation, and expulsion from the mainstream of community life were the fate of people who were idle, deviant, or otherwise without the necessary resources to deal with their circumstances in life. These people no longer were considered worthy of membership in the human family. One of the first holding cells for these marginalized members of the human group was Bethlehem Hospital in London, later known as "Bedlam" because it was little more than a prison where the use of manacles and iron chains was common. Treatment was consistently harsh and cruel, supported by the Protestant Reformation's foreboding perspective that persons whose mental functioning deviated from the norm meant moral decay from within. The Protestant ethic's emphasis on individual responsibility for admission into God's kingdom drew heavily on one's capacity for disciplined contemplation, purposeful action, and productive outcome. Persons lacking these were lost. Failing to act rationally was a sign of being possessed by the Devil—views that became entrenched in popular conceptions of mental disability. Not only were idiocy and dementia deemed incurable, but they were also seen as indicators of being less than human. Consequently, the reasoning went, people so identified would be insensitive to cold, heat, hunger, and pain and could do with less, and they did. The Hôtel Dieu in Paris designated by the King for all persons who were mentally ill or mentally retarded was described as follows:

> "The patients were herded together in rooms crowded with miserable beds in which they were put without distinction of disease; there were two, four, six, and even twelve people bedded together in various positions; one can

easily imagine how sanitary this was! Owing to the conditions of the time, the medical assistance was limited, as was the religious assistance despite the large number of priests and nuns; half of the priests were busy with the church and office work; half of the nuns were so absorbed in their devotions that they overlooked their work, while the other half were too busy to take care of the spiritual needs of the sick." (Scheerenberger, 1983, p. 43)[6]

Treatment of children with disabilities worsened as well, perhaps because of the recurring plague of that era, the deteriorating economic conditions brought on by religious and political conflicts, and the increasing failure of poor families to care for their children. Soon after the establishment of the Hôpital Général, replica "hospitals" were established throughout France. In England, a similar trend developed, although the origins of that wave of institutional confinements began with an act of 1575 that provided for the "punishment of vagabonds and the relief of the poor" through the construction of houses of correction. In the 17th century, these houses also included factorylike facilities so residents could work to support the institution that imprisoned them. This system was so economical and socially therapeutic for communities seeking to rid themselves of deviants that it spread throughout Europe. By the end of the 18th century, when John Howard investigated their operations and functions in England, Holland, Germany, France, Italy, and Spain, he found that " 'the same walls could contain those condemned by common law, young men who disturbed their families' peace or who squandered their goods, people without profession, and the insane' " (quoted in Foucault, 1965, p. 45).

The purpose of confinement was to remove the poor, the homeless, and the misfits from the streets of the community. It was to reduce idleness in the general population. This trend was most unfortunate for the least well positioned during this period because as factory work became more efficient it required fewer workers, which increased unemployment and expanded the ranks of the idle and the poor. Consequently, as communities became less tolerant of idleness, the transformation from agrarian to industrial means of production actually increased idleness. In many cities in Europe, the unemployment problem became so acute the poor and idle were systematically rounded up and driven from town. The establishment of the Hôpital also helped with this increasingly difficult problem. According to Foucault (1965),

> For the first time, purely negative measures of exclusion were replaced by a measure of confinement; the unemployed person was no longer driven away or punished; he was taken in charge, at the expense of the nation but

at the cost of his individual liberty. Between him and society, an implicit
system of obligation was established: he had the right to be fed, but he
must accept the physical and moral constraint of confinement. (p. 48)

What followed were policies and practices based on the premise that
idleness was evil and work was salvation. In England, the King ordered
strict enforcement of the Poor Laws, which resulted in aggressive pursuit
and prosecution of beggars and vagabonds and "all those who live in
idleness and will not work for reasonable wages or who spend what they
have in taverns . . . for these people live like savages without being married,
nor buried, nor baptized; and it is this licentious liberty which causes so
many to rejoice in vagabondage" (Foucault, 1965, p. 50).

Just below the surface of this idleness-is-evil ideology was the economic and political reality created by the transformation of the workplace.
On the one hand, increased unemployment was a source of political unrest,
and on the other hand, it was a source of uncommitted capital. In that there
was no thought that unemployment was a consequence of declining economic conditions, then unemployment must be due to the moral decay of
the unemployed. Persons without work had failed a basic tenet of religious
doctrine. In that labor was penance for the fall of man, then failing to work
was equivalent to rejecting God's salvation. "Labor in the houses of
confinement . . . assumed its ethical meaning: since sloth had become the
absolute form of rebellion, the idle would be forced to work, in the endless
leisure of a labor without utility or profit" (Foucault, 1965, p. 57).

This was the context within which disability acquired meaning. During
the centuries that preceded city life, the collective response to the condition
was mixed. But now there was this moral reasoning connecting idleness with
damnation. Consequently, the purpose of confinement was to correct the moral
decrepitude of the idle. In both Protestant and Catholic countries, mental
illness became a problem of sin for which instruction and obedience in spiritual
matters was the only solution, as suggested by Saint Vincent de Paul:

The principal end for which such persons have been removed here, out of
the storms of the great world, and introduced into this solitude as pension-
ers, is entirely to keep them from the slavery of sin, from being eternally
damned, and to give them means to rejoice in a perfect contentment in this
world and in the next. (quoted in Foucault, 1965, p. 62)

The result for people least advantaged in life was physical separation
from community life, confinement in institutions, and inhuman treatment

while being confined. Conditions at institutions were so deplorable in England during the 18th century that Parliament nearly passed a bill for the "Regulation of Private Mad-houses" in 1773. Humanitarian reformers such as Vincenzo Chiarugi, Joseph Daquin, and William Tuke freed patients from chains in 1774, introduced humanitarian reforms at the hospital in Chambery in 1787, and recommended the establishment of a more humane mental hospital for relatives of the Society of Friends in 1793. In France, Philipe Pinel, who became administrator of the Bicêtre in 1793, reported that in that institution " 'It is impossible to pass over in silence that which they call the cell service, where 600 mentally sick were massed together without order and left to the rapacity and ineptness of subalterns. It was a picture of disorder and confusion' " (Scheerenberger, 1983, p. 45).[7] The practice of the period had been to admit persons with mental illness to the Hôtel Dieu for baths, bleeding, and medications and to transfer men to Bicêtre and women to Salpétrière if they failed to improve at the Hôtel Dieu. By the 18th century, there were 7,000 women at Salpétrière, with 1,000 who were mentally disturbed living in only one wing of the building. Their conditions were as follows:

> "[They were] in the most deplorable condition. . . . Though the rooms are washed twice a day, these poor souls live in indescribable filth and are like the lowest animals." (Scheerenberger, 1983, p. 46)[8]

So it went into the 19th century. People who lacked the capacity and opportunity to adjust to city life idealized by self-directed, productive activity consistent with religious calling were institutionalized. Increasingly, the society of the good and the proper distanced itself from asylums of the evil and immoral. The only contact between the two occurred when visitors paid to see these creatures who were defined as being physically, mentally, and spiritually less than human. According to Foucault (1965),

> As late as 1815, if a report presented in the House of Commons is to be believed, the hospital of Bethlehem exhibited lunatics for a penny, every Sunday. Now the annual revenue from these exhibitions amounted to almost four hundred pounds; which suggests the astonishingly high number of 96,000 visits a year. In France, the excursion to Bicêtre and the display of the insane remained until the Revolution one of the Sunday distractions for the Left Bank bourgeoisie. Mirabeau reports in the *Observations d'un voyageur anglais* that the madmen at the Bicêtre were shown "like curious animals, to the first simpleton willing to pay a coin." One

went to see the keeper display the madmen the way the trainer at the Fair
of Saint-Germain put the monkeys through their tricks. (p. 68)

Life in the asylum was as subhuman as was its public displays.
Residents lived in cramped, cold, wet cells with nothing but straw pallets
as furniture. In the La Salpêtrière during the winter, living conditions
worsened when the waters of the Seine rose to allow sewer waste to enter
the cells, and rats to attack the residents causing them sickness and even
death (Foucault, 1965, p. 71). Then there was the additional pain for those
whose behavior was violent or threatening. According to Foucault, treatment at La Salpêtrière was especially egregious:

> Madwomen seized with fits of violence are chained like dogs at their cell
> doors, and separated from keepers and visitors alike by a long corridor
> protected by an iron grille; through this grille is passed their food and the
> straw on which they sleep; by means of rakes, part of the filth that
> surrounds them is cleaned out. (p. 72)

At the hospital of Strasbourg in 1814, Francois-Emmanuel Fodéré

> "found a kind of human stable, constructed with great care and skills: 'for
> troublesome madmen and those who dirtied themselves, a kind of cage,
> or wooden closet, which could at the most contain one man of middle
> height, had been devised at the ends of the great wards.' These cages had
> gratings for floors, and did not rest on the ground but were raised about
> fifteen centimeters. Over these gratings was thrown a little straw 'on which
> the madman lay, naked or nearly so, took his meals, and deposited his
> excrement.' " (quoted in Foucault, 1965, p. 73)

All in all, this was treatment for animals, not humans. Indeed, as
Foucault argued, the belief system supporting this treatment defined them
as such. To make matters worse, the only route to restoration of that lost
humanity was punishment through rigorous discipline, stern treatment, and
spiritual rejuvenation. Mental deviance was an "unchained animality" to
be "mastered only by discipline and brutalizing" (Foucault, 1965, p. 75).
It was also a condition to be feared.

TECHNICAL CONTROL

The 19th century was no more auspicious for the poor and the disabled
than the 18th century. By then, another need-problem-solution cycle was

underway to create a new round of sociocultural change that would again disadvantage those lacking strategic position and resource to secure what they needed and wanted in life. This century was the crucible for the industrial age, stimulated by Newtonian problem solving that had spread throughout the scientific community to create innovative means of producing technological gain. This round of sociocultural change commenced when James Hargreaves introduced the spinning jenny and when James Watt built the steam engine. These inventions catalyzed a need-problem-solution condition that had been building within a handicraft industry still dependent on the spinning wheel and hand loom for textile production. By the 18th century, production gridlock had developed within the handicraft industry because the guilds could not keep pace with the demand for textiles in British controlled India. Consequently, freelance merchants bypassed the guild system in favor of cottage labor that they supplied with bulk fibers (linen or wool) to spin yarn and dye fabric.

This system broke down in 1733 when John Kay invented a flying shuttle loom, which wove faster than workers could produce and caused shortages in yarn. James Hargreaves's 1770 spinning jenny solved this problem because it produced yarn faster, although it could produce only one of the two types needed. Richard Arkwright solved this problem with a water frame that produced the other type of yarn but in the process created yet another problem: The water frame was too large and expensive for cottage use. So Arkwright built a factory to house the water frame, starting the factory system and commencing the industrial revolution. Factories spread all over Europe, and innovations in machined-based power followed. James Watts' steam condenser and Matthew Boulton's rotary power enabled steam engines to power other machines, which resulted in the first steam powered cotton mill in Papplewick, Nottinghamshire. By 1785, the industrial revolution had transformed England; it transformed France 30 years later, and it transformed Germany and the United States 20 years after that.

The chief beneficiaries of these technological transformations were, of course, those in positions of control over the new technological means of production—the Kays, the Hargreaves, the Arkwrights, the Watts, and the Boultons. Those left out were the same groups as before—the poor and the disabled. But this time being left out meant experiencing new hardships due to the accelerated pace of this new version of sociocultural change that, in the final decades of the century, created problems far more complex and socially challenging than any confronted in the past. By 1795, for example,

England was forced to experiment with social programs such as the Speenhamland Act that provided welfare (dole) relief for the poor who were surviving on low-paying, low-skilled jobs. The rapid pace of industrialization had increased the number of cities with a population of more than 50,000 from three in the 1780s to over 30 by the 1850s. Manchester, the seat of industrialization in England, grew from 25,000 to 455,000 during the same period.

The typical small English city was ill-prepared for this rate of change. Consequently, police protection, water distribution, and garbage and sewage disposal services were rendered inadequate, as was housing, which was shabbily built and expensive. Whole families were forced to live in single rooms, working 14 hours per day and longer. Children either worked or wandered in the streets unattended. There was no job security, no community, no family, and no hope because the automated factory had reduced jobs and tasks to routine movements any unskilled person could perform. The only winners in this period of social change were factory owners who controlled the means of production in the new economy. They epitomized the Protestant ideology of determination and sacrifice in pursuit of productive gain. The losers were everyone else, especially children who had little chance of pulling themselves from the poverty that engulfed them.

Moreover, the prevailing ideology explaining the forces responsible for this round of sociocultural change was in accord with "natural law" as described by Adam Smith's laissez-faire doctrine of supply and demand. The assumptions undergirding this and other theories of social process were anchored to the ideology of natural science. From Adam Smith's laissez-faire economics to Louis Balanc's socialism, and Karl Marx's communism, belief in natural law prevailed. Doctrines that science was the foundational wellspring for all inquiry emanated from positivist French philosopher Auguste Comte who founded sociology and argued that the development of human knowledge began at a theological or imaginative stage of divine explanation, evolved to a metaphysical or abstract stage of philosophical explanation, and then culminated with positivism, which employed scientific law to explain and predict all naturally occurring phenomena. In the eyes and minds of most 19th-century intellectuals, stage three had arrived, even though that stage had dislocated many from the mainstream of community opportunity.

By the middle of the 19th century, therefore, there was little to challenge the control of productive gain through science. Perceptions of efficacy that developed from the Renaissance to the 18th century now translated into technologies of scientific control in the 19th century. Newtonian thinking that had reordered ultimate sources of truth could also produce practical understanding through technical control. The potential for human achievement seemed infinite. Newton was right, the universe was orderly; and the positivist methods were right, pragmatic gain was unlimited.

Finally, Charles Darwin's *The Origin of Species* offered new insights on the application of science in social affairs, for example, by sorting the able from the disabled on a more systematic basis. Because by the time Darwin originated his evolution of the species, others offered the services of science to identify those who deviated from the norm of humanity. In *Mental Maladies: A Treatise on Insanity,* Jean Etienne Dominique (1845) defined two levels of mental retardation; Edouard Seguin suggested differences between simpleness or superficial retardation, backwardness or feeblemindedness, imbecility, and idiocy; and in 1858, John Langdon Hayden Down described congenital, accidental, and developmental causes of retardation. In 1877, the American Association on Mental Deficiency identified three categories of intellectual functioning—idiocy, imbecility, and feeblemindedness; and in 1884 Kerlin added moral imbecility, which meant lack of will-power " 'to be other than they are, or to do otherwise than they do' " (Scheerenberger, 1983, p. 111).[9]

Soon to follow were psychologists such as Cattell, Johnson, and Binet, who measured human behavior by constructing standardized tasks and conducting laboratory experiments. Cattell introduced mental testing in 1890, using college students to study psychological constructs; Johnson followed in 1897 with laboratory studies of boys with mental retardation, showing them to be more able to make simple objective associations than complicated logical ones; and Alfred Binet observed in 1899 that "less intelligent" children failed to adapt to change as quickly as "more intelligent children" (Scheerenberger, 1983, p. 111). These applications of scientific measurement set the stage for sorting the able from the disabled. They gave governmental agencies the means of counting and recording the incidence of mental disability in their country. By 1890, the United States reported 95,571 persons with mental retardation in the general population, with 15,534 receiving institutional support—5,254 in institutions for persons with mental retardation, 2,469 in asylums for persons with mental illness, and 7,811 in almshouses for the poor (Scheerenberger, 1983). Along with these tracking procedures came policies to confine and control the deviant.

This began in Europe, where laws were enacted that assigned responsibility for the care of those persons lacking position and capacity to satisfy their own needs. England's Poor Law Amendment Act of 1834 ensured care and treatment of "idiots and imbeciles" detained in workhouses. The Poor Law Act of 1844 permitted local agencies to provide workhouse detainees with educational services. The Lunatic Asylum Act of 1853 established public supported asylums for persons with disabilities. The Elementary Education Act of 1870 also required school boards to provide education for children with mental retardation. And the Idiots Act of 1886 allowed for public support for educational services for children so classified (Scheerenberger, 1983).

Comparable policies were slow to develop in the United States because institutionalization had to compete with home-based service, the preferred mode of caring for disabled children who were from wealthy families. For this group, keeping the disabled child at home in a supportive environment was superior to placing him or her in an institution where treatment was inadequate. Unfortunately, this was not an option for poor families who depended on support from state and local government to keep family members at home or, if that was not possible, for another family to assume responsibility for their care. This eventually led to an auctioning system connecting poor families with services offered by other households, a practice that encouraged the abuse described by Dorothea Dix in her address to the Kentucky legislature:

"In Kentucky I found one epileptic girl subject to the most brutal treatment, and many insane in perpetual confinement. Of the idiots alone, supported by the State at a cost of $17,500.62, in indigent private families, and of which class there were in 1845 four hundred and fifty, many were exposed to the severest treatment and heavy blows from day to day, and from year to year. In a dreary block-house was confined for many years a man whose insanity took the form of mania. Often the most furious paroxysms prevented rest for several days and nights in succession. No alleviation reached this unhappy being; without clothes, without fire, without care or kindness, his existence was protracted amidst every horror incident to such circumstances. Chains in common use." (quoted in Scheerenberger, 1983, p. 100)[10]

In time, this system of caring for disabled children from poor families became so corrupt that children were auctioned off to the lowest bidder on the first of May each year, a practice unseemly close to slavery, and it was.

Care in service-providing households deteriorated to a point in which the disabled person received only the minimum needed to survive. Unfortunately, when state and local government intervened to correct these abuses by building almshouses, poorhouses, and county homes, they simply replicated the misery experienced by the disabled on a larger scale. In 1851, the Joint Committee on Public Charitable Institutions approved the establishment of the Massachusetts School for Idiots and Feeble-Minded Youth, and this encouraged other states to do the same. By 1880, there were publicly supported institutions serving 4,216 persons with mental retardation in California, Illinois, Indiana, Iowa, Kansas, Kentucky, Massachusetts, Minnesota, Nebraska, New Jersey, New York, Ohio, and Pennsylvania (Scheerenberger, 1983).

The principle gain from this new system of institutional services was security, order, predictability, and control. Resident life was designed to be safe, productive, obedient, and respectful—an ideal set of expectations for the closing decades of the 19th century in which concern about mental retardation had shifted from charity to fear. The popularity of explanations for deviance based on some variant of social Darwinism and the growing belief that persons with mental disorders were inclined to deviance focused public attention on the hereditary influence and its threat for the future of the human species. Richard Dugdale's 1877 report on *The Jukes: A Study in Crime, Pauperism, Disease, and Heredity* concluded that the Juke family origins, when traced back six generations, exhibited higher proportions of offspring with social, psychological, and physical problems than offspring with "non-Juke blood." This suggested that social devolution was increasing, that there was " 'an ever increasing army of incompetents becoming as they breed, still more incompetent and irresponsible, still more destructive; ever more and more debasing and depressing alike on the body politic' " (Sheerenberger, 1983, p. 117).[11]

Segregation and confinement were attractive solutions to these mounting concerns. Consequently, it was not long before the goal of institutionalization changed from enlightened treatment and progressive education to paternalistic custody and segregated control. Children originally enrolled to receive an education grew to adulthood only to discover their parents were unwilling to assume responsibility for their care and wanted them to extend their stay. Institutions were, after all, secure and predictable. Soon administrators were combining treatment programs to serve the more capable residents with custodial programs that served persons identified as incapable of learning. They also established policies of gender segregation for fear that women with mental retardation would "reproduce their kind."

The upshot of all this was a dramatic increase in the scope and purpose of institutionalization. Rather than preparing residents for lives of self-directed fulfillment, the purpose was to prepare them for self-sufficiency within the institution. In 1897, Johnson wrote, " 'We have no desire to make our child self-directing as he must always be under the direction of the institution. What we do wish is, to make him as nearly self-supporting as possible in the institution' " (Scheerenberger, 1983, p. 125).[12] This amounted to a sentence of life imprisonment, and it evolved into a system of slave labor as well. Residents became solutions to the very problems they presented in that by performing the day-to-day work of the institution, they kept themselves occupied, eliminated the need for supervision, and reduced the cost of running the institution. Everyone was happy—except, perhaps, the residents. The master strategy epitomizing this approach was the "colony plan," eventually adopted by the largest of the state institutions. It included a training school with industrial, custodial, and farm departments supervising resident labor for purposes of " 'colonizing lads, as they grow into manhood, in properly-arranged houses, as farmers, gardeners, dairy-help, etc' " (Scheerengberger, 1983, p. 128).[13]

In sum, the consequence of failing to fit into a social order defined by one's position and capacity in the industrial structure of productive work was segregation and confinement through institutionalization. This process, which began in the 17th century and extended through the 20th century, led to policies and practices that treated people as less than human. Segregation and confinement meant being taken care of and being told what to do. What was most predictable about institutional life for those who were institutionalized was that there was no opportunity to choose and to act on behalf of their own needs and interests. It meant they had no chance for self-determination.

In fact, the prevailing viewpoint was that people who were in institutions were there for their own sake as well as for the sake of their families and the community. Too often, this exclusion from the mainstream was an out-of-sight, out-of-mind solution to a most difficult social and moral problem. It was a solution that only families had to deal with as they experienced the pain that came with institutionalization. Many times families forgot this pain, as the following letter from one resident attests in his plea for an opportunity to visit his father (Scheerenberger, 1983, p. 159):[14]

My Dear Father:

   I wish you would leave me come home for my birthday which is not
far off. It comes on the 25th of September, which is Thursday. There is
one question I wish to ask you and it is this: if I ask you to take me home,
you say you haven't the money and if I run away why you seem to have
it to bring me back, and that is what puzzles me. I only wish I could spend
just one month with you, I would be more than satisfied, and you know I
have been here exactly 9 years and haven't been home in a decent way
yet, and I guess I never will. If you can't give me a little change, I will
have to make it myself, I will never show my face near home, and you can
depend on it. From

                                          Your unthought of Son
                                          "H.F.W."

Social Selection Theory

   History informs us that the needs-problem-solution cycle that drives
sociocultural change in all human communities stimulated major transformations in how humans optimize their opportunities over the millennia.
During each of three major transformations, some members of the community increased their capacity and enhanced their opportunity to the extent
they were able to position themselves favorably with respect to a new
means of producing desirable gain. For example, during the transformation
from nomadic and sedentary life, some individuals and groups gained
advantage for themselves by securing positions of control over other
people's time and behavior. During the agrarian era, some individuals and
groups gained advantage for themselves by securing positions of control
over economic transactions of others. And during the industrial era, some
individuals and groups gained advantage for themselves by securing positions of control over the technical means of producing gain.
   In each of these sociocultural transformations, those well positioned
in the community's structure of productive output were able to optimize
their opportunities for pursuing their own ends and, as a consequence, to
improve their prospects for freedom. On the other hand, those less well
situated socially, economically, and technically suffered because they
lacked access to these means of improving their circumstances. Lacking
control over other people's time and behavior during the horticultural era,
they were unable to improve their prospects for living the self-directed life

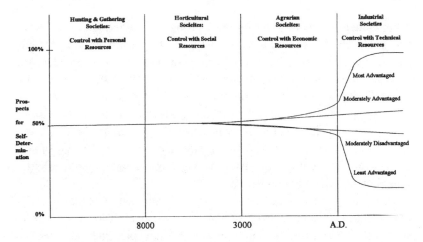

Figure 4.3. The Evolution of Prospects for Self-Determination for Four Groups of Individuals—Most Advantaged, Moderately Advantaged, Moderately Disadvantaged, and Least Advantaged

on their own; lacking advantage in economic transactions with others, they lost capacity to pursue their own ends when they attempted to improve their economic circumstances by engaging in daily exchanges with others; and lacking control over the technical means of producing gain, they were unable to keep up with the technological pace of gain production.

In sum, individuals who occupied positions that provided access to valuable resources and who had the capacity to use those resources effectively and efficiently were able to use these advantages to improve their circumstances in life. They were able to build on their positional advantage by using their capacity to alter their circumstances to improve their prospects for getting what they wanted in life. Moreover, this improvement in prospects produced a feedback effect that enhanced subsequent capacity and subsequent positional advantage. The interaction between favorable personal capacity and favorable positional opportunity accelerated the accumulation of gain to produce gross differences in opportunity and outcome among members of the community.

Figure 4.3 illustrates this dynamic. It highlights the transformations in resource control that occurred when human groups altered their mode of adaptation from nomadic hunting and gathering to the sedentary activities of horticultural, agrarian, and industrial periods. As indicated in the figure, prospects for self-determination were comparable among various members of the human community during the hunting and gathering period. After that, prospects differentiated as inequalities of opportunity and outcome increased somewhat during the agrarian era and then accelerated in the industrial era. These trajectories illustrate the point that, during these periods, prospects for self-determination accelerated on different trajectories to the extent the same individuals and groups experienced the same optimalities of adjustment and optimalities of opportunity. Some groups consistently experienced favorable circumstances of capacity and opportunity and some groups consistently experienced unfavorable circumstances of capacity and opportunity.

According to social selection theory then, the factors responsible for these differential effects were social, not biological. They were due to social selection factors, not natural selection factors. Natural selection produced its effect prior to the human transformation from nomadic to sedentary modes of production—when *Homo sapiens sapiens* was differentiated from *Homo sapiens, Homo sapiens* was differentiated from *Homo erectus,* and when *Homo erectus* was differentiated from *Homo habilis.* Also, the natural selection effect was physiological and morphological, not psychological and social. Social selection effects, therefore, describe those adaptive variations occurring within the species *Homo sapiens sapiens* that are social, not natural. *Homo sapiens sapiens* has not been on earth long enough for natural selection to produce the variations in social adaptations that we have observed over the last 10,000 years.

The propositions of natural selection theory explain why different species produce different numbers of offspring and, by implication, why some have a better chance of survival than others.[15] Proposition 1 accounts for these differential survival rates by noting differences in biological and physiological makeup of different species; Proposition 2 explains that these differences are passed from generation to generation. Proposition 3 concludes that, as a result, there are likely to be different numbers of offspring based on these variations in physiology, morphology, and behavior.[16] This differential production of offspring is what we know as the natural selection effect. Some species survive in greater numbers than others due to these variations and the perpetuation of variants. Proposition 4 concludes that when the numbers of one species increase and the numbers of another species decrease, there is a natural selection effect.

Social selection theory follows a similar logic, although it explains why some individuals and groups are selected by psychological, social, and cultural factors. Individuals and groups vary in their prospects for getting what they need and want in life because their adjustments and opportunities vary. Social selection theory explains how this occurs with Proposition 1 stating that individuals vary in how well they adjust to opportunity for gain and Proposition 2 stating that individuals experience variations in their optimalities of opportunity for gain. Consequently, within a community of actors, prospects for self-determination will vary according to the distribution of these optimalities. Proposition 3 states that when the same individuals experience the same optimalities of opportunity and optimalities of adjustment, then gain accumulates according to these optimalities. Proposition 4 states that when this occurs, the social system produces a social selection effect favoring some individuals and groups over others by consistently providing them with more favorable circumstances for getting what they want in life.

This explains the inequality of opportunity and outcome in civilized life. Concentrations of advantage defined as *favorable adjustment to favorable opportunity* have accelerated the accumulation of gain and its distribution among members of the group in direct proportion to their optimalities of adjustment and opportunity. This means that individuals and groups making optimal adjustment to optimal opportunity receive greater shares of the cooperative produce than those making suboptimal adjustment to suboptimal opportunity. Furthermore, this social stratification effect accelerates over time, as optimal opportunity is increasingly associated with individuals making optimal adjustments and suboptimal opportunity is increasingly associated with individuals making suboptimal adjustments. This is what has happened for more than 5,000 years. It is a natural consequence of freedom as power.

The Problem of Freedom as Power

This chapter began by describing how three theories of justice have addressed the question of what is fair treatment for people least well situated in society. Justice as fairness claims those least advantaged in society deserve to gain in proportion to the gain experienced by the most advantaged members of society. Being least advantaged is sufficient to entitle them to benefit from the success of the cooperative endeavor. Justice as entitlement claims individuals deserve to benefit to the extent they produce or receive gain through fair exchange with others. They deserve no more. They do not deserve gain produced by others unless it is given to them voluntarily or is part of a voluntary transaction. Charity, not subsidy through governmental transfer, is the only means of helping persons least able to produce gain through the voluntary exchange. Any redistribution of gain that takes from one and gives to another is a violation of the right of the first to keep what is his or hers.

Equal opportunity theory's claim for fair treatment of the least advantaged rests on an understanding of the factors responsible for unequal prospects for self-determination. The theory claims that an individual's chance of living the self-determined life depends on his or her capacity and his or her opportunity to self-determine. Constraints on either of these circumstances diminish prospects for pursuing the self-determined life. This argument shifts the debate from deciding whether to redistribute material gain among members of society to determining what combinations of capacity and opportunity are most likely to improve an individual's prospects of pursuing the self-determined life.

Figure 4.1 demonstrated the cogency of this line of reasoning by describing four trajectories for prospects for self-determination, one that accelerated gain production, a second and third that netted incremental gain and loss over time, and a fourth that produced accelerated loss. All four trajectories leveled, after initial increases and decreases, to maintain at different prospect levels, one group (also referred to as cell 1 prospects from Table 3.1) experiencing the highest chances of self-determination, two groups (cell 2 and cell 3 prospects) experiencing moderately favorable and unfavorable prospects for self-determination, and a fourth group (cell 4 prospects) experiencing the least optimal prospects. This analysis demonstrated that interaction between capacity and opportunity was responsible for the acceleration of gain and loss for two of the four trajectories—those most and least advantaged in society. The analysis also suggested that these two trajectories occurred independently of individual effort. This is because interaction between the optimalities of adjustment and opportunity can produce an acceleration effect for any person who finds himself or herself in a circumstance of favorable capacity and favorable opportunity. Consequently, the gain resulting from this circumstance is outside the domain of moral desert and cannot be justified on the basis of freedom as personal power.

Notes

1. Excerpted from *The social case: Human nature and the evolution of society,* by Alexandra Maryanski and Jonathan H. Turner, with the permission of the publishers, Stanford University Press. © 1992 by the Board of Trustees of the Leland Stanford Junior University.

2. This point is described as well in Lenski and Lenski (1974).

3. This is the argument Maryanski and Turner (1992) make, arguing that human nature is genetically linked with patterns of survival that are individualistic first and social second. The social resulted when civilization became a necessary consequence of declining prospects for survival in small groups that permitted maximum freedom and autonomy.

4. Reprinted from *Human societies: An introduction to macrosociology,* by G. Lenski & J. Lenski, with the permission of the publishers, The McGraw-Hill Companies. © 1974.

5. Mann (1986) and Maryanski and Turner (1992) argue convincingly that the transformation from hunting and gathering to sedentary life created the "social cage" effect that was contrary to human nature and preferences for freedom and autonomy.

6. Excerpted from *A history of mental retardation,* by R. C. Scheerenberger, with permission of the publishers, Paul H. Brookes Publishing Co. © 1983. Scheerenberger is quoting from I. Giordani (1961). *Vincent de Paul* (pp. 76-77). Milwaukee: Bruce.

7. Scheerenberger is quoting from G. Zilborg (1941). *A history of medical psychology* (pp. 326-327). New York: Norton.

8. Scheerenberger is quoting from C. Manceron (1977). *Twilight of the old order* (Trans. P. Wolf, p. 431). New York: Alfred A. Knopf.

9. Scheerenberger is quoting from I. Kerlin (1887). Moral imbecility. *Proceedings of the Association of Medical Offices of American Institutions for Idiotic and Feebleminded Persons,* p. 5.

10. Scheerenberger is quoting from D. Dix (1848). *Memorial soliciting a state hospital for the protection and cure of the insane submitted to the General Assembly of North Carolina* (p. 23). Raleigh, N.C.: Seaton Gales.

11. Scheerenberger is quoting from A. Osborne (1894). President's annual address. *Proceedings of the Association of Medical Officers of American Institutions for Idiotic and Feebleminded Persons,* p. 392.

12. Scheerenberger is quoting from G. E. Johnson (1897). What we do, and how we do it. *Journal of Psycho-Asthenic, 2,* 98.

13. Scheerenberger is quoting from W. Fish (1892). Custodial care of adult idiots. *Proceedings of the Association of Medical Officers of American Institutions for Idiotic and Feebleminded Persons,* p. 209.

14. Scheerenberger is quoting from M. Barr (1904). *Mental illness and social policy: The American experience* (p. 334). Philadelphia: P. Blakiston's Son.

15. See Table 5.3, p. 194.

16. The theory was adapted from Levins and Lewontin (1985, p. 32).

Freedom as Right

When freedom is solely a function of an individual's capacity to get what one needs or wants in life, then the expression of that freedom is directly proportional to Person's personal, social, economic, and technical power to change the unfavorable circumstances of an opportunity into favorable circumstances for a desirable pursuit. As indicated in the previous chapter, this has been the dominant experience of freedom throughout history. From the beginning of human civilization, persons well situated in their community had access to resources unavailable to others that enabled them to enhance their own capacity to optimize opportunity for themselves and for their families. This created gross differences between those with capacity, opportunity, and accumulated gain and those without any advantage in capacity, opportunity, or gain. Only in the last three centuries has the ideology of freedom for all come to affect the direction of sociocultural evolution to encourage persons lacking capacity and opportunity to improve their own prospects for self-determination. The reason it took so long for the ideal of freedom as right to compete with the historical experience of freedom as power is that the *decentralization* of social, economic, and technical power, which was a precondition for this generalized expectation for freedom, took several thousand years to evolve.

The full explanation for how this transformation came about begins with the needs-problem-solution cycle that accelerated the process of sociocultural evolution when humans adopted a sedentary mode of adaptation and organized themselves into elaborate divisions of labor. The consequence of this concentration of human capacity on producing commonly valued gain was a surplus of output that could be reinvested in new opportunity for gain. This reinvestment of surplus to optimize the circumstances for producing additional gain accelerated the needs-problem-solution cycle to create new opportunity, and this, in turn, enabled some members of the human group to improve their prospects by positioning themselves more favorably in the social structure. This occurred gradually as social structures evolved to decentralize access to the social, economic, and technical means of producing gain that were once concentrated in the hands of the few.

This decentralization of power had the secondary effect of shifting the locus of control over productive gain, leading to the development of new ideologies legitimating the advantages of those individuals and groups who found themselves in these new positions of control. In this way, belief systems that explained and legitimated how the social and physical world worked evolved as a consequence of and in congruence with each new redistribution of freedom as power. This meant that new ways of perceiving and explaining the social world tended to legitimate the status quo by making the newly evolved social structure the basis for a new moral order for community life. In other words, how the social structure actually functioned would eventually produce a belief system about how it ought to function, and this, in turn, would legitimate what already existed.

Given this evolutionary history, it is not surprising that ancient ideologies of right did little to advance the idea of freedom for all. When freedom as power determines who deserves what control over what resources, individuals with power deserve their power by virtue of having it. This was the effect of ideologies explaining and legitimating what already had come to be. They discouraged those lacking capacity and opportunity from attempting to enhance their own resources to pursue their own ends by reinforcing the existing distribution of advantage and disadvantage in the community. Individuals lacking resources had no choice but to accept their station in life by channeling their energy into other areas, for example, by engaging in self-development to achieve moral perfection. This, too, was reinforced by beliefs that claimed the present life in the material world was preparation for something better in a spiritual life. In the ancient world, those least well positioned in the community simply had to adjust to the prospect that their pursuit for more desirable ends in their lives would never occur. This changed in the modern world, at least in principle, in that there was the expectation that all persons should have a right to pursue their own ends in life.

But the transformation from ancient ideology of freedom as power to modern ideology of freedom as right took centuries, awaiting as it did for a pattern of decentralized power to yield an ideology based on a *negotiated* distribution of rights and responsibilities that presumed a *condition of equality* among power holders. These circumstances developed in the West where the fall of Rome produced equally powerful competitors who had a common need to legitimate their gains to avoid an otherwise chaotic condition of all against all. The feudal society that emerged from this unique condition of decentralized power was based on negotiated agreements between equally powerful actors defining various divisions of rights and responsibilities that would yoke them in mutually beneficial social relationships. The ideology for right emerging from this condition of equal power was based on an expectation for *reciprocal benefit*.

The feudal order that evolved from this principle of reciprocity lasted an entire millennium until the transformation from agrarian to industrial means of production unleashed another needs-problem-solution cycle that gave the commercial classes access to economic resources that they used to improve their own prospects by forcing feudal monarchs to guarantee them a new set of rights, as specified in the Magna Carta. The social contract ideology that evolved from this great document justified this new set of rights on a basis different from the reciprocal benefit rule that legitimated the feudal order. This new ideology claiming freedom as a right was based on human nature and natural law.

The immediate beneficiaries of this new ideology were, of course, members of the ascendant commercial classes of the preindustrial era who employed this belief to their advantage during the industrial revolution by further enhancing their capacity and opportunity for pursuing what they needed and wanted in life. The ideology of freedom as right helped them argue for their own interests against the feudal nobility who controlled resources that maintained their positions of power and advantage in the community. The ideology of individualism that developed from this new belief claimed that individuals were responsible for their destiny. Consequently, they deserved that set of fundamental rights that was necessary to pursue their own ends in life. No external force had the right to intervene between Person and his pursuit—given that pursuit harmed no one. John Locke argued for the right to be free from external interference; John Adams argued for the right to be free to pursue economic gain; and Jeremy Bentham argued for the right to pursue happiness. These claims were legitimate because they were grounded in human nature and natural law.

There were unintended consequences attached to this new ideology, as well, because it raised expectations for those lacking the experience and the right to self-determination. In fact, the idea of basing the right to freedom on human nature and natural law was fundamentally destabilizing because it provided no basis for excluding those who lacked the capacity or opportunity to determine their own way in life. Any individual or group could perceive their situation as being discrepant from the ideal of freedom for all and demand restitution to ameliorate the discrepancy—and they did. The leaders of the American and French revolutions of the 18th century pushed this demand to its logical limit when they claimed freedom for all, arguing that social institutions ought to be constructed to serve the interests of the governed rather than the authority of the government. This destabilizing effect has extended into the postmodern era in that it continues to *raise expectations* among those lacking the experience of self-determination.

This was not a problem in the ancient world because the prevailing ideologies of that period produced the opposite effect; they lowered expectations. The ancient view claimed individuals were fated to live out their lives as they began them to fulfill a divine plan that was consistent with cosmic harmony. Under this system, individuals were expected to fit into fixed positions in life—positions that were consistent with individuals' fixed capacities and fixed opportunities. The result was stability and predictability. The social stratification ideology of the modern world inverted this worldview and the causality it presupposed. Modern ideology was based on a premise of human causal agency functioning within a material world governed by knowable natural law. It elevated the value of actions taken by individuals relative to the compliance expected and sanctioned by institutions. No longer were individuals considered passive reactors to the will of external authority.

In the modern world, individuals increasingly saw their institutions as a *means* to those ends in life they defined as valuable. This meant that as individuals grew in capacity to optimize new opportunity, their institutions were expected to change to reflect that growth and to accommodate their demands for new opportunity. This turned out to be fundamentally unstable, as compared with ancient social stratification ideologies. There were fewer *ideological checks* against the *indeterminate* rate of change that resulted from freewheeling interaction among multitudes of individuals pursuing their own ends in life, from the development of new ideologies justifying these pursuits and outcomes within an evolving division of labor in the community, and from an ever changing environmental circumstance challenging these human adjustments to change.

In sum, this new set of social circumstances increased uncertainty because it allowed individual actors to generate their own ideologies governing the distribution of rights and responsibilities freely negotiated with each other. Of course, these new ideologies functioned as in the past by constraining the opportunities and outcomes of some while enhancing the opportunities and outcomes for others. This, in turn, created new demands for redress by those left out of the mainstream of that newly stratified opportunity. Finally, all of this affected the external environment in unexpected ways by producing unintended consequences that affected the adjustments of individuals and groups to create yet another cycle of change begetting change.

In effect, this interaction between individuals, their ideologies, and their environmental circumstances accelerated the rate of change while it decreased the predictability of how that change would affect individuals, their ideologies, or their circumstances in life. The end result was a new baseline of social experiences in a postmodern world characterized by increased numbers of individuals freely expressing their various capacities to optimize new opportunity, increased variations in ideologies permitting new pursuits and justifying the new opportunities they created, and an increased frequency of unintended environmental consequences that both constrained and enhanced the pursuit of individuals and the development of attendant ideologies.

Given these dramatic changes in human adjustment and its understanding, it is not surprising that new explanations for social stratification emerged to account for the new forms of social inequality that resulted. Theories of individual determinism, for example, identified the individual as the principle force in the production of variations in opportunity and outcome among members of the community, theories of collective determinism identified the group as being responsible for social inequality, and theories of environmental determinism claimed that the forces of nature caused some individuals and groups to adjust more successfully than others. These explanations were modern to the extent they were empirical rather than metaphysical; they all claimed that sociocultural evolution produced differences in opportunities and outcomes because of *empirical events* associated, for example, with individuals, with their groups, or with observable circumstances in their environments.

Based on these different causal theories, there were different recommendations for reducing the discrepancy between the ideal of liberty for all and the empirical fact of liberty for some. For example, the redress recommended by individual determinism usually came down to some form of voluntarism in that anything else would interfere with the individual's freedom of pursuit. This would be unfair because it would prevent individuals from enjoying the results of their efforts. The redress recommended by collective determinism, on the other hand, usually invoked some form of governmental intervention on behalf of the least advantaged, which came at the expense of the most advantaged. This was justified because it was considered unfair for any member of society to be denied a share of the cooperative surplus produced by a division of labor involving everyone. The solution to social inequality recommended by environmental determinism was to do nothing that would interfere with the inexorable flow of social evolution functioning in accordance with natural law. Because no amount of redress could change the course of nature, it would be better to prevent those least able to adjust from overpopulating the community.

Of course, none of these theories improved the lives of those least advantaged in society. In fact, during the modern era, treatment of the poor, the disenfranchised, and the disabled actually worsened. For example, when ideologies of individual determinism were evoked to judge individuals who failed to live up to the moral ideal of initiative and independent resourcefulness, blame and punishment were likely. On the other hand, when ideologies of collective determinism influenced social policy, decisions to care for the least advantaged led to institutionalization and imprisonment—for their own good and for the good of society. Finally, when community sentiment was governed by beliefs of environmental determinism, the public reaction was fear that legions of incompetents would infect the gene pool of the majority. In this climate, policies of sterilization and even extermination were likely.

So at one end of the ideological continuum, there were belief systems that blamed individuals who failed to succeed, at the other end there were beliefs that offered paternalistic care for those unable to fit the productive mold of the most able, and at all points in between there was an undercurrent of suspicion that those least advantaged in society were a threat because they would pollute the hereditary prospects of future generations. The fundamental problem with all of these ideologies was their attribution of a unifactor, unidirectional course for social evolution that was expected to yield outcomes that were inexorable and determinate. Instead of focusing on the *interaction* among individual pursuits, ideologies for collective action, and environmental circumstance, each theory focused on one factor to the exclusion of the others, and rather than specifying those interaction effects responsible for the accumulated gain and loss that differentiated prospects for freedom among individuals, they focused on unidirectional effects. This, of course, obscured the harm that emanated from bidirectional causes.

In this sense, the three ideologies were closer to the ancient assumption of determinism than to the postmodern world of probability. Both the modern and ancient world saw cause as unidirectional and inevitable, rather than bidirectional and probable. In the ancient order, the belief was that change emanated from external forces that caused individuals to react to their circumstances by finding where they fit with cosmic intent, but in the modern order, individuals were agents of their own destiny. The ancient and modern belief systems assumed causality to be *one-way*—with ancient causality originating distally and modern causality originally locally. The result was that they encouraged expectations for *determinate* and *inevitable outcomes* that, incidentally, worked conveniently for the advantaged when assigning responsibility for the failures in life experienced by the disadvantaged. In the ancient world, if you were poor, you were so because the cosmic force determined you should be so, and in the modern world if you were poor, you were poor because your own failures in life made you poor. Either way, the explanation and judgment you deserved were unequivocal.

In the postmodern world, no explanation or judgment is certain in that explanations for success are multicausal and bidirectional reflecting as they do interactions among several classes of variables. We know, for example, that we change our environments and are changed as a consequence of those changes. We know that our beliefs systems affect how we act on our environments to get what we want in life and that the results of our actions, in turn, affect the confidence we have in our beliefs and their utility in explaining and justifying how the world works and what we can expect from it in the future. We also understand that our actions, our beliefs, and

our environmental circumstances interact to affect our prospects of experiencing the self-determined life. In sum, we recognize that the outcomes
of these interactions are probable rather than certain, and that this uncertainty in predicting the direction and course of future opportunity is what
makes the postmodern experience indeterminate rather than determinate
and future outcomes probable rather than inexorable.

To explain how this postmodern worldview came to be, we need to
understand how freedom as power produced social stratification ideologies
that constrained the hopes and aspirations of some while liberating the
hopes and aspirations of others. We also need to understand that as power
decentralized to give more individuals opportunity to build their capacity
to self-determine, these newly empowered individuals created their own
ideologies to legitimate their newly acquired resources to optimize opportunity in their communities. In the modern world, the watershed event
symbolizing this social transformation from freedom as power to freedom
as right occurred when the barons of King John's court leveraged their
positions of power to establish their rights contractually guaranteed in the
Magna Carta. This precedent encouraged others to negotiate opportunity
guarantees by constructing similar social contracts. In that the resultant
ideology justifying these contractual arrangements was based on human
nature rather than divine law, there developed a generalized expectation
for freedom as a right for all persons, even those lacking a power base for
negotiating a more favorable set of opportunities (rights) for themselves.
A consequence of this generalized expectation for freedom was, inevitably,
the creation of a discrepancy between the right and the experience of
self-determination among those lacking the power to negotiate more favorable circumstances on their own.

This created a paradox of freedom in the modern world because the
decentralization of power generated new opportunity for self-determined
pursuit for those who already had sufficient capacity (power) for self-
determination—for people who were already self-determined. This chapter
explains how this occurred, using the following general argument. When
individuals negotiate the distribution of rights and responsibilities with
each other, the resulting agreement reflects the power balance that exists
before the negotiation—which tends to increase the advantage for the more
powerful and decrease the advantage for the less powerful person. When
this pattern is repeated with the same individuals experiencing the same
power imbalance with others, the resulting interaction exacerbates rather
than ameliorates inequalities in the distribution of rights and responsibili-

ties. In other words, freely negotiated distributions of rights and responsibilities between parties of unequal power accelerate power imbalances between parties.

The paradox of the modern experience with freedom as power was that this condition led to a generalized expectation for freedom for all; that, in turn, produced the discrepancy between the right and the experience of freedom. This is what made the ideal of the modern social contract so different from the ideal of the ancient community. There, expectations for personal freedom were obviated by beliefs that individuals had fixed capacity, fixed opportunity, and fixed outcomes throughout life. By the time the ideal of freedom for all had become a unifying value for the social contract, the concept of person had changed to correspond with that ideal. The argument put forth in this chapter is that the feudalism of the Middle Ages provided the crucible for this transformation in the concept of person because it provided an opportunity for individuals to define their relationships with their community in terms of mutual benefit.

This transformation in the concept of person occurred gradually as new groups of individuals negotiated social contracts with their governments to justify their gains in the modern era, and this, in turn, set the occasion for the discrepancy between the universal claim for freedom and the experience of freedom among those lacking the capacity and opportunity to negotiate a better contract for themselves. The effect of this discrepancy on the social theorizing of the modern world was to generate different ideologies of determinism either to explain away the discrepancy (as was the case for individual determinism and environmental determinism) or to offer paternalistic solutions for its amelioration, as was the case for collective determinism.

The problem with the modern solution to the discrepancy problem is that it was based on a conception of causality that was unicausal and unidirectional. Equal opportunity theory offers a postmodern solution by basing its propositions on the assumption that individual pursuits, ideologies for collective action, and environmental circumstance interact to produce probable or prospective outcomes. Consequently, the theory claims that the best one can expect in equalizing the distribution of freedom among a population of actors—given that such an ideal is central to the institutional ideals of the society—is for each person to have a *fair chance* of pursuing individually defined ends in life that are fulfilling for that person. When this condition is present, then the institutions of that society reflect the ideal of freedom for all because they promote fairness in liberty for all.

Negotiating Freedom as Right

The transformation that gave us this ideal of fairness in liberty for all took more than a thousand years, spanning that period that began with the fall of Rome and ended with the modern era. Prior to this transition period we call the Middle Ages, the only experience and expectation for freedom was freedom as power. For the longest period of civilized life, individuals and their kinship groups optimized their adjustments to the extent they were able to secure access to positions of control over the social, economic, and technical resources necessary for producing desired gain for themselves and for their families. By passing the advantages they acquired to their offspring, the same groups of individuals maintained optimal adjustments for long periods. This accelerated the accumulation of advantage for some in that it produced an exponential enhancement of their capacity and opportunity to self-determine relative to others. This enhancement also affected the distribution of opportunity and outcome of less fortunate members of society to create systems of social stratification reflecting these differential accumulations. This meant that the distribution of capacity and opportunity to self-determine among all members of the community corresponded to those differential accumulations of gain favoring individuals most advantageously positioned in society, with prospects for self-determination being optimal for those with the greatest capacity to self-determine, prospects being moderately optimal for those with moderate power to self-determine, and prospects being least optimal for those with the least power to self-determine. Moreover, the acceptance of these stratification systems by all members of society legitimated the unequal distribution of freedom prospects, giving truth to the observation that what becomes the right is simply a recognition and acceptance of what has been the might.

CREATING INEQUALITY

Even in the absence of overt conquest of one human group by another or in the absence of enslavement of the vanquished by the victorious and the legitimization of unequal prospects for freedom by the dominant group, therefore, "might" still affects "right" through accumulated advantage generated from social exchange. This suggests that Nozick's just society in which free exchange of resources is protected by a minimal state would, in the end, reflect the existing power imbalance defined by the original condition of capacity and opportunity attached to various parties engaging in exchange. Although rights and responsibilities may develop from specific transactions initiated and consummated between individuals voluntarily entering into exchange relationships where Person gives a portion of his resources to Other in exchange for a portion of Other's resources given to Person, the outcome of these transactions will at least maintain and, more often, exacerbate the existing power imbalance between the parties. If Person, who has greater capacity and more opportunity for getting what he needs in life than Other, enters into an exchange with Other, Person is likely to leave the exchange with the additional resources he needs and, at the same time, leave with greater capacity than Other. Other, by contrast, is likely to get the resource she bargained for but, at the same time, leave with less capacity for future opportunity than Person. Moreover, if these exchanges are repeated, they have the potential of creating harm for the less advantaged member of the exchange.

This is the nature of exchange between parties who have unequal capacity and opportunity to self-determine. The stronger party experiences a greater gain than the weaker party experiences a net loss. The only difference between the harm produced through voluntary exchange and the harm produced from physical domination is that the differential prospects for future pursuits are concealed by the voluntary nature of the exchange but not by the involuntary nature of the physical domination. During exchange in the marketplace of social life, the declining prospects for self-determination experienced by less well situated individuals occur gradually over time, which can affect generations of offspring who suffer inexorable declines in capacity and opportunity to pursue what they want in life. That Person's net capacity is diminished, whereas Other's is enhanced, or that Person will have fewer opportunities in the future, whereas Other will have greater opportunities, is not of immediate concern, nor is it immediately evident at the moment of exchange.

Nevertheless, the agreement reached about how much should be given and received by the parties to an exchange *legitimates* the result and makes the agreement about what was transacted *right*. Consequently, the question of justice appears answered in that Person agrees to respect Other's claims in one area in return for Other's agreement to respect Person's claims in another area. What Person and Other agree to distribute between them legitimates their mutual claims. The result seems fair because it divides different claims on resources into entitlements and responsibilities, with Person's entitlement to X depending on Other's responsibility for permitting Person's access to X, and Other's entitlement to Y depending on Person's responsibility for allowing Other's access to Y. Person and Other agree to respect each other's rights with regard to this distribution of resources, and their agreement legitimates the distribution. What ends in Person's possession is justly his because it was obtained through fair negotiations with Other—because he obtained it in accordance with Nozick's theory of entitlement. Similarly, what ends in Other's possession is fairly hers for the same reason. No resource redistribution occurred in violation of what Person or Other believed to be fair for them according to their agreement.

For that moment in time, there is no argument about the particulars of the exchange. If Person and Other agree to terms, fine. After all, who can second-guess judgments of independent, rational actors consenting to interact a given way? Looking beyond, however, there may be a question about what is fair when the *same parties* engage frequent exchanges with each other under the *same conditions of power imbalance,* in which one party consistently experiences greater capacity and opportunity than the other. Then, there is potential for harm through an *accumulation* of advantage attaching to the party with an initial advantage.

The problem of defining one person's right and another person's responsibility in terms of transactions agreed to voluntarily does not appear to be problematic for a given exchange or to constitute the potential for harm, for example, when levels of capacity or power and optimalities of opportunity attached to each party to the transaction are equal. The potential for harm is present, however, when one party has a power advantage over the other *and* when the parties engage in frequent exchanges over time. Then the distribution of power is likely to produce a corresponding distribution of rights and responsibilities.

This is why Nozick's justice as entitlement ultimately comes down to freedom as power determining freedom as right. When individuals with greater capacity and opportunity to self-determine exchange resources with individuals having lesser capacity and opportunity, then those with greater capacity and opportunity end up with more rights and fewer responsibilities, whereas those with lesser capacity and fewer opportunities end up with fewer rights and greater responsibilities. The cycle of power begetting rights occurs in proportion to the cycle of capacity begetting optimal opportunity. Power accumulations legitimate unequal distributions of freedom in proportion to the rate at which capacity-opportunity interactions benefit the few at the expense of the many.

Unfortunately, cumulative harm is not easily recognized when deriving principles of justice from thought experiments on original state conditions presuming rational choice between actors of equal power. Rawls, for example, used thought experiments to formulate his theory of justice as fairness as did Nozick in deriving his theory of entitlement. In the following passage, Weinreb (1994) illustrates the approach once again to explain how individuals might behave in original state conditions prior to a conception of justice:

> Suppose there were only one human being. Living alone, she learns that sometimes good or bad things happen to her that she can repeat or prevent from being repeated, whereas other good or bad things happen to her no matter what she does. If she puts seeds in the ground in a certain way, plants, which she can eat later, grow in the same place. But sometimes they die. Pouring water onto the ground where the plants are growing keeps them alive. But just when they are ready to be picked, they turn black and die after a night when it is cold. If she covers them during the night, some survive. But animals eat them. . . . She thus becomes aware of her own causal agency. Over time she extends her agency and explores its limits. Also, observing that the behavior of other beings and things is variably opposed to her own, she attributes concrete causal agency to them and supposes that they, like herself, are trying to obtain outcomes favorable to themselves. Perhaps, insofar as she identifies specific reactions like anger, pleasure, or pain in herself, she projects them also onto other supposed agents. Stretching all that as far as it will go, she envisions what happens around her as a contest of wills in which sometimes she and sometimes they gain the upper hand . . .
>
> Now add to her universe another human being. If she and he were unable to communicate beyond giving signals of something about to happen and she contemplated him only as another causal agency, the actions of which affected and were affected by her behavior, nothing would be changed. So far as his actions were concerned, she would still conceptualize "good" and "bad," if at all, only in terms of her will or his. Suppose, however, that she and he are able to communicate with each other in some form that allows them to be aware of one another's purposes, not only as reflected in what happens but independently, as possibilities or projects entertained but unrealized. As before, they are both aware that some occurrences are good for one and bad for the other, and vice versa. If the agency of neither can affect such an occurrence, that is the end of the matter, each perceiving it as the case may be. But if the agency of both, or even one, can alter the outcome in a way more favorable to one or the other, they will now be able jointly to entertain that possibility. Thinking only in terms of causal agency, they will eventually become aware that they can adjust their various efforts in a way that makes the eventual outcomes taken all together more favorable to both. Each using her and his respective advantages and taking account of the other, there will be some equilibrium that is better for each than she or he could achieve alone.

> The leap from individual purposive action to cooperative action for a joint
> purpose would be a large one; but if there is communication between them,
> it need not be radically different from using other objects as tools to
> achieve one's own purpose. (pp. 142-144)

The logic suggested by this passage is seductive because it implies a
general principle for justifying a division of labor and a distribution of
entitlements and responsibilities similar to that suggested by Nozick's
theory of entitlement. Consequently, it appears to be fair. But is it?

To answer this question we are reminded that in the original condition
there was *equality* of capacity and opportunity between Person and Other.
This allowed either party to withdraw from the negotiation to pursue
alternative means of getting what they wanted. Consequently, neither party
was in greater need of the exchange. Both were interested in consummating
the agreement. Before we infer a general principle of justice from the
original position, therefore, we should ask if this conditions of equal power
is likely to persevere in subsequent transactions. Will the parties have equal
capacity and opportunity on their second, third, fourth, and nth contact?
Probably not, principally because Person and Other will be different people
on subsequent occasions and their capacities and opportunities will reflect
these differences. Person may have acquired surplus capacity and increased
opportunity for his pursuits, whereas Other may have experienced a decline
in her capacity and opportunity for her pursuits.

This is what happens in life, and the empirical fact of social inequality
warns us of the potential for harm when the same individuals bring to the
marketplace of exchange the same inequities in capacity and opportunity. It
warns us about the fairness of distributing entitlements and responsibilities
according to agreements made between parties with differential advantage.
Moreover, it reminds us of the history of inequality in social power and how
this inequality created ideologies about what is fair and just in the distribution
of freedom among various individuals in society. Finally, it reminds us of the
long struggle for equal rights to self-determination and how this struggle has
reflected power imbalance in the negotiation of greater opportunity for self-
determination for individuals previously denied that right.

JUSTIFYING INEQUALITY

Rawls's theory of justice as fairness and Nozick's theory of justice as
entitlement are insensitive to the social dynamic created when one person's

capacity affects another person's opportunity. This is because both theories assume that human capacity and social opportunity are fused and invariant conditions either attached to or detached from the individual. For example, Rawls conflates human capacity and social opportunity and then separates the result from the individual to conclude who is morally entitled to social redress through redistribution of cooperative surplus, whereas Nozick conflates human capacity and social opportunity and then attaches the result to the individual to conclude who is morally entitled to everything gained through legitimate exchange in the marketplace. So, depending on the definition of a person that is most appealing, one can conclude with equal justification that social redress should be delivered or withheld and feel morally secure with the result. Those convinced by the argument that individuals are distinct from their capacities and opportunities will agree with Rawls's difference principle for organizing the just society; those swayed by the argument that individuals are attached to their capacities and their opportunities will believe with Nozick that individuals are entitled to what they get on their own and that gain obtained any other way is unjustified.

Unfortunately, this does little to improve our understanding of the accumulated disadvantages experienced by the least well positioned members of society. In fact, conflating capacity and opportunity is perhaps a step backward in time when we consider that the postmodern view of the individual and society distinguishes the capacity of individuals from the opportunities afforded them due to their position in the social structure. Moreover, it is a step backward to the extent it ignores the empirical reality that human capacity and social opportunity are variable, not fixed entities, and that they function in an indeterminate rather than a determinate social circumstance.

Compare this postmodern conception of person with the Platonic conception of the individual in which all social entities were unified in perfect harmony with the cosmos. People and things were properly placed and fixed according to their fundamental nature. In Plato's *Republic,* humans were to be ordered in the ideal division of labor according to capacities that fixed them in occupations according to their nature. Those with capacity for appetite were to be the workers, farmers, merchants, doctors, and actors; those with capacity for courage were to be the class of fighters; and those with capacity for wisdom were to be the rulers (see Garraty & Gay, 1981, p. 99). In this system, the only change in capacity and opportunity to be expected was within the parameters defined by one's potential for perfectibility as a person slotted for a particular station in life.

Perfectibility within one's station was also encouraged in Hinduism, in which relief from life's misery was always available through self-improvement. The static material world was contrasted with a more hopeful spiritual world. If your position in life caused you earthly pain, you could hope for something better in another life. The Hindu caste system fixed the individual's capacity and position within one of several social strata at birth and then justified this arrangement with promises of transmigration of the soul following death. The Aryan social stratification system based on hereditary background, occupation, and economic status determined opportunities and responsibilities of all by discriminating and stratifying according to skin color (Garraty & Gay, 1981, p. 99). Personal capacity was limited to one's ability to choose the correct moral path to emancipation and freedom in a later life. This was self-determination for the most distant of opportunities. Those who chose well by observing socially acceptable caste behavior would be rewarded with a caste upgrade in a subsequent life.

Religion offered emotional relief for individuals suffering from their lifetime anchor to misery by promising emancipation should they *develop themselves psychologically.* According to Hinduism, misery in the material world was not a problem of limited capacity or constrained social opportunity. It was a problem of psychological immaturity. Every person could find enlightenment by withdrawing from the material world to connect with the universal world. Through this path of self-development, they could undergo repeated cycles of rebirth as they progressed to higher levels in the caste system. What is interesting about these ancient ideologies is that they placed responsibility for the harm wrought by social stratification *on the individual.* If you believed your treatment in life to be unfair, you had only yourself to blame. The social order was not unjust in that if you thought and acted morally, you, too, could assuage the experience of hopelessness and despair. You, too, could experience psychological emancipation. The great religions of the world played on this theme repeatedly to offer solace to the masses who found themselves without the social, economic, and technical resources needed to get what they needed and wanted in life.

The Social Construction of
Rights and Responsibilities

This ancient worldview came to an end in the West when the Roman Empire fell, cutting off western Europe from the cultural influence of the

East. During this period, commonly referred to as the Dark Ages, there was no trade, few cities, and no money. Self-sufficiency reached an uncivilized low. Security was gone, too. Survival of the fittest replaced rule of law, and protection from aggression required knights in armor. Relations between villagers and protectors were *reciprocal* and *contractual* as lord-servant bonds gradually and painstakingly evolved into new social structures. The only light in this land of dark was the Church, which maintained contact with the East and with the distant reaches of the West. It also provided safe haven for persons of intellect and contemplation who shrank from the barbarism and violence of survival subsistence. Monastic houses, governed by abbots holding allegiance to the pope and church in Rome, provided a network of connective ties throughout the West and, at the same time, provided a staging area for converting barbarians to Christian life. By the year 1000, the countries that made up Europe, France, Germany, northern Spain, several city-states in the Italian peninsula, the kingdoms of England, Scotland, Denmark, Norway, and Sweden, and the great kingdoms of Poland, Bohemia, and Hungary in the east, were out of the Dark Ages.

The emergence of Europe from the rubble of the Roman Empire is significant in that with the destruction of that order went the ancient ideology for justifying the distribution of opportunity and responsibility in the community. What emerged was a new system of stratification and a new belief about the proper relationship between individuals and the collective. But coexistent with these new forms were remnants of the ancient world maintained by the Church through its ideological dualism connecting present life with afterlife. The human experience, according to the Church, was still fixed and limited in capacity and opportunity and could be emancipated only in the afterlife. Between this conception of the present and the promise of the future, the Church reigned preeminent because it was the sole gatekeeper between enslavement in the material world and freedom in the spiritual world.

Herein lay the fundamental contradiction between the new and the old. Although the emergent social forms of Europe produced socially stratified opportunity as in the past, they were *less centralized,* depending as they did on *differentiated centers of political and military power.* In the West, social structures gradually evolved toward a division of rights and responsibilities based on negotiated agreements for mutual benefit. For opportunistic individuals, this amounted to a substantial occasion for gain. But for many others, it simply meant another system based on power, control, and cumulative advantage.

The new structure for defining social opportunity among members of the community was *feudalism*—a complex network of social exchange developed from mutual need. Given the warlords of the West were not sufficiently powerful to control all segments of the population at once, local potentates emerged to provide protection for their communities in return for food and shelter. The exchange pattern connecting the players in the new system was based on land controlled by a king or duke who granted fiefs to barons who pledged oaths of homage and fealty to the king backed by political and military service according to the terms of the grant. Barons, in turn, granted portions of their fiefs to knights who also swore homage and fealty to barons according to their grants, and so on. In this way, kings and vassals created reciprocal relationships defined by mutual need and bilateral support. All relationships were contractual, mutually agreed on transactions consummated by free men and social peers (Microsoft Encarta, 1993a).

The new hierarchy of rights and responsibilities based on exchange extended from kings at the top through various lord-subject ranks in the middle to the mass of peasantry and serfs at the bottom. Unfortunately, those on the lowest rungs of the hierarchy suffered as before in that they had little with which to negotiate an improvement in their opportunity in this evolving community of mutual benefit. Instead, they were attached to the resource being negotiated among the powerful, which was the land they were unable to leave without permission. This was the harm created by negotiated settlements among the powerful. It was the social cost of a stable social structure that coupled serfs to nobles to kings in a community defense system that minimized disruption to feudal life.

These self-sufficient, monolithic, manorial units of the Middle Ages punished and constrained behavior violating the norms of reciprocal rights and responsibilities properly connecting each member to the feudal community. The economic system of divided work that made up the craft industries of these units were controlled by a merchant-producer class that formed guilds or unions to control who could produce what for how much. This new group of entrepreneurs increased the players in an evolving network of entitlements and obligations that created a pervasive sense of conformity that cemented and anchored all opportunity to fixed positions in the emergent structure. The system worked for everyone except those lowest in the social order. Consequently, no one had an interest in change. Serfs did not want change that would threaten their security, guild members did not want change because they monopolized control over the market, nobles wanted to maintain what they had by keeping serfs working the land, kings wanted to maintain what they had by keeping the nobility defending the community, and the Church wanted to maintain spiritual control over feudal life by determining how each person should choose and act to gain grace in God's kingdom.

The new system also re-created the ancient conception of fixed capacity anchored in immutable opportunity. Being born into a position in the feudal system determined your prospects for improving your capacity or altering your opportunity. As in the ancient world, so in the feudal world, opportunity was stratified and capacity was fixed. The two concepts were invariant in a system that eschewed change and beatified stability. Only in the spiritual world could you hope for something more. There, you were free to improve yourself in ways consistent with Church doctrine. Because only through improved compliance to the moral questions of life could you hope for relief from the pain and suffering created by stagnant opportunity. Again, an ideology of self-perfection was available to assuage life's misery.

THE FEUDAL CONTRACT

At least in this sense, the feudal stratification of opportunity was similar to systems of the past. Social inequality was present as before, rulers monopolized and abused power as before, the poor and disabled suffered as before, and their prospects for improved life were as dismal as before. Moreover, religion offered the same promise of an afterlife as before. Yet there was a difference in the way the new system became legitimate in the eyes of the people. In the Middle Ages, what became a right or a responsibility did so through a negotiated agreement, and this was different from the process of legitimating rights in ancient society. There, what was right was what had always been right. No negotiation could make it otherwise. In feudal Europe, the negotiated agreement created bonds of loyalty connecting individuals in different positions located throughout the social structure. Responsibilities between king and baron, baron and knight, vassal and lord, and merchant and king were assumed *voluntarily* in exchange for promises received. Individuals occupying different positions were dependent on each other through *consent*. This left the door ajar, at least in principle, for a few daring individuals to enhance their capacity in hopes of improving their opportunity. There was space in this system for entrepreneurial activity to alter circumstances and improve the distribution of rights and responsibilities for the daring.

This was the new opportunity afforded by the feudal contract that became the basis from which the ideology of equal rights would eventually evolve, although this evolution would take nearly a thousand years. The contract afforded new opportunity in that each time there was another decentralization of power, there was a new occasion to negotiate another distribution of rights and responsibilities. In this sense, feudalism—and its succession of contractual agreements connecting various power holders— was a transition in the evolution from the ancient to the modern era. By the 16th century, when the transition was nearly complete, King John of England had agreed to a charter drafted by his English barons giving them constitutional liberties and protections from encroachment by his royal authority, and Martin Luther had protested the sale of Church indulgences by posting his 95 Theses on the door of Palast Church in Wittenberg, Germany, to begin the Protestant Reformation.

The erosion of centralized sociopolitical power that these two events symbolized also led to a demise in the universal ideology guiding secular and religious thought. In its place were new beliefs about the proper relation between the individual and supreme authority. From the Magna Carta came ideologies of self-government in secular affairs, and from the Protestant Reformation came ideologies of individualism in spiritual affairs.

These changes made the onset of the modern era fundamentally liberating in that they replaced external authority of the collective with internal responsibility of the individual, and this reversed the relationship between the individual and society. For the first time, collective authority was to serve as a *means* to the fulfillment of *individual ends*. This had profound effects on attitudes about freedom. Gone forever was the security and comfort of knowing the only path to God was through the Church. Now, choice making for personal salvation was an individual responsibility requiring decision making in matters previously directed by church clerics. Moreover, decision making carried ultimate consequences in that choosing rationally in pursuit of one's interest was expected to be consonant with the will of God. The only way of knowing how best to fulfill this responsibility was to seek it through hard work and constant devotion to a productive calling.

No wonder devotion to moral conduct in everyday living and working persevered. Protestants took their new freedom seriously because God rewarded those who chose well and punished those who chose poorly. Individuals lacking self-disciplined thinking and acting deserved the life they created for themselves. Luther's uncharitable attitude toward persons with mental disabilities reflected this view, too. If you were unable to express yourself rationally, you were possessed: " 'The Devil sits in such changelings [persons with severe mental disabilities] where their soul should have been there!' " (quoted in Scheerenberger, 1983, p. 32). For Protestants, freedom was not just choosing any action. It was choosing correct action in accordance with ultimate, natural law.

This change in the relationship between laity and church and between man and God was as much political as it was religious because, in the final analysis, it was a *shift in power*. In the centuries before the Reformation, there was one religious entity and one political entity, and in the centuries following the Reformation, there were many religious entities and many political entities. By the end of the 17th century, there had been religious and political revolutions in the Netherlands, France, and Germany, and the resulting differentiation in spheres of influence gave individuals greater freedom in their personal, civic, political, and religious affairs. No longer did the assumption of unity between the moral and the political prevail, either. Niccolò Machiavelli disposed of this notion in his analysis of the formation of the state in which rational calculation of self-interested gain determined who succeeded and who failed. The successful were utilitarian and rational rather than humanitarian and ideal. They chose rationally in pursuit of their own interests.

Undergirding these sociopolitical changes was an *economic power shift* that contributed to the decentralization of control over the means of producing economic gain by loosening the commercial stranglehold the feudal guild system had held over the economic life for centuries. This shift commenced in the 15th century when explorers from the West discovered that resources available in the New World were in demand in the East and could be traded there for profit. Nation-states such as England, France, and Spain competed with each other for market shares by harnessing their populations to create new products for export. The profit incentive for worldwide trade was so great that governmental policies favored merchants and their entrepreneurial activities because success in commerce improved the balance of trade in the form of gold imports for local exports. Soon worldwide commerce replaced the guild system in a dispersal of economic power and hastened the decline of feudalism.

It also benefited peasants living on feudal estates in the West because they enjoyed a system of fixed payment for use of the land they occupied, and when the market value of products they produced increased 1,500% between 1500 and 1650, as shiploads of precious metals poured into

European capitals creating excess money chasing limited goods, they made an inflated profit on all they produced. Their landlords, by contrast, suffered a decline in net wealth because their fixed-lease incomes purchased less and less, forcing many to sell their land. The net effect was greater economic freedom for peasants in the West, but no such advantage for peasants in the East, whose relationships with landlords were not as favorable. This meant that in the West there was a marked change in the distribution of wealth and advantage due to this net increase in the capacity of previously left out groups to optimize their economic circumstances. Add to this the governmental cooperation of western European powers in various commercial ventures by underwriting merchant groups such as the East India Companies (operated by English, Dutch, and the French with franchises to monopolize trade in various parts of the world), and you have additional capacity building for entrepreneurial dominance in the emerging world market (Palmer, 1963, p. 104).

By the 17th century, western Europe had acquired a major portion of the world's wealth as peasant farmers and city merchants joined with state monarchies to dominate the import-export business of the world. The loser in this new alliance was the feudal nobility, which had come to depend on fixed revenues from land they leased to peasant farmers in perpetuity. When inflation eroded their earnings and their declining economic resources eroded their political influence, they lost social and political control to farmers and middle-class entrepreneurs, and this, in turn, accelerated the decline of feudalism in western Europe.

If this were not enough to hasten the transition to the modern era, there was, at the same time, a *technological power shift* that gave yet another group of individuals an opportunity to expand their capacity for self-determined pursuits. This time it was scientific inquiry that had become legitimate in its own right because of the growing sentiment in the West that rational decision making was necessary and sufficient for resolving the major ethical and secular problems of the human condition. Increasingly there was a new confidence in human potential—a belief that humans were capable of choosing in accordance with the laws of nature and of God and that this independent choice making could lead to untold heights of practical and moral accomplishment.

Evidence to reinforce this view had been mounting since Nicolaus Copernicus introduced his heliocentric theory that the earth and planets revolved around the sun, since Johannes Kepler confirmed Copernican theory by showing how planets rotated about the sun in elliptical orbits, and since Galileo revealed details of other orbiting planets through his telescope. These discoveries proved that the laws of nature could be known through active, positive inquiry rather than through passive contemplation, and this liberated secular thinkers and inquirers from religious dogma as they sought to explain the nature of the universe and the material world through scientific problem solving. Seventeenth century rationalists such as Francis Bacon and René Descartes published influential books rejecting medieval philosophy and religious doctrine in favor of scientific inquiry; and Newton's scientific method unified Baconian and Cartesian perspectives on empirical truth seeking by combining induction and deduction in a dramatic discovery of gravitational force. Newton demonstrated that the mysteries of the universe could be discovered and understood by the rational mind. He proved that what moved naturally in the cosmos fell naturally on earth, that cosmic truth was a thing knowable and verifiable through reason. This encouraged reform minded social theorists to conclude that what was natural in the universe was natural to society and its institutions. From here, it was a short distance to claiming that freedom to choose rationally and in pursuit of one's happiness was a right that was natural to all humans possessing rational thought.

THE SOCIAL CONTRACT

Given these aforementioned shifts in the distribution of sociopolitical, economic, and technical power, it is not surprising that ideas about freedom would soon correspond to the new opportunities these changes provoked—ideas about being *free from* external threat and oppression, ideas about being *free to pursue personal gain* through the acquisition and accumulation of gain, and ideas about being *free to find happiness* through the development of a rational self.

Freedom from oppression of course was a central concern during the decentralization of sociopolitical power in the 15th and 16th centuries when the power monopoly held by the monarchy and church evolved into a system of shared governance involving the monarchy, the nobility, and the merchant class of the West. This new distribution of rights and responsibilities produced new conceptions about the proper order in society, and the basis for these new ideas of the just society was the *nature of being human* rather than the nature of being divine. This, in turn, created a new set of problems for theorists attempting to justify the social order because for the first time they had to anchor their ideologies of justification in discoverable facts of human nature rather than in revealed facts of divine nature.

Thomas Hobbes took on this challenge by claiming human nature was the source of all social conflict in that humans pursued their own interests by seeking pleasure and avoiding pain. Consequently, when left unfettered by social custom, they engaged in "war of every man against every man" (Garraty & Gay, 1981, p. 595). In that this condition would be perceived as intolerable over the long term, Hobbes claimed that humans would voluntarily give up a portion of their freedom to a sovereign guardian— " 'that great Leviathan . . . that mortal God' "—*in exchange* for a promise of peace and order (Garraty & Gay, 1981, p. 595). This, he claimed, would legitimate the state in the eyes of the people because it was born of a contact between them and the Leviathan. John Locke based his ideology of justification on a similar theory of human nature that he claimed had " 'basic self-persevering tendencies to avoid pain and seek pleasure.' " From these tendencies, he inferred a set of " 'innate practical principles' " which included the capacity to choose and act *morally* (Yolton, 1985, p. 472). Locke concluded from this that because the self-interest of the Leviathan would ultimately threaten the freedom of the individual, a balance of power was necessary to protect individual rights.

These new approaches to legitimating the social order turned past ideology of authority and tradition on its ear because it placed institutions in the service of needs and rights of individuals. Jean-Jacques Rousseau captured this new orientation in his *Discourse on the Origin of Inequality Among Mankind* that claimed that the natural state of humans was morally superior to the civilized state of society. In the *Social Contract,* Rousseau wrote "Man is born free, and everywhere he is in chains. Many a man believes himself to be the master of others who is, no less than they, a slave." Rousseau argued that social inequality was an unnatural consequence of birth and for that reason was fundamentally unfair. No person had a right to control another. He concluded that the social contract was the only morally acceptable means of institutionalizing fairness in social life. "Since no man has natural authority over his fellows, and since Might can produce no Right, the only foundation left for legitimate authority in human societies is Agreement" (Rousseau, 1962, p. 173).

Another conception of freedom was that individuals ought to be *free to pursue their own gain* in life, given that they did not infringe on the free pursuit of others. This idea was perhaps a consequence of new opportunities for economic gain that came about during the decline of the feudal economy, the rise in state mercantilism, and the expanding free market economy of the 18th century. Theorists such as Adam Smith claimed that individuals ought to freely participate in the market for their own gain because this would achieve the greatest good for the greatest number. He theorized that because human productivity depended on specialized divisions of labor requiring free flow of human resources to meet the demand of specialized industries and activities *and* because the mechanism providing this flow of resources was the marketplace in which individuals exchanged labor for wages through voluntary exchange, then it followed that the market should be left to regulate itself toward an optimal accumulation of gain for the community. In other words, unregulated freedom in pursuit of personal gain would optimize the benefit for all in accordance with the natural law of the marketplace:

> "As every individual . . . endeavours as much as he can both to employ his capital in the support of domestic industry, and so to direct that industry that its produce may be of the greatest value; every individual necessarily labours to render the annual revenue of the society as great as he can. He generally, indeed, neither intends to promote the public interest, nor knows how much he is promoting it. By preferring the support of domestic to that of foreign industry, he intends only his own security; and by directing that industry in such a manner as its produce may be of the greatest value, *he intends only his own gain,* and he is in this, as in many other cases, *led by an invisible hand to promote an end which was no part of his intention"* [italics added].[1] (Routh, 1989, p. 87)

This reasoning became the basis for *laissez-faire* ideologies that claimed that government should be confined to maintaining security, enforcing the law, and adjudicating disputes. All other institutional functions such as education and charity should be conducted privately. According to this thinking, poverty was an inevitable outcome of a free market economy because the "iron law" of wages stated that the higher the wages earned by the poor, the greater their tendency to have children whose needs, in turn, drained their parents' meager resources and further reduced their levels of subsistence. The laissez-faire solution was to build a robust economy through the invisible hand of the marketplace:

> "It deserves to be remarked, perhaps, that it is in the progressive state, while the society is advancing to the further acquisition, rather than when it had acquired its full compliment of riches, that the condition of the labouring poor, of the great body of people, seems to be the happiest and

the most comfortable. It is hard in the stationary, and miserable in the declining state. The progressive state is in reality the cheerful and the hearty state to all the different orders of society. The stationary is dull; the declining melancholy." (Routh, 1989, p. 95)

Of course there was sparse evidence regarding the effects of the invisible hand and the expectation that unregulated pursuits of gain produced a better life for the poor than what was possible through regulated exchange. But evidence was not necessary to advance this idea of freedom. All that was necessary was for people to want it, and they did. Moreover, those who succeeded in their acquisitive pursuits benefited from the idea that their success could be claimed a virtue, as John Kenneth Galbraith (1987) explains in the following:

> The reference to the invisible hand has for many a mystic overtone: here is a spiritual force that supports the pursuit of self-interest and guides men in the market to the most benign of ends. So to believe [this] does Smith a grave disservice; the invisible hand, the most famous metaphor in economics, was just that, a metaphor. A man of the Enlightenment, Smith did not resort to supernatural support for his argument . . .
> Yet as a purely secular matter, it was a huge step that Smith here took. The person concerned with self-enrichment had hitherto been an object of doubt, suspicion and mistrust, feelings that went back through the Middle Ages to biblical times and the Holy Scripture itself. Now, because of his self-interest, he had become a public benefactor. A major rescue and transformation indeed! Nothing in all history has so served personal inclination. And so it continues in our own time. (p. 64)

The idea that individuals ought to be free to pursue happiness was, of course, consistent with the notion they ought to be free to acquire wealth. The latter was simply an extension of the former, focusing as it did on what *all* humans had in common—the desire to find happiness. Whereas freedom for gain focused on the pursuit of a *means* for achieving various ends in life, freedom to pursue happiness focused on an *end* all humans valued. Consequently, all institutions ought to be instruments enabling individuals to engage this pursuit. Moreover, the social constructivism required for this freedom to be realized was believed by many to be within the grasp of human endeavor. Many believed society could be improved by constructing institutions to the satisfaction of all citizens. This was fostered by growing beliefs of the period that everyone functioned under the same laws of right and reason, that all should participate in promoting civil progress, and that all should do so through logical, reasonable inquiry. The projected end of these activities and pursuits would be a just society fostering equality and liberty for all.

Jeremy Bentham led the movement to create institutions in this vein by determining what government should do in accordance with what individuals wanted to be done. He concluded, "It is for them [individuals] alone to point out what we ought to do, as well as to determine what we shall do. On the one hand the standard of right and wrong, on the other the chain of causes and effects, are fastened to their throne" (Bentham, 1961, p. 17). In other words, only individuals could determine "what we ought to do," what the government is obligated to do according to the "standard of right and wrong" and according to the empirical world, "the chain of causes and effects." The moral rule derived from this analysis was the *principle of utility* (Bentham, 1961):

> By the principle of utility is meant that principle which approves or disapproves of every action whatsoever, according to the tendency which it appears to have to augment or diminish the happiness of the party whose interest is in question: or, what is the same thing in other words, to promote or to oppose that happiness. I say of every action whatsoever; and therefore not only of every action of a private individual, but of every measure of government. (pp. 17-18)

The end toward which that rule applied was the *pursuit of happiness,* which depended on rationality and moral judgment, as Shields (1955) explains in the following:

> The pursuit of pleasure non-rationally is self-defeating. To achieve the greatest possible amount of happiness an individual must act rationally. Fortunately, men are, by nature, rational animals. What distinguishes rational action is (a) a conception of a desired end and (b) an understanding of the best means to attain it. The rational individual first calculates the desirability of an end, then he calculates how he could best achieve the end through action. Not the character of an act, nor the intent of the individual, but rather the actual consequences determine the moral validity of an act. Since the amount of happiness it yields in practice is the measure of the utility of an act, rational calculation of its probable effects is required to judge an act's morality. When an individual in the pursuit of his self-interest acts according to the principle of utility, he acts to achieve the desired end of happiness by the desirable means of "reason." (p. 10)

In this conception of the just society, happiness was the ultimate end or purpose of human pursuit, and reason was the *means* necessary for fulfilling this purpose. Through its application, a just society could be constructed in accordance with the principle of utility. Bentham set out to construct such a society by reforming the British legal system so that its laws and policies would yield the greatest happiness for the greatest number.

The American and French revolutions were in large measure a consequence of this conception of the just society in which institutional regulation of social relations were expected to reflect the needs and interests of individuals rather than needs and interests of the state. So conceived, government should *serve* individuals in their pursuit of happiness, as stated in the Declaration of Independence: "We hold these truths to be self-evident that all men are created equal, that they are endowed by their creator with certain unalienable rights, that among them are life, liberty and the pursuit of happiness." In this phrase, the words *life* and *liberty* were listed as necessary means for pursuing happiness. Consequently, they were to be guaranteed for all persons. Again, the implication is the same as in Bentham's thinking—that institutions were constructed by humans to be used by them for their ends in life. In other words, institutions were intended to help people *pursue* their own happiness. Jefferson underscored this reasoning when he wrote in the Declaration that government is " 'instituted among men . . . to effect their safety and Happiness.' " Mortimer Adler (1987) explains this more fully in *We Hold These Truths:*

> Let me sum up what we have learned so far in our attempt to understand the Declaration's assertion that "among these [unalienable] rights are life, liberty, and the pursuit of happiness."
>
> 1. The *primary right is the pursuit of happiness,* having its foundation in our moral obligation to make good lives for ourselves.
> 2. The rights to life and liberty are subordinate rights because *they are rights to means indispensable for the pursuit of happiness* and also because security of life and limb, freedom of action, and political liberty are dependent on external circumstances that are within the power of an organized society and its government of control.
> 3. *All other rights,* those so far not mentioned or, if mentioned, not discussed, *are also subordinate to the right to pursue happiness,* either as supplementing the rights to life and liberty or as implementing these rights [italics added]. (p. 59)

The Discrepancy Problem

By the 19th century, it was evident that the powerful would be the chief beneficiaries of the revolutions in America and France, which established *freedom from* oppressive government; that the entrepreneurs would be the chief beneficiaries of the industrial revolution, which legitimated *freedom for* personal gain; and finally that the educated would be the chief beneficiaries of the scientific revolution, which legitimated and sanctioned *freedom in pursuit of happiness* through rational self-development and personal fulfillment. It was also obvious that poor working people would fare less well with respect to these new freedoms. Any increase in freedom from oppression by the state they might experience would be matched with the oppression experienced by urban living and factory toil; any new opportunity for economic gain would be matched by new ways of experiencing poverty, and any new opportunity to pursue happiness would be overshadowed by the more likely prospect of feeling misery and despair.

Once again history repeated itself, this time with a new set of players positioned to take advantage of the new freedoms and the same set of players positioned to experience new disadvantages in life. In the modern world of the 19th century, the poor and the disabled were in the same positions they were before any expectation for freedom in pursuit of happiness. Their prospects for living a self-determined life were the same as before because the means of gaining resources to expand capacity and to optimize opportunity were the same as before. They were still inaccessible. The access gains experienced by members of the entrepreneurial middle class had done nothing to change the access gains of individuals who were least advantaged in life.

The plight of these less well situated in society is what created the moral dilemma among those claiming a better world had arrived. How could this claim be true when the contradiction between the promise and the experience of freedom was palpably self-evident for many in society? The 19th century was ripe for explanations for why this discrepancy between the right and the experience of self-determination persisted in a social context claiming freedom and equality for all. Benjamin Franklin's self-made individualist provided an explanation based on the Protestantism of the 17th century; Karl Marx's theory of class warfare offered an explanation based on ownership of the means of production; and Herbert Spencer's theory of environmental determinism offered an explanation based on the evolution of inherited advantages and disadvantages.

So when interest in constructing institutions to serve human needs came of age in the 19th century, there were ready-made explanations for what should be done with this expectation for freedom and equality for all. Theories of *individual determinism,* for example, argued that this expectation could be realized when individuals had maximum protection from governmental interference in private affairs, theories of *collective determinism* claimed it would be realized when economic hardship was distributed equally among all members of society, and theories of *environmental determinism* claimed that realization of the ideal was constrained naturally by differences in inherited capacities of individuals. The implication of these theories was that failure to self-determine among some members of society was (a) due to individual failure to take initiative in pursuing opportunity and assuming responsibility for results (individual determinism), (b) due to society's failure to alleviate unjust social and economic hardship preventing the least well situated in society from getting what they need and want in life (collective determinism), or (c) due to the genetic inadequacies of individuals that caused them to adjust poorly to life's circumstances (environmental determinism).

INDIVIDUALISM

The first of these theories was a product of the Protestant Reformation, which claimed that individuals were directly responsible for their success and failure in life. Through self-discipline, hard work, and careful self-management of one's moral life, they could learn the choice-making skills necessary for entering God's kingdom. The Puritans were an advance guard in promoting this idea of the individual's moral capacity for self-disciplined living. The New England colonies institutionalized John Calvin's doctrine of predestination that claimed that only the righteous would be saved (read "freed"), which translated into an ideology of salvation that required being educated, hard-working, diligent, frugal, and law-abiding. The Puritans believed the young began life in a state of savagery that could be ameliorated only through a rigorous regime of training and discipline (see Gutek, 1988, pp. 9-10).

By the 18th century, this ethic of self-disciplined self-help was on its way to defining the meaning of freedom in America, the land of opportunity; and Benjamin Franklin's *Poor Richard's Almanack,* issued between 1732 and 1757, articulated this new ideology. According to Gutek, the *Almanack* was read "by Americans who eagerly accepted his emphasis on the values of frugality, diligence, thrift, hard work, and inventiveness."

Franklin's philosophy exalted the common sense of the self-made and largely self-educated person (Gutek, 1988, p. 17). A century later, the same ethic appeared in best-selling books for boys describing how Franklin's philosophy helped the disadvantaged succeed in life. Horatio Alger (1834-1899) wrote more than 100 such books about the American dream and about young heroes, such as Ragged Dick, Luck and Pluck, and Tattered Tom, who surmounted poverty and misfortune to find fame and fortune by practicing honesty, diligence, perseverance, and self-discipline. Similarly, 19th-century Englishman James Allen (1989) wrote how health, wealth, and well-being came to those who were "self-made":

> Man is made or unmade by himself; in the armory of thought he forges the weapons by which he destroys himself; he also fashions the tools with which he builds for himself heavenly mansions of joy and strength and peace. By the right choice and true application of thought, man ascends to the Divine Perfection; by the abuse and wrong application of thought, he descends below the level of the beast. Between these two extremes are all the grades of character, and man is their maker and master. (p. 14)

Individuals were responsible for their successes and their failures. The idea that social oppression was a factor in explaining failure in life as espoused by Marx was alien to the ideology. Only individuals could determine their future because class identity and class conflict in the Marxist sense had no place in America. According to Christopher Lasch (1979),

> The Protestant work ethic stood as one of the most important underpinnings of American culture. According to the myth of capitalist enterprise, thrift and industry held the key to material success and spiritual fulfillment. America's reputation as a land of opportunity rested on its claim that the destruction of hereditary obstacles to advancement had created conditions in which *social mobility depended on individual initiative alone.* The self-made man, archetypal embodiment of the American dream, owed his advancement to habits of industry, sobriety, moderation, self-discipline, and avoidance of debt. He lived for the future, shunning self-indulgence in favor of patient, painstaking accumulation; and as long as the collective prospect looked on the whole so bright, he found in the deferral of gratification not only his principle gratification but an abundant source of profits [italics added]. (p. 106)

COLLECTIVISM

At the other end of the continuum of explanations for success and failure in social life were theories of collective determinism that claimed class differences and socioeconomic hardship accounted for the misery experienced by those least well situated in society. Karl Marx's *Das Kapital* (1867), which appeared nearly a century after Adam Smith's *Wealth of Nations* (1776), described the egregious side of the free market industrial economy at the same time collective interventions were being instituted to ameliorate the misery of the working poor. For example, in 1802, Robert Peel attempted to get the Health and Morals of Apprentices Act passed to regulate conditions of work for poor children in the textile mills; in 1819, England established a maximum 12-hour working day for juveniles; in 1824, it passed a Combination Law of 1799-1800 repealing laws prohibiting workers from unionizing; in 1833, the British Factory Act was passed to provide factory inspections; in 1847, England's British Factory Act restricted the working day to 10 hours for women and children between the ages of 13 and 18; in 1869, British debtors' prisons were abolished; from 1840 to 1850, Connecticut, Massachusetts, and Pennsylvania passed laws to limit the hours minors could work in textile factories; in 1850, France provided workers with old-age insurance; and in 1883, Bismarck introduced sickness insurance in Germany.

Part of the impetus of these interventions came from workers themselves who acted on their own behalf by leaving England for the United States and Canada during the 1816 economic crisis in England, by rioting over wages in Derbyshire, England, in 1819, by expanding the Trade Union movement in Britain in 1825, by founding the Working Men's Party in New York in 1828, and by establishing the American Federation of Labor in the United States in 1886. These actions anticipated, as did Marx, that as workers improved their access to resources, they too would eventually enhance their collective capacity to improve their prospects for pursuing their own ends in life and that this enhanced capacity and improved prospects would eventually be reflected in a new distribution of rights and responsibilities connecting them with their employers.

By the end of the 19th century, there were these two competing theories explaining socioeconomic change. There was Smith's theory of the free market economy claiming that free exchange among individuals in the marketplace would maximize wealth for society, and there was Marx's theory of collective determinism claiming the economic forces functioning *within* all societies created class conflict due to accumulation of wealth among the few. For Smith, the marketplace must be left alone if a nation was to prosper, and for Marx, access to control over the means of production must concentrate in the hands of the few if society was to devolve into war between the classes:

Hitherto, every form of society has been based, as we have already seen, on the antagonism of oppressing and oppressed classes. But in order to oppress a class, certain conditions must be assured to it under which it can, at least, continue its slavish existence. The serf, in the period of serfdom, raised himself to membership in the community, just as the petty bourgeois, under the yoke of feudal absolutism, managed to develop into a bourgeois. The modern laborer, on the contrary, instead of rising with the progress of industry, sinks deeper and deeper below the conditions of existence of his own class. He becomes a pauper, and pauperism develops more rapidly than population and wealth. And here it becomes evident, that the bourgeoisie is unfit any longer to be the ruling class in society, and to impose its conditions of existence on society as an overriding law. It is unfit to rule because it is incompetent to assure an existence to its slave within his slavery, because it cannot help letting him sink into such a state, that it has to feed him, instead of being fed by him. Society can no longer live under this bourgeoisie, in other words, its existence is no longer compatible with society. (Marx & Engels, 1955, p. 22)

For Smith the ultimate consequence of the free market economy was improvement of prospects for all members of society relative to what was possible in a controlled economy; and for Marx the ultimate consequence of free market economy was class warfare with the proletariat overthrowing the bourgeois to control all the means of production:

The development of modern industry, therefore, cuts from under its feet the very foundation on which the bourgeois it produces and appropriates products. What the bourgeoisie therefore produces, above all, are its own gravediggers. Its fall and the victory of the proletariat are equally inevitable. (Marx & Engels, 1955, p. 22)

The policy implication of Smith's theory of laissez-faire economics was against collective intervention in any of the economic affairs of the nation to ensure maximum gain for the nation, and the policy implication of Marx's theory of collective determinism was for collective intervention in all the affairs of the nation to hasten the inexorable evolution toward the classless society.

ENVIRONMENTALISM

A third explanation for the discrepancy between the right and the experience of self-determination was belief that nature and the physical environment determined the course and content of social evolution.

Although individuals and groups can determine their own direction in life within limits defined by their physical makeup and environment circumstance, over the long term these relatively more powerful forces separate the able from the unable through survival-of-the-fittest sorting that yields moot any short-term amelioration attempted on behalf of the less able. In other words, the social and economic disadvantages experienced by those least well situated in society were, in fact, valid indicators of what was an inevitable and inexorable outcome in life. So why forestall the inevitable? Such efforts were, in the final analysis, a waste of time and scarce resources.

Although evolutionary explanations such as this one had been around since Ionic philosopher Anaximander postulated life originated from the sea, they had not become significant in modern social theory until Darwin's 1859 publication of *On the Origin of Species by Means of Natural Selection or the Preservation of Favoured Races in the Struggle for Life.* This work gave scientific credence to strongly held views that change in the natural and social world moved inexorably toward perfection—a view consistent with Darwin's theory of change (see Levins & Lewontin, 1985, p. 83). It was not long, therefore, before the theory, along with its philosophical underpinnings, became the intellectual bedrock for fledgling social sciences such as anthropology, which set about discovering which "races" proved superior; cultural anthropology, which tried to discover those cultural practices that were superior for different groups; and Spencerian sociology, which argued that evolution in human activity moved toward greater perfectibility and that interrupting "natural" selection through social intervention would only "coddle the weak and unfit." Then, of course there was German philosopher Friedrich Nietzsche (1957) who extended this thinking in his philosophy of the will to power:

> Let us acknowledge unprejudicedly how every higher civilisation hitherto has *originated!* Men with a still nature, barbarians in every terrible sense of the word, men of prey, still in possession of unbroken strength or will and desire for power, threw themselves on weaker, more moral, more peaceful races (perhaps trading or cattle-rearing communities), or on old mellow civilisations in which the final vital force was flickering out in brilliant fireworks of wit and depravity. At the commencement, the noble caste was always the barbarian caste: their superiority did not consist first of all in their physical but in their psychical power—they were *complete* men (which at every point also implies the same as "more complete beasts"). (p. 367)

The Problem of Social Redress

The effect of these three theories on the social redress recommended for people in need cannot be underestimated. For one thing, they promoted new understandings of the cause of social inequality. For another, they recommended social policies reflecting those new understandings. Finally, the very existence of these social policies promoted the legitimization of these new understandings, demonstrating once again that an "is" frequently becomes an "ought."

In this way the 20th century became a crucible for reifying 19th-century theories claiming to explain the discrepancy between the right of all persons to self-determination and the experience of self-determination among least advantaged members of society. Individualist theories of determinism argued that the greatest good for the greatest number was possible only through unregulated pursuits of self-interested individuals in free market economies; collectivist theories of determinism argued that the problem of social and economic inequality emanated from the relationship between class membership and access to the means of productive gain and could be corrected only through social and economic reforms that abolished these relationships; and evolutionary theories of environmental determinism argued that the greatest benefit for the most able was possible by permitting the laws of evolution to follow their natural course in perfecting the human species and its institutional forms.

Moreover, all three theories postulated simplistic causal forces to explain social inequality, with each theory identifying a different agency responsible for inequality in the distribution of social and economic outcomes. Theories of individual determinism identified the individual as the principle causal agent in social life and claimed that the right to self-determination maximized freedom for individuals to the extent that the right protected those pursuits from interference from others, including the state. The only restriction on this right was for the purpose of maintaining order and legitimacy of transaction according to the rule of law. Robert Nozick's theory of entitlement was based on this premise. It posited the marketplace of social exchange as the locus for individuals to interact freely with each other to acquire resources and opportunities needed for their pursuits. Here individuals' *power* (capacity) to exchange with others determined the *right* (opportunity) to exchange with them. Accordingly, there would be no occasion for social redress on behalf of the least advantaged because there could be no interference in that free zone of social exchange.

Collectivist theories identified the cause of inequality in the class structure, arguing that since the beginning of human civilization inequality in opportunity and outcome associated with different social strata created social injustice in need of rectification. Some argued this should be accomplished by starting from scratch with experiments in utopian living such as those attempted by British socialist Robert Owen in Illinois and Indiana. Others argued class conflict between the haves and have-nots was necessary for a classless society to emerge from the rubble of the inexorable revolution. Still others sought to reform the social structure through governmental redistribution of gain in accordance with principles of equality. This was the solution offered by John Rawls's (1971) *A Theory of Justice,* which recommended application of the difference principle to reduce egregious inequalities in outcomes experienced by individuals most and least advantaged in society. Rawls's justice as fairness demanded that all members of society receive a reasonable share of the cooperative surplus produced by a division of labor involving all members of society.

Evolutionary determinism claimed that environmental circumstance produces a natural selection effect by favoring individuals whose adaptive behaviors improve their prospects for survival. The implication was that individuals could control their fate only to the extent their behaviors were adapted to or selected by the conditions imposed by the environment. Another implication was that social policy should follow this inexorable evolutionary trend rather than to counter it with social redress, which, in the final analysis, would be futile. A more rational approach would be to limit the number of individuals whose maladaptive behaviors, which are hardwired to their hereditary circumstance, doom them in the long run.

Understanding the causal assumptions undergirding these ideologies of determinism is important in that these theories affect how we think about the discrepancy between the right and the experience of self-determination for least advantaged members of society. For example, arguments based on the causal assumptions embodied in individual determinism usually claim unregulated choice making in the market of exchange is the best of all those possible social constructions because it depends on self-interested pursuit by multitudes of autonomous individuals interacting with each other in accordance with the laws of supply and demand. Governmental intervention in that free zone is rejected as a mode for social redress because it would have long-term negative consequences for all through lowered productivity gain and job prospects that always affect most adversely those least able to adjust to economic shortfall. On the other hand, arguments based on the causal assumptions of collective determinism usually claim that nothing less than a restructured society based on principles promoting greater equality can compensate for the injustice experienced by those least well situated in society. Finally, arguments based on assumptions of environmental determinism usually claim that social selection based on merit anchors prospects for pursuing the good life to evolutionary forces that in contemporary life give selective advantage to those with greater cognitive skills. This means that positions in the social structure are, in the final sort, hardwired to genetic makeup, and they prevent social redress from altering the inevitable outcome of social differentiation positioning the cognitive elite at the top and the cognitive subnormal at the bottom.

But, of course, these debates are waged within a historical context of governmental intervention deeply wedded to an ideology of the state welfare that is at odds with the causal assumptions of any of these theories considered alone. The justification for government interventionism in the 20th century was the result of a set of circumstances that did not fit very well with any single-cause theory of social process or moral redress. Central to those circumstances was the Great Depression of the 1930s that forced unemployment on large numbers of working people who fit poorly into categories of most and least advantaged and who demanded governmental assistance to shore up their life prospects through protection from income loss caused by disease, disability, lack of employment opportunity, old age, or death. This established a precedent for governmental activity in other areas as well, which challenged simplistic accounts for how the social world worked and what ought to be done if it failed to function as expected.

These new circumstances affected each of the ideologies differently. For example, post-1930s thinking about the role of government was in one sense compatible with the collectivist view that government was responsible for the well-being of its citizens, but in another sense the new thinking fell short of the strong argument for social redress on behalf of least well situated persons, especially if they had never been in the mainstream of competitive work. From the beginning, welfare ideology was intended for those who had worked and, consequently, *deserved* to be protected from the risks of living in the industrial age. It was a response to the needs of the majority population that had no option but what the modern economy offered by way of pursuing a decent livelihood that promoted and sold welfare ideology. According to this reasoning, government had an obligation to cover these risks, as it did through payroll taxes deducted from wages of the working to finance benefits of those no longer working. Initially at least, welfare policy had little to say about persons who never worked, and consequently, had not earned and did not deserve the right to unemployment insurance, disability compensation, or retirement benefits.

Welfare ideology also deviated from the ideal of individual determinism and its central idea that individuals are responsible for their own opportunities and outcomes in that free zone of social exchange for individual advantage. The government practice of requiring workers to pay into a protection system violated the minimal state concept Nozick's theory of entitlement justified. Welfare ideology also deviated from policies suggested by evolutionary determinism because support of the old, the disabled, and the poor only encouraged their longevity and propagation, which could be considered contrary to the natural trend toward human perfection. In fact, the Aid to Dependent Children program included in the Social Security Act of 1935, which grew into the AFDC today, provided payment to mothers who were unable to support their children through other means. This meant that the poorest members of society would receive governmental subsidies to raise their young who, on reaching maturity, could then have children in poverty and dependence who would also be eligible for support.

Perhaps the reason for these imperfect matches between determinism ideology and 20th-century governmental policy had less to do with the content of the arguments they posed than on the *causal bases* that supported those arguments. Welfare policy was based on a conception of cause that was more complex than those undergirding any of the three ideological views. Welfare ideology reflected *multiple* causal factors emanating from personal capacity, social opportunity, and environmental circumstance. It presumed that covariation between worker capacity, job opportunity, and environmental change created conditions that were unpredictable and at times threatening to one's prospects for pursuing the good life. Consequently, the government was responsible for providing a baseline of support in times of need, for example, when *personal capacity* declined due to illness, injury, or old age, when *social opportunity* changed through the elimination of jobs, or when *environmental circumstance* changed because businesses failed or moved out of town or out of the country. Government was responsible for securing the social basis necessary for working people to have a reasonable chance of fulfilling their own pursuits over a lifetime, which meant that social security was a fallback position guaranteeing protection for all workers from potentially devastating disruptions in their capacity or opportunity for getting what they needed and wanted in life.

In sum, unifactor causal explanations for social inequality are simply inadequate for understanding the postmodern world. Consequently, their recommendations for social redress are inadequate, as well. By emphasizing one source of influence rather than the interaction among all three, they yield conclusions about what ought to be that contradict what experience and history tell us. For example, we know there is support for the claim that individuals have a hand in determining their future, and that they act on their social and physical environment to make it more favorable for securing what they want. But we also know there is support for the claim that social and physical environments limit their capacity and their opportunity to succeed in life, and that oftentimes these limitations seem unfair. So the problem of justifying social redress comes down to understanding how these forces may interact to produce different prospects for self-determination. It is not predicting what outcomes will inevitably result, because we cannot do that.

This is what deterministic presumptions encourage us to do. They urge us to bet on *predetermined* future states that have only a *probability* of occurring, and they encourage us to attempt to satisfy our need for predictability and our desire for control. In sum, they lead us to expect too much from collective action, too much from individual initiative and responsibility, and too much from natural cause. The policy options derived from these presumptive states lead us to error at the extremes when we attempt to ameliorate the situations experienced by people who are least well-situated in society.

Table 5.1 illustrates the types of options likely to be considered when we focus on single-cause explanations of social inequality. Table 5.1 presents four types of explanations. The first cell is a multicausal theory of indeterminism that attributes causal agency equally to the individual, the collective, and the environment. The remaining three cells present single-cause theories, with individualism in cell 2, collectivism in cell 3, and environmental determinism in cell 4. The policy options typically associated with these four types of causal attributions correspond to this four-fold classification. For example, the policy expectation generated by indeterminism is to *empower* autonomous individuals by optimizing their prospects for self-determination (equal opportunity theory), the expectation associated with individualism is to *pity* the unfortunate through acts

Table 5.1 Classification of Treatment Approaches for the Disadvantaged According to Four Types of Causal Attribution

		The Collective as Primal Cause	
		High	Low
Individuals as Primal Cause	High	Indeterminism *Empower* Autonomous Individuals by Optimizing Prospects	Individualism *Pity* Hapless Individuals through Voluntary Acts of Charity
	Low	Collectivism *Rescue* Helpless Individuals through Paternalism	Environmentalism *Constrain* Worthless Individuals through Segregation

of charity (Nozick's theory of entitlement), the policy expectations associated with collectivism is to *rescue* helpless individuals through acts of paternalism (Rawls's difference principle), and the expectations associated with environmental or evolutionary determinism is to *constrain* population growth among worthless individuals who are incapable of adjusting to the changing world (Herrnstein's meritocratic theory).[2]

Table 5.2 advances this analysis by comparing the end states implied by the four theories, beginning with their causal assumptions, the ideologies emanating from those assumptions, the conclusions they reach regarding what is fair, and the policy options they suggest for treating individuals adversely affected by the discrepancy between the right and the experience of self-determination. The first column of Table 5.2 summarizes evolutionary theory, which postulates environmental causes—the genetic makeup of individuals and selective forces in the environment—for determining the course and direction of sociocultural evolution. It argues that society ought to function in accordance with these forces because no amount of social redress can change the inevitability of social differentiation of opportunity and outcome that unfolds according to natural law. Consequently, no amount of social redress on behalf of the least advantaged in society will alter the inevitable result that will always yield winners and losers. Better to reduce the number of people born as losers and increase the number of people born as winners than to try to tinker with nature.

Table 5.2 Comparison of Assumptions and Consequences of Four Theories on Social Redress

Environmental Theory	Individual Theory	Collective Theory	Opportunity Theory
Given:	**Given:**	**Given:**	**Given:**
1. That the environment is the principle causal agent in sociocultural evolution; and	1. That the individual is the principle causal agent in sociocultural evolution; and	1. That the group is the principle causal agent in sociocultural evolution; and	1. That interaction between environments, individuals, and groups is the principle causal agent in sociocultural evolution; and
(diagram: E → I, E → G)	*(diagram: I → E, I → G)*	*(diagram: G → E, G → I)*	*(diagram: I ↔ E, I ↔ G, E ↔ G)*
2. That rights to individual freedom are limited by parameters defined by changing environmental circumstance.	2. That rights to individual freedom maximize to the extent rational individuals are free to pursue their own interests in the absence of obstruction from others.	2. That rights to individual freedom maximize for all when disinterested individuals rationally choose principles that are in the long-term interests of everyone.	2. That rights to individual freedom maximize when interactions between individuals, groups, and environments produce optimal prospects for self-determined pursuits for all.
Then:	**Then:**	**Then:**	**Then:**
Individuals maximize the experience of freedom within boundaries defined by these natural environmental circumstances. Consequently:	Individuals maximize the experience of being free when they pursue their own interests rationally and when they experience the consequences of those pursuits. This is consistent with the argument that:	All members of the group will maximize the experience of freedom when the principles chosen state that:	The experience of freedom depends upon interaction between individual capacity to self-determine and social and environmental opportunity for expressions of that capacity. Consequently if:
1. If differences in mental abilities are inherited, and 2. If success requires those abilities, and 3. If earnings and prestige depend on success, 4. Then social standing (which reflects earnings and prestige) will be based to some extent on inherited differences among people.	1. People are entitled to their natural assets. 2. If people are entitled to something, they are entitled to whatever flows from it (via specified types of processes). 3. People's holdings flow from their natural assets. Consequently, 4. People are entitled to their holdings. 5. If people are entitled to some thing then they ought to have it (and this overrides any presumption of equality there may be about holdings.)	1. Each person is to have equal right to the most extensive basic liberty compatible with similar liberty for others. 2. Social and economic inequalities are to be arranged so that they are both (a) reasonably expected to be to everyone's advantage, and (b) attached to positions and offices open to all.	1. All individuals have the right to self-determination, 2. All societies have some individuals who lack the capacity to self-determine, 3. All societies generate unequal opportunities to self-determine, and 4. Some individuals do not exercise their right to self-determine because they lack capacity and opportunity to self-determine, then 5. All societies should optimize prospects for self-determine for these least advantaged individuals by improving their capacity and optimizing their opportunity to self-determine.
Therefore:	**Therefore:**	**Therefore:**	**Therefore:**
Society ought to function in accordance with natural and biological law.	Society should not interfere with individual pursuits by taking resources from the most successful to give to the least successful.	Society should intervene on behalf of the least fortunate in society by assuring that gains by the most advantaged members of society are matched by commensurate gain by the least advantaged in society.	When societies claim the right to self-determination for all, they create a social obligation to back that claim by assuring optimal prospects for self-determination for all.
Because:	**Because:**	**Because:**	**Because:**
No amount of social redress can change the inevitability of the social differentiation of opportunity and outcome produced by the forces of bio-socio-cultural evolution.	From a moral point of view, it is unfair for any member of society to be prevented from enjoying the results of individual pursuits freely and legitimately engaged.	From a moral point of view, it is unfair for any member of society to be denied a fair share of the cooperative surplus produced by a division of labor involving everyone.	The claim of rights to self-determination for all sets up a discrepancy condition defined by perceived differences between the right and the experience of self-determination that demands social redress for its reduction.

Hence, the policy goal of "constrain," as indicated in Table 5.2. Herrnstein's meritocracy theory connects this conclusion with these causal assumptions.

Individualism postulates the individual to be the principle determinant in sociocultural evolution. Therefore, society should not interfere with personal pursuits by taking gain produced by the most successful and giving to the least successful. Nozick's theory of entitlement presents this logic with its causal assumptions. The implication is that it is unfortunate, though not immoral, for some to succeed in their self-determined pursuits, whereas others do not. This is life. Consequently, voluntary acts of charity for the less fortunate are the best way of ameliorating suffering as indicated by the policy of pity through charity.

Collectivism postulates that the group is the principle causal agent in sociocultural evolution, and, therefore, it has moral authority to intervene on behalf of the less fortunate. Accordingly, the collective should ensure that gain produced by the most advantaged in society is matched by commensurate gain allocated to the least advantaged in that from a moral point of view it is unjust for any member of society to be denied a fair share of the cooperative surplus made possible by a division of labor involving everyone. Rawls's theory of justice as fairness recommends the difference principle, which accomplishes this end by yoking gain produced by the most successful with failure to produce gain by the least successful. This redistribution of outcomes is fair because it guarantees gain for those who are most helpless and who must be rescued through policies of paternalism administered by the successful.

Equal opportunity theory claims *interaction* between the environment, the individual, and group ideology is responsible for change during sociocultural evolution. Moreover, when these conditions prompt the collective to agree that the right to self-determination should be extended to all its members, then there is an obligation to back that claim by ensuring optimal prospects for self-determination for all. In other words, the *claim* for self-determination for all, not some natural or metaphysical condition, is what creates the obligation to give every individual a reasonable chance of living the self-determined life. Finally, this claim becomes a *motivational force* for social action when there is a *discrepancy* between the right and the experience of self-determination. Then the demand for social redress on behalf of those most adversely affected by the condition of social inequality intensifies, and the probability of redress in the direction of equalizing prospects for self-determination increases.

Equal opportunity theory presents the logic of this conclusion—which is based on the assumption of interactive cause—by showing how individual capacity and social opportunity contribute to the experience of self-determination when interactions evolve in the direction of increasing the discrepancy with the ideal of self-determination for all. It is this drift toward increasingly greater social difference between rights and experiences that increases the probability of collective intervention to increase capacity to self-determine or to improve opportunity for the expression of that capacity. In other words, the discrepancy between the right and the experience of self-determination is itself a force for change toward equalization of prospects for self-determination among those least well situated in society.

Although this conception of cause in sociocultural evolution yields substantively different interpretations of freedom and what should be done to equalize its experience among individuals, it nevertheless takes into account the same causal factors as the other three ideologies. But it does more, too. Equal opportunity theory specifies *how* the three factors interact to differentiate prospects for self-determination among individuals in a group. This helps us to understand that persons who are least advantaged in society are no less intrinsically worthy or helpless than others. They simply lack the capacity and social circumstance needed to jump-start their own self-determined pursuits. They are as intrinsically autonomous as anyone else, and as a consequence, are as deserving as anyone else to experience an optimal prospect for self-determination.

Table 5.3 shows the relationship between the assumption of interdependent cause and the selection theory that explains its effects. The first column of Table 5.3 lists the three causal assumptions under discussion: (a) that environments affect the characteristics of individuals and groups that in turn affect the success of individuals, (b) that characteristics of individuals affect characteristics of the physical and social environment, which also affect the success of individuals, and (c) that characteristics of groups affect the characteristics of individuals and environments, which also affect the success of individuals. The second column of Table 5.3 explains how interaction between environments and individuals over evolutionary time (millions of years) produce a natural selection effect, and how interaction among individuals, groups, and environments over generational time produce a social selection effect. In other words, natural selection theory describes how biological evolution has affected the lifetime of the species, whereas social selection theory explains how sociocultural evolution has affected prospects for self-determination in the lifetime of individuals.

Social selection theory explains this differentiation of prospects among members of a group by describing three relationships. The first relationship

Table 5.3 Explanations for Causal Assumptions of Equal Opportunity Theory

Assumptions	Explanations
Assumption 1 Characteristics of environments <u>affect</u> characteristics of individuals and groups to produce variation in success of individuals: $E \longleftarrow \begin{array}{c} I \\ \updownarrow \\ G \end{array}$	<u>Natural Selection Theory</u>: 1.0. Individuals within a species vary in physiology, morphology, and behavior. 2.0. Offspring resemble their parents on the average more than they resemble unrelated individuals. 3.0. Different variants leave different numbers of offspring. 4.0. Differential accumulations of various offspring within and across spepcies produce a <u>natural selection effect</u>.

Assumption 2
 	
Characteristics of individuals <u>interact</u> with characteristics of physical and social environments to produce variation in success of individuals:
 	
$I \longleftarrow \begin{array}{c} E \\ \updownarrow \\ G \end{array}$
	<u>Social Selection Theory</u>:
	
	1.0. Individuals vary in the optimality of their adjustments to produce gain
	   1.1. Differences in optimalities of adjustment produce differences in gain.
	   1.2. The closer to optimal the adjustment, the closer to maximum the gain and the more likely the availability of time, behavior, and gain for pursuing subsequent opportunity.
	   1.3. The greater the time, behavior, and gain available for pursing an opportunity, the more likely the control over the means of producing gain during that opportunity.

Assumption 3
 	
Characteristics of groups <u>interact</u> with characteristics of individuals and envrionments to produce variation in success of individuals:
 	
$G \longleftarrow \begin{array}{c} E \\ \updownarrow \\ I \end{array}$
	2.0. Individuals vary in the optimality of their opportunities for producing gain.
	   2.1. Opportunity to control the means of producing gain varies according to its location in the environment.
	   2.2. The greater the probability of controlling the personal, social, economic, and technical means of producing gain from a given position in the environment, the more often the optimal adjustment and maximum gain experienced by individuals while occupying that position.
	   2.3. The more often an individual optimizes adjustment and maximizes gain while occupying a position in the environment, the more that individual accumulates surplus time, behavior, and gain for pursing subsequent opportunity while in that position.
	   2.4. The more time, behavior, and gain an individual accumulates to pursue new opportunity while occupying a position in the environment, the more likely that individual will acquire control over the personal, social, economic, and technical means of producing gain while in that position.
	
	3.0. The more often the same individuals have optimal opportunities to optimize adjustments within a group's division of labor, the more likely all optimalities of opportunity and adjustment in the group will be stratified according to the surplus time, behavior, and gain produced by those members of the group.
	
	4.0. The stratification of optimallities of opportunity and adjustment according to the differential accumulation of surplus time, behavior, and gain among a population of actors produces a <u>social selection effect</u>.

is between individual adjustment and the physical and social environments, and is explained by the proposition that the better the present adjustment, the more likely the availability of resources for optimizing subsequent adjustments. The second relationship is between individuals' present adjustments and their opportunities, and explained by the proposition that the more favorable the opportunity, the more likely individuals will make optimal adjustments and have surplus resources to improve subsequent opportunities and adjustments. The third relationship is between the frequency of individuals' optimal adjustments and the frequency of their favorable opportunities, and indicated by the proposition that the more frequently the same individuals experience optimal adjustments and favorable opportunity, the more likely a social stratification effect will accelerate the accumulation of advantage for those adjusting optimally to favorable opportunity. The evolutionary end state of these interactions is a perpetuation of gain and advantage for some and a perpetuation of loss and disadvantage for others—the social selection effect we call social stratification.

This focus on *interactive effects* created by covariation among individuals, group ideologies, and environments anticipates outcomes that are *indeterminate* and descriptive rather than determinative and prescriptive. For example, when all actors have relatively equal capacities to adjust optimally to get what they need and want and when their opportunities are relatively equal with respect to their prospects for success in those endeavors, then the specific outcomes of these interactions will be indeterminate, although the prospects for self-determination for the actors will be equal. Under these conditions, everyone will have an equal chance—an equal probability—of engaging opportunity to get what they need and want in life. When capacities and opportunities interact to create unequal outcomes among a population of actors, however, and when these inequalities accumulate because the same individuals experience the same optimal or suboptimal opportunities for gain repeatedly over time, then the resulting social stratification tends to match these accumulated advantages and disadvantages, and the prospects for self-determination decline for some and increase for others along patterns indicated by this stratification.

This is the implication drawn from an assumption of interactive cause: Social stratification is not due solely to individual capacity, solely to environmental circumstance, or solely to collective ideology. It is a consequence of interaction among all three. Individuals bear only partial responsibility for their lot in life, especially when they find themselves positioned at the very top or at the bottom of the hierarchy. In these positions, prospects for self-determination are unlikely to change because, as indicated in Chapter 3, in these locations in the social structure, prospects for self-determination tend to be influenced more by optimalities of opportunity than by optimalities of adjustment. They tend to be more a function of the favorability of the social circumstance than they are due to the optimality of the individual's adjustment. Stated more simply, nearly anyone can succeed when conditions are exceptionally favorable, and conversely, nearly everyone can fail when conditions are exceptionally unfavorable. What they do or how they adjust is less influential in determining their success than is the environmental circumstance in which they pursue their ends.

Equal opportunity theory builds on this understanding of how sociocultural sorting works. Its justification for collective intervention on behalf of the least advantaged is not based on an inherent immorality of social stratification per se—an argument posed by the Marxist perspective—rather, it is based on a social obligation emanating from the group's ideology of equal freedom. Consequently, when a claim of freedom for all is made—that is to say, when an ideology of equal freedom has legitimacy in the group—then discrepancy conditions produced by social stratification create an impetus to equalize prospects for self-determination for all members of society, including those least well situated.

Notes

1. Routh's quotations of Adam Smith are from Smith's "An Inquiry Into the Nature and Causes of the Wealth of Nations."
2. See Herrnstein, R. J. (1973) *IQ in the meritocracy* (Boston: Atlantic-Little Brown) 197-198.

Optimal Prospects

One problem of fairness in social life yields judgments about an individual's prospects for living a decent life in a group and the other yields judgments about the compensation an individual can expect for one's contribution to the group. In the modern world, these judgments are embodied in notions of social and allocative justice, the former focusing on the decent life a society promises its citizens and the latter focusing on the rewards a society provides its citizens for contributions to the group. When both conditions are satisfied, everyone believes they are treated fairly by the collective and by their peers. In these circumstances, there are no feelings of social injustice because the rules governing the group favor some over others and there are no feelings of excusable envy because some members of the group receive more than they deserve for their contributions. Justice prevails and everyone is happy. When these conceptions of justice are applied to freedom, one can argue as Rawls does that everyone has the right to a basic set of liberties simply for being a member of the human group, and one can also argue as Nozick does that every individual in the group deserves an opportunity to pursue their own ends in life.

In Chapter 3, we saw that for the longest period of history, the rules of justice did not apply to the distribution of rights or experiences of freedom. Perhaps this was because there was no concept of freedom in the earliest hunting and gathering societies. This is not surprising given the egalitarian structure of those communities maximized freedom for all (Patterson, 1991).[1] The problem of unequal distributions of freedom did not arise until the emergence of human civilization, which produced gross inequality in the distribution of opportunity and outcome. Chapter 3 chronicled these differential increases in power for some and declines in capacity and opportunity for others. Even then, there was no equality-of-freedom problem because there was no expectation for freedom for all—there was no conception of equal rights to liberty. Consequently, there could be no discrepancy between the expectation and the experience of freedom. With no discrepancy to attract attention and concern on the part of those suffering from its denial, there could be no basis for advocating change in social institutions to extend freedom to those denied. The only concept of freedom was freedom as power.

Nevertheless there was a conception of fairness in the distribution of valued goods in society. As social stratification effects became more pronounced due to the accumulated gain for the few, gross discrepancies in social and economic advantage among different groups in the population demanded explanation. So the idea of fair treatment due to one's member-ship in and contribution to the group *predated* the idea of freedom as a *distributable primary good* that might also accrue to one's desert for being a contributor in the cooperative effort. In fact, the idea of adding freedom to distributable primary goods governed by rules of justice did not even come to light until well into the second millennia. Perhaps this is why fairness in liberty for all was not a problem until then. In that before the second millennia, the distribution of goods according to rules of justice meant distributing the gain and loss attached to various outcomes of self-determined pursuit. The idea of distributing the right and the experi-ences of self-determination—which are means to produce gains—never came up. Consequently, the idea of freedom as a distributable commodity never came up.

Of course, this changed when that concept of freedom as right finally came into being. As Chapter 4 described, this idea emerged when control over the sociopolitical, economic, and technical bases of power shifted from church and state to diverse groups of religious reformers and secular entrepreneurs who had their own ideas about the opportunities they wanted to pursue to achieve desirable ends in life. The compromise mechanism for the resultant power sharing among these emergent forces was the rationally negotiated social contract that gave each power broker protection from encroachment, abuse, and unfair advantage inspired and pursued by every other power broker. The resultant balance emerging from these negotiated settlements served to check the egregious accumulation of gain and advantage of one group at the expense of other groups.

But the problem with this organizing principle for society was its instability, awaiting as it did another power shift and another alignment of interests to establish a new contract and a new social order. More problematic than this even was the widespread perception among political theorists of the time that the social contract could not capture the minds and hearts of a citizenry long accustomed to believing governmental legitimacy depended on connections with a higher morality such as one identified with God and mediated by the church. The ideology of divine right of kings was more appealing because at least it could claim moral linkage between the governing head and God.

What social contract theorists offered to counter ancient doctrine of divine right was a claim that the social contract connected *human nature* with *natural law*. Thomas Hobbes and John Locke argued that humans shared a common nature that was rational pursuit of pleasure and avoidance of pain and that the social contract was the only political instrument that permitted the expression of this capacity for rational thought and self-determined pursuit. Locke claimed that by virtue of this common humanity, all humans were endowed with certain inalienable rights enabling them to pursue their own interests and that these rights could not be abridged by any governmental authority that was itself derived from consent of the governed through the contract.

This was the foundation for the ideology of *freedom for all*. It was a logical consequence of human nature and natural law as conceived in thought experiments about humans functioning in the original state. It was an ideology as legitimate as the doctrine of divine right in that it too was hardwired to God. What was different in this conception of legitimacy was that this alternative circuitry reversed conceptions about the proper relationship between individuals and their institutions. Rousseau's claim that man was born free but everywhere in chains captured the essence of the new wiring. All social institutions, especially church and state, were now conceived as means not ends, because everyone had a right to be free by virtue of a common humanity. For the first time in human history, institutions were to serve as means to guaranteeing the right of self-determination.

Of course, this conception created a new set of social problems never before encountered. First of all, it presumed liberty to be a means to be fairly distributed among all citizens and that social institutions should protect and sustain this fair and just distribution. This expectation for equal distributions of liberty in turn set the occasion for discrepancies between the right and the experience of freedom. So much of the 19th century was spent reacting to problems created by this expectation, with *environmental determinism* arguing that discrepancies between the right and the experience of self-determination among members of the human group were due to inexorable forces of nature over which humans and their institutions had no control, with *individual determinism* arguing that the discrepancy condition had no moral significance because variation in the expression of freedom would inevitably yield different outcomes that justly accrued to those responsible for their production, and with *collective determinism* arguing that those suffering from the discrepancy between the right and the experience of self-determination deserved social redress because all cooperative surplus was outside the domain of individual desert. Chapter 4 identified the limitation of these arguments to be anchored in their assumptions of unifactor, independent cause that is contrary to the dynamic of social life that functions in accordance with multifactor, interdependent cause.

Yet even if we accept this postmodern assumption that social life evolves according to dynamics created by the interdependence among individual capacity, group ideology, and environmental opportunity, we are still left with the problem of explaining how social redress on behalf of the least advantaged members of society came to affect social life as it has in the latter half of the 20th century. To say it was an accidental confluence of interdependent causal forces is only partly true. Equally influential in this explanation of sociocultural evolution is the transformation in the *concept of fairness* contained in the West's ideology of right and how this new conception came to redress claims made by the least advantaged members of society.

In the distant past, fairness dealt only with the *distribution of outcomes* of self-determined acts rather than with the *distribution of rights or opportunities* responsible for those outcomes. Hence, there was no confusion about how to distribute rights to self-determination between members of society with grossly different advantages and disadvantages. Persons with advantages had more rights and opportunities to pursue their goals than persons without advantages. In the last few hundred years, however, the distribution of rights and opportunities for freedom has come under the purview of social and allocative justice because of the claim that everyone deserves to be free. This has given us different theories of justice on the proper distribution of freedom along with wealth, income, status, prestige. Rawls argues for a theory of social justice that combines the distribution of freedom with the distribution of outcomes of those self-determined pursuits enabled by that distribution of freedom, whereas Nozick argues for a theory of allocative justice that combines the distribution of freedom with the distribution of its outcomes according to rules of acquisition. As we have seen in the previous chapters, these conceptions of justice create rather than resolve problems of fairness. This is because this new concept of fairness must deal with the different problems associated with distributing the two types of primary goods: fairness in the distribution of *outcomes* and fairness in the distribution of *opportunities*. Rawls's and Nozick's theories of justice are insensitive to this distinction.

Equal opportunity theory avoids this conflation by focusing on the distribution of the right to freedom that is the means of producing outcomes, not on the distribution of outcomes produced by the expression of freedom. Equal opportunity theory justifies intervention on the means rather than on the ends of self-determined pursuits. Whereas, both Rawls's and Nozick's theories of justice deal with the entire bundle of rights, experiences, and outcomes of freedom taken together, equal opportunity claims that all that an individual deserves is an equally optimal prospect for getting what one needs and wants in life. Everyone deserves the means necessary for pursuing the self-determined life. Everyone deserves a fair chance in the self-determined pursuit. This does not mean everyone deserves an equal starting point or an equal ending. It only means that everyone deserves an equal chance in life. This can be defined as a *reasonably favorable match* between their capacity and their social opportunities.

Equal opportunity theory backs this claim by showing the cause of unequal experiences of self-determination to be interaction between capacity and opportunity (social and environmental). Because variation in either capacity or opportunity affects prospects for a self-determined pursuit, frequent and persistent declines in either or both decrease prospects for self-determination and justify social redress. The significance of the discrepancy between the right and the experience of self-determination is the measure it provides for declines in life prospects for various individuals and groups in society. Consequently, equal opportunity theory bases its recommendation for social redress on this discrepancy, not on some external principle claiming what the distribution of primary goods in human society ought to be in some future end state. When social life evolves toward increased discrepancies, redress is necessary. The collective responsibility is to empower those experiencing loss in capacity and opportunity so they can regain capacity to pursue the self-determined life.

This is consistent with the theory's empirical explanation for how differences in accumulated advantage came to be, how the concept of equal rights to freedom came to be, and finally, how discrepancies between rights and experiences create a sense of injustice that produces arguments for redress on behalf of those least advantaged in society. Equal opportunity focuses on the fair distribution of rights and expressions of self-determination, not on the distribution of other primary goods that flow from self-determined acts. In this sense, the theory is based on a conception of freedom as a distributable primary good that differs from other primary goods to the extent it is a means to gaining access to those primary goods. Membership in the human group, therefore, entitles everyone to this means in that without it, access to any of the other primary goods in life is jeopardized. Accordingly, "fairness in liberty for all" argues for an equal chance at the self-determined life. When everyone has a similar chance of being self-determined—when each person has that right and can express it—then everyone is equally likely to live the self-determined life. The ideal of fairness in liberty for all is achieved.

Extending the Franchise

The advantage of this conception of fairness is that it yields the same conclusion whether viewed from the point of view of social justice or from the point of view of allocative justice. When viewed as social justice, fairness in liberty for all means that freedom is a good to be distributed to all members of society. When there is a discrepancy between this right and its expression among a population of actors, therefore, social redress is justified. When viewed as allocative justice, fairness in liberty for all affirms the expectation that everyone deserves a reasonable chance of getting what they need and want in life. Consequently, those who engage risky opportunity successfully are entitled to benefit from the success of that engagement; just as those who are unsuccessful or who avoid its risk are obliged to live with the consequences of those choices. In neither case, is collective intervention justified simply because individuals fail to get what they seek in that this would separate them from the results they produce. Equal opportunity theory claims that only when prospects for producing individually determined outcomes are reasonably favorable for all do all persons deserve the results they produce.

This conception of fairness in liberty for all is not without its problems, however. Since the birth of democratic government in the Western world, there have been long-standing discrepancies between rights and experiences of self-determination for some groups in society. Given the presence of social differentiation and stratification since the earliest civilization, this is not surprising in that in all societies advantage tends to accumulate for some and disadvantage tends to accumulate for others. This creates an additional set of social problems for those societies claiming equal liberty for all because it obligates them to reduce discrepancies between the right and experience of self-determination—it obligates them to adjust the distribution of rights and responsibilities toward equality of prospects for all.

The source of this problem was the social contract between the people and the state, which promised equal rights for all members of society even though some members were less powerful socially, economically, and technically. The inequality in power that existed at the inception of the original contract continued its evolutionary drift toward differentiation of opportunity and outcome according to that imbalance that created the same discrepancies between rights and experiences of self-determination for disadvantaged populations that had been in place before the social contract was in effect. This is the equal rights paradox of the social contract. Although the claim of equal liberty for all may include everyone in the original contract, the empirical fact of unequal power in social life eventually creates conditions of unequal prospects for freedom due to the evolution toward greater differentials in power. So even in the best of all possible worlds in which contractual claims for equality of rights are based on equal power among all participants—as in Rawls's thought experiment involving the veil of ignorance—resource exchange among individuals and groups will eventually devolve into a condition of unequal power. Any adjustment of the social contract after this evolution toward inequality, therefore, will be reflected in inequality of rights and experiences of self-determination now legitimated by the contract.

The only way social contracts claiming equal liberty for all can ensure equal liberty for all is by ensuring all parties to the contract maintain equal power, because as soon as power is unequally distributed the resulting contractual rewrite will reflect and legitimate that unequal distribution of power. Not only is the discrepancy between the right and the experience of self-determination likely to persevere in human societies no matter how democratically constructed they are in principle, but this tendency to legitimate unequal distributions of power through new versions of the social contract will also tend to prevent the development of institutional mechanisms (e.g., Rawls's difference principle) from operating automatically and inexorably to redress inequalities of opportunity and outcomes.

In sum, achieving fairness in liberty for all is unlikely from a practical point of view because the process of equalization requires adjustments in the social contract that are contrary to the interests of those who have the power to rewrite it in favor of equalization. In that revision toward equalization will require a renegotiation of who needs and deserves what to gain access to the primary goods in life, no member of society who already has access to primary goods has an interest in changing his situation. In other words, those with sufficient capacity or power to get what they want in life have no need or interest in engaging in transactions that reduce their own prospects. Consequently, if a rewrite of the social contract is to favor the least advantaged in society, it will do so only to the extent there is shift in the balance of power in favor of those who are least advantaged.

This means that social contracts guaranteeing rules for fair play for all—including the least powerful in society—are likely only if agreed to by equally powerful signatories to the contract, which is perhaps why Rawls invoked the veil of ignorance as a precondition for constructing the just society. This suggests that the only way to adequately explain why fairness for *all* was included in the original social contract is that it was a side condition necessary for the powerful to secure fairness for themselves. It was a consequence of equalization in social, economic, and technical resources held by newly advantaged groups in society and the result of a desire on the part of those groups to consolidate and legitimate their newly acquired gains. In short, the "all" was not intended to benefit the least powerful members of society—the disenfranchised, the poor, or the disabled. The benefits these groups were to receive centuries later were secondary and accidental to the primary benefit accruing to the nouveau riche who *were* the intended beneficiaries of the idea of liberty for all.

This leads to the conclusion that the social contract and its connection with human nature and natural law legitimated the positions of power occupied by these new groups in the social structure, and the side effect of this legitimization through the human nature connection was that every person, regardless of position in the power structure, was entitled to the same guaranteed opportunity because they too were human; they too were governed by laws of nature. Guarantees of liberty attached to those with social, economic, and technical power also applied to those without those sources of power. By virtue of human membership, every person had a right to the self-determined life. The human nature connection with the social contract legitimating the claim of self-determination for all applied to the powerful and the powerless equally.

There was no way to escape the logic implied by the human nature connection, except perhaps to suggest some members of society were less human, as was suggested for the enslaved, the poor, and the disabled. By excluding these "undesirable" members of society on grounds they lacked the essence of being human, that they were immoral, irrational, or too stupid to qualify as human, one could justify denying them human rights. They did not deserve to be treated as human because they lacked the essential characteristics of morality and rationality. Descriptions in previous chapters of the treatment these least well situated members of society experienced is evidence of this facile conclusion about who was human, who was not, who was entitled to rights and who was not.

Nevertheless, the universal claim of liberty for all did become consequential, eventually. In the short run, it was consequential to the extent it established an expectation to be realized in the just society. Because all persons deserve a say in the social contract due to their membership in the human species, fairness in liberty for all should be the basis for the construction of the just society. Locke's claim of inalienable rights for all was one such consequence of rising expectations for reducing discrepancies between rights and experiences of freedom. In the long run, therefore, the universal claim of liberty for all was also consequential, even though this time period was in centuries involving as it did more than a moral claim and desire for a just society.

That "more" that was involved turned on the paradox of reconciling expectations for individual rights with the evolution toward differential access to social power. The experience of democratic government captures the rights paradox at work. On the one hand, democracies are built on the claim of fairness in liberty for all, and on the other hand, the mechanisms they employ to adjust social relationships toward greater equality require adjustments in power by those who have a hand in producing that inequality in the first place. Unfortunately, the solution to this problem is also contained in the condition of unequal power. To adjust the social contract to favor the weak, the weak and the powerful have to renegotiate the contract in favor of the weak. But this is unlikely in that when the powerful and the powerless negotiate, the powerless usually become less powerful and the powerful more so.

The social contract works toward fairness when the person claiming a right to be respected by another has sufficient power to enforce that claim, either by evoking terms of a contract or by forcing a renegotiation of the contract. When these conditions are present, Person and Other work together to distribute rights and responsibilities in accordance with the power relationship connecting them. Of course, this leaves unresolved the problem facing the powerless who are at a disadvantage when entering the zone of free exchange with individuals substantially better situated. This condition is likely to increase advantage for the powerful and disadvantage for the weak because Person will have less capacity to secure the means of producing gain through claims on Other's resources than Other has in securing the means of producing gain through claims on Person's resources. Should these exchanges continue between Person and Other, they would decrease Person's resources and increase Other's.

This is the pattern of accumulated gain and loss we expect when transactions in the marketplace of free exchange connect the *same* individuals with the *same* accumulations of gain or loss over time. Social contracts resulting from these relationships legitimate conditions of inequality in capacity and opportunity to make them seem fair. But this appearance of fairness rests on the theory there can be no claim for social redress that lies outside the distribution of rights and responsibilities defined by the most recently legitimated social contract, the one justifying inequality. This is how social stratification systems function to reinforce and justify social inequality—regardless of whether that legitimization resides with the doctrine of divine right or the doctrine of the social contract. Social selection works the same in all societies because what defines rights and responsibilities are power relationships connecting individuals with each other and with their groups. These relationships work toward maintaining advantage for those who are already advantaged by their access to greater resources.

This analysis of the balance of power in social relationships leads to the conclusion that the problem of unfairness is unlikely to be resolved by those best situated to resolve it, even when there is substantial moral justification for social redress in the interest of fairness for all. This is because the solution to be implemented requires equalization of capacity and opportunity through a new division of rights and responsibilities among members of society. Such a redistribution would require that the more powerful bargain away their advantage so the less powerful can build their capacity (power) and enhance their opportunity to succeed in life. Such voluntary redistribution of advantage (power) is contrary to one's self-interest as claimed by Hobbes and Locke, which takes us back to Nozick's argument for voluntary social redress through charity.

The problem created by the demand for social redress also helps us understand the fundamental contradiction between *power imbalance*—which affects the distribution of rights and responsibilities in all social contracts—and the *political ideal* of fairness—which claims liberty for all in social contracts such as the American Declaration of Independence and the French Declaration of the Rights of Man and of the Citizen. It reminds us that the moral impetus for responding to the demand for redress is the discrepancy between the right and the experience; that this impetus, in turn, is a function of rising expectations among all members of society that optimal prospects for pursuing the self-determined life be shared equally. The practical political problem develops, however, when it is time to respond to the moral impetus for fairness because then we must confront the paradox of social redress—that those in control of the means necessary for creating a more just society are usually the ones least likely to benefit from making good on that obligation.

This leads to the conclusion that the ideal of fairness in liberty for all is unlikely to be realized through the natural course of sociocultural evolution, whether that evolution is influenced by rights and responsibilities negotiated by autonomous individuals acting in their own interests and legitimated by the social contract or whether it is influenced by rights and responsibilities determined by higher authority and justified by the doctrine of divine right. Because in both systems of deciding rights and responsibilities, freedom as power is determinate. Individuals least well situated in society, therefore, will continue to be left out of the mainstream of community life. They will continue to be marginalized by declining prospects for living the self-determined life in that they have the least capacity and the fewest opportunities for expanding their rights and reducing their responsibilities.

Whether we like it or not, the proposition that *power defines right* is still a robust predictor of the distribution of opportunities and outcomes in social life. Even today, the distribution of power defines rights and responsibilities, as it has in the past. Nevertheless, social redress on behalf of the disenfranchised, the poor, and the disabled has occurred, and this apparent contradiction with the analysis presented here compels us to examine how this can be so. What we will discover from this examination, unfortunately, is that the social redress of the past decades was a side effect of a redistribution of power affecting the rights of the powerful. We will see, as we have seen before, that the social redress on behalf of the disenfranchised and the disabled was a *secondary consequence* of a redistribution of rights and responsibilities first favoring those who have already gained a measure of power in social life.

A good example of this secondary-effect explanation is what happened to persons of color who were still bound into slavery a century and a half ago and who most people believe were freed by Lincoln's Emancipation Proclamation of 1863 and the Thirteenth Amendment to the Constitution. A closer reading of this history tells us that freeing the slaves did not come about because the president and Congress finally decided to act on a moral impulse. Freeing the slaves was a consequence of a shift in power that eventually favored the disenfranchised. This should be no surprise in that from the beginning, the movement to abolish slavery was secondary to the more influential economic and political competition between the North and the South that finally led to a war to preserve the Union. Abolishing slavery was secondary to this balance of power struggle that focused on preserving the economic interests of power holders in the North and South. If Lincoln and Congress could have saved the Union at the moral cost of maintaining slavery, they would have. In fact, they attempted to do just that when Congress passed the Missouri Compromise of 1820, establishing the 36th parallel that divided land acquired in the Louisiana Purchase into free and slave states, and also when Congress passed the Fugitive Slave Act of 1850, prohibiting aid for slave fugitives and penalizing U.S. marshals for refusing to arrest and return them to their masters. These actions were intended to preserve the distribution of rights and responsibilities connecting the economies of the North and the South. Had the South not seceded from the Union or had it won the war, slavery would have persisted long after, perhaps until mechanized farming rendered it uneconomical to support the interests of the powerful. Slavery was an economic and social resource benefiting those individuals most advantaged in the South.

This is not to say there was not moral outrage over the institution of slavery either—there was. From the 1830s on, small groups of aggressive antislavery advocates called abolitionists marshaled public opinion against

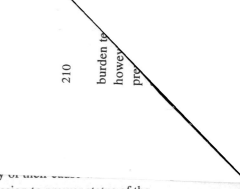

the practice, organized opposition to fugitiv
politicians to end the institution. They even
slave owners. Nevertheless, they were not su
their ends. But they were able to create tens
South competition for social, economic, and
underway before slavery became a moral is
the South rebuilt itself based on Jim Crow le
oppressed socially, politically, and econon
nowhere to be found, even though the morality of their cause
then as it was before the war. This moral regression to prewar status of the
rights of African Americans infected North and South alike. There was
little concern then about the obvious discrepancy between the Fourteenth
Amendment that ensured equal protection under the law for all citizens and
the enactment of Jim Crow laws that deprived persons of color equal
protection under the law. Moreover, this discrepancy between the right and
the experience of freedom for African Americans persisted into the second
half of the 20th century.

A similar story can be told for disabled students who benefited from
schooling as a secondary consequence of compulsory school attendance,
which was intended for nondisabled students. Here again, there was no
intent to provide social redress because no one thought these children
deserved a fair chance at the self-determined life. Compulsory attendance
was intended to serve the educational needs of nondisabled children. Prior
to this new policy, parents enrolled their disabled children in private
schools or institutionalized them. When states required all children to
attend school, they enthusiastically complied, causing dismay among public school officials (Lazerson, 1983, p. 17).[2]

From 1890 to 1915, school enrollment increased 55%, average daily
attendance increased 84%, the average number of days in school increased
18%, and the total school expenditures increased 329% (Lazerson, 1983,
p. 18). These trends in educational opportunity for all students were a
special benefit for children with disabilities who were more expensive to
teach. A 1909 study by Leonard Ayres reported that 33.7% of all students
in the elementary grades were "retarded," which led states to institute
systematic testing procedures to identify those who needed special classes.
The goals of this initial sorting of children were mixed. Some believed
children with disabilities should be in classes designed to meet their needs,
whereas others worried the presence of these students in regular classes
would adversely affect the education of other students and would unduly

achers who would have to deal with them. Both groups agreed, er, that special class placement was the answer because this would vent disabled students from interfering with the progress of nondisabled students and at the same time, it would prevent them from becoming wards of the state (Lazerson, 1983).

But increasingly, the dominant concern was fear that the presence of feebleminded students in the public schools would contaminate the learning opportunities of other students. Leaders in the intelligence testing movement of that period fed this fear; the comments of testing guru Lewis Terman (1917) illustrate the point:

"Feeble-mindedness has always existed, but only recently have we begun to recognize how serious a menace it is to the social, economic and moral welfare of the state. Extensive and careful investigations in large numbers and in diverse parts of the United States have furnished indisputable evidence that it is responsible for at least one fourth of the commitments to state penitentiaries and reform schools, for the majority of cases of chronic and semi-chronic pauperism, and for much of our alcoholism, prostitution and venereal disease."[3] (quoted in Lazerson, 1983, p. 25)

What began, therefore, as an opportunity to include students with disabilities with all students in a universal provision for public school education ended as an occasion to exclude them from the definition of "all" children enrolled in general education, to prevent them from contaminating "normal" students through their presence in the same classes, and to educate them separately to reduce their tendency toward social deviance after they left school.

This was the status of special education schooling during the first half of the 20th century. Although the number of students enrolled in special classes in the United States increased from 26,000 to 162,000 from 1922 to 1932 (see Lazerson, 1983, p. 28), the education they received was substandard: "Classes [were] in basement rooms and former closets with the least trained teachers, children with different handicaps [were] lumped together and no real effort [was] made to teach them" (Lazerson, 1983, p. 34). Teachers and administrators did not feel these students were worth the time, effort, and money to educate. Even the White House Committee and Child Health and Protection concluded that, " 'it must be remembered that the state is responsible to the taxpayers for the use of public moneys and that in consequence the state tends to look on all education as an investment that will pay justifiable dividends' " (quoted in Lazerson, 1983, p. 35).[4]

Attitudes about special education classes among educators were negative as well, leaving no mistake that the purpose of the segregated class was to exclude those who could not benefit from the educational opportunities in the mainstream (Lazerson, 1983, p. 36).[5]

By midcentury, special education had become a dumping ground for students who failed to fit in mainstream instructional practice. It became a second-class tracking system that ensured whoever went in would never get out. The humanitarianism that once drove special education into the foreground of public concern had long since receded. In its place was fear of the subnormal backed by policies of segregation through special class placements, as Lazerson (1983) explains in the following:

> Its humanitarian thrust had always been *secondary* to the fear generated by the mentally subnormal. Once the current of fear had declined, replaced by other concerns, once a structure had been established to place and thus control the deviants, special education seemed to have little to offer [italics added]. (p. 37)

The Equal Opportunity Principle

The ideal of fairness in liberty for all, therefore, remained an ideal for those least advantaged in society well into the 20th century. The temporary social redress persons of color and individuals with disabilities received in the late 19th century and early 20th century was incidental to the power advantage gained by other members of society who had benefited from a redistribution of rights and responsibilities during this period. Any collateral gain these left out groups experienced was short-lived depending as it did on the meager access to resources these groups had in pursuing their own ends at the turn of the century. Consequently, their prospects for self-determination actually declined from then on. People of color languished under the oppression of Jim Crow laws preventing them from pursuing the same opportunities afforded white people, and people with disabilities languished under similar conditions of constrained opportunity due to widespread perceptions they lacked capacity to benefit from opportunity routinely afforded nondisabled people. Paternalism and pity wrapped in an oppressive shroud of social, political, and economic discrimination sealed their fate by depressing their hopes and limiting their prospects. Color and disability were as effective predictors of poverty and despair as poverty itself, so intertwined were perceptions of cause and consequence in linking capacity with opportunity.

Social redress for these two groups came about in the last half of the 20th century when the idea of fairness in liberty for all finally came to mean *all* persons. This unusual period that followed World War II constituted a brief moment in human history when the truly powerless were finally included in the social and political definition of *all*. Today, thanks to our own era that has operationalized the equal opportunity principle so that all actually means all, we are often reminded of the tendency of the powerful to view neglected members of society as not fully counting in any politically significant way when deciding who deserves fairness in the distribution of rights and responsibilities in society.

Historically, this tendency to omit various groups from the conception of all was the rule rather than the exception. Although in principle the concept was inclusive, in practice, it was exclusive. This prevented the weak and powerless from mounting an effective claim against unfair treatment when that claim required institutional redress based on who counted and who did not in the concept of fairness for all. If you did not count in the definition of *all* in any political sense, then your claim was not worth consideration in any social or moral sense. You simply had no claim to the entitlements attached to "all persons."

With our long history with the exclusive rather than the inclusive all, it is of interest how we finally came to value the latter at all, given the transformation from the former to the latter would require a different understanding of the social contract and a different distribution of rights and responsibilities according to that understanding. Today's inclusive version is politically correct. Accordingly, public discourse gives the inclusive all an ascendant normative ring that is expected to reverberate in our minds and hearts as an ultimate good. To be exclusive rather than inclusive is to suggest a value contrary to what we claim is appropriate in democratic life. Morally, we have difficulty advocating the inclusive conception of all while practicing the exclusive conception, at least in public policy debate.

But again, history reminds us how different this climate is from what it was prior to the Civil War when slavery was legal and shortly after the war when discrimination took its place to produce the same exclusionary effect (Jackson, 1992). Recall the Supreme Court's 1857 decision in *Dred Scott v. Sanford* that " 'Negroes' could not become citizens because at the time of the writing of the Constitution they were considered a 'subordinate and inferior class of beings.' " Chief Justice Taney's conclusion reminds us of this conception of the exclusive "all" in the following:

> They had for more than a century before been regarded as being of an inferior order; and altogether unfit to associate with the white race, either in social or political relations; and *so far inferior, that they had no rights which the white man was bound to respect;* and that the Negro might justly and lawfully be reduced to slavery for his benefit. He was bought and sold, and treated as an ordinary article of merchandise and traffic, wherever a profit could be made of it. This opinion was at that time fixed and universal in the civilized portion of the white race. It was regarded as an axiom in morals as well as politics, which no one thought of disputing or supposed to be open to dispute [italics added]. (quoted in Jackson, 1992, p. 30)

This prewar "all" excluded African Americans because they were considered less than human, and this lesser moral, political, and social status meant they were not entitled to the rights guaranteed under the constitutional all. What resulted was one standard of fairness for white populations and another standard for black populations. This permitted all institutions to discriminate between the two groups because one group was less human than the other. The prevailing belief was that one group had less capacity for rational thought and autonomous action and consequently, was less deserving of the full set of human rights. People with these inferior levels of humanity needed protection much as children needed oversight and direction because they were incapable of self-determination. They lacked capacity to think on their own, to make intelligent choices on their own, and to pursue desirable ends in life on their own. But unlike children, people of color could never mature because they were fundamentally lacking by nature. They would never achieve, therefore, a status equal to white Americans, and they did not belong in the definition of all. Hence, there was no logical or moral inconsistency in proclaiming liberty for one group but not for another because only those qualifying as fully human deserved the right to self-determination under the constitutional all.

Given this historical grounding in an exclusive all, it is noteworthy how the inclusive all finally came to control policy discussions on the legitimacy of social redress for least well situated individuals. How could a transformation of the magnitude required to alter public thought and attitude regarding the rights of people who were so thoroughly marginalized ever occur at all, much less bring about redress on their behalf? According to the proposition of power affecting right, a precondition for this transformation would be for those left out to be included in the mainstream at least long enough for them to negotiate a rewrite of the social contract on behalf of their own claims for fairness.

But this precondition is itself unlikely. Prior to the Civil War, those included in the Constitution had the power to advance their rights and legitimate their control over the means of producing what they needed and wanted in life, whereas those excluded had no rights to counter this expanding hegemony. The evolution of rights and responsibilities toward differential advantage separating the included and the excluded was ensured, and institutional discrimination on this basis affected judgments about what was fair and what was just. Discrimination became a central tenet in belief systems about how the social world should function as well. It became a way of life. This was the effect of slavery on public attitudes about left out groups. Slavery created belief systems that classified people according to who was fully human and fully deserving of rights guaranteed by the Constitution and who was not. The Civil War may have abolished slavery, but it did not abolish the belief system supporting the practice. Those beliefs remained in the minds of Americans in the South as well as in the North.

So when the social contract was finally rewritten by adding the Fourteenth Amendment to the Constitution, which included former slaves under its protection, the expectation was not to alter the fundamental idea of fairness through social inequality. It was only to provide freed men and women *legal equality*. Nevertheless, this change opened the door for redefining who was eligible for inclusion in the constitutional all because the amendment read "All persons born or naturalized in the United States, and subject to the jurisdiction thereof, are citizens of the United States and of the State wherein they reside." It opened the door to a new interpretation of the meaning of fairness as well, in that every person was entitled to the same rights. "No State shall make or enforce any law which shall abridge the privileges or immunities of citizens of the United States; nor shall any State deprive any person of life, liberty, or property, without due process of law; nor deny to any person within its jurisdiction the equal protection of the laws."

The net effect was to abolish the legal basis for two standards of fairness—one for the white majority and another for the black minority. In the eyes of the Constitution, fairness meant treating every person the same under the law. If a white person deserved a privilege bestowed by the collective, then a black person deserved the same privilege. It also meant that if one person violated the law, that person would be punished under the same rules of due process that applied to another person. There could be no preferential treatment, nor could there be egregious discrimination in enacting or enforcing law. The rules of the contract applied equally to all.

Beyond this contractual change from the exclusive to the inclusive all, the amendment also reflected another set of forces at work to affect the course of social evolution toward an inclusive fairness. For example, the Radical Republicans—who were responsible for the Thirteenth Amendment abolishing slavery, the Fourteenth Amendment providing equal protection under the law, and the Fifteenth Amendment affirming the right to vote for all persons—were also interested in improving the social, economic, and political condition of former slaves. This interest stemmed, in part, from the hope that some day all black citizens would become fully accepted members of a society that would enable them to secure a greater share of the resources and opportunities in the South, thereby alleviating economic competition from white southerners.

As Harvie Wilkinson (1979) explains, the Radical Republicans acted for purposes of "elevating southern Negroes to humiliate southern whites, of enfranchising the Negro to entrench the Republican party in the South, and of using blacks to forestall seating southern delegations in Congress hostile to northern business interests" (p. 12). In other words, the *power shift* in play before the war continued well after it ended, with those in control seeking gain from the advantage they afforded former slaves through the constitutional amendments they expected would ensure former slaves a place in the political process that would counter any resurgence of competition from southern whites in Congress.

By helping former slaves become full citizens, Radical Republicans prevented former plantation owners from regaining political power in Congress. Toward this end they enacted a full set of laws designed to pave the way toward legal and social equality. The Civil Rights Act of 1866 gave former slaves the same rights to make contracts and hold property as whites; the Civil Rights Act of 1870 prohibited the harassment of former slaves as they moved from place to place; the Civil Rights Act of 1875 prohibited restrictions on " 'equal enjoyment of the . . . facilities and privileges of inns, public conveyances on land or water, theaters, and other places of public amusement' " (quoted in Wilkinson, 1979, p. 12).

The plan for empowerment of southern blacks and for the political containment of southern whites seemed foolproof. On the one hand, the Constitution included former slaves in the "all" by providing them full legal protection and political equality as stipulated by the three amendments to the Constitution, and on the other hand, the Civil Rights acts provided social equality in areas that were essential for acquiring the personal, social, and economic resources necessary for pursuit of the self-determined life. Taken together the package of protections and assurances for political and social equality was similar to that passed a century later, and was similarly intended to secure full citizenship and full participation in American life for people of color. But this did not happen, which accounts for why the effort was repeated a century later. It did not happen because the prevailing belief among white Americans did not change, even though the social contract describing the legal basis for distributing rights and responsibilities among white and black Americans had changed. The revised social contract now claimed all rather than some humans had the right to self-determination in social, political, and economic life; but this had little effect on attitudes toward former slaves.

REDRESS FOR PEOPLE OF COLOR

For the next century these deeply held beliefs created substantial obstacles to the realization of freedom for all Americans. They also created a moral dilemma because they contributed to the growing discrepancy between the right and the experience of self-determination for African Americans. No longer was it possible to justify the discrepancy by examining constitutional intent. Before, that was a source of solace for segregationists because the exclusive all of the Constitution permitted second-class citizenship for those excluded. But now the inclusive all eliminated use of the social contract to justify discrimination. This problem could not be corrected easily because neither the Constitution nor Federal law was likely to be rewritten with the exclusive all, nor was it likely that prejudicial attitudes of the white majority would change quickly. To complicate matters, the power imbalance between white and black Americans exacerbated the discrepancy condition because the personal, social, economic, and technical means necessary to equalize opportunity were aligned to forestall that from ever happening. Justice demanded redress but those with the power to authorize that redress were themselves constrained by their own beliefs.

When it came time to make good on the moral claim of equal protection under the Constitution, therefore, nothing happened. For a century, the discrepancy between the right and the experience of self-determination worsened for African Americans. What happened instead was consistent with the prediction based on power imbalance. Those with the social, economic, and technical means of getting what they wanted wrote their own version of the social contract and this new version separated the judicial arena of the body politic into two parts—the smaller and less important one functioning in accordance with federal law governed by the Constitution, and the larger and more important part functioning in accordance with local law and state constitution. Fearing a showdown between judicial power and legislative and executive power would resolve in favor of the latter, the Supreme Court interpreted constitutional intent narrowly so as to permit this bifurcation between federal and state authority in dividing social and political rights and responsibilities among the white and black populations. The result was a system of rights and responsibilities that matched prevailing attitudes and beliefs about two classes of humans.

The Supreme Court, in effect, dismantled the package of constitutional rights guaranteed in the 1860s and 70s by interpreting the Constitution so narrowly that no ruling would contradict the wishes of the powerful white population in the South. In effect, it avoided a showdown between federal and state government and between the judiciary, the executive, and legislative branches at all levels of government. It surrendered to majority will on a conception of fairness that was in direct contradiction with the Constitution (see Wilkinson, 1979, pp. 20-21). The Court believed its decisions would be ignored if they contradicted the mood, attitude, and wishes of the powerful majority in the South. It feared that if it acted and failed to be heard and to be heeded, its subsequent decisions would be ignored as well, which would further sap its strength and erode its authority as the final court of the land. So the Court ignored the discrepancy between the right to self-determination and the expression of that right, at least when that discrepancy applied to black Americans (see Wilkinson, 1979, pp. 21-22). Repeatedly, it ignored the interests of the powerless by ruling on the side of the powerful. In using the Fourteenth Amendment to aid employers in labor contract negotiations with employees, for example, the Court defined a new purpose of the amendment—which was to "resist venturous public action on behalf of the disadvantaged of whatever race (see Wilkinson, 1979, pp. 23).

But foremost in the mind of the Court in its rulings on equal protection under the Fourteenth Amendment was to avoid confrontation with the southern white interest in segregation. In seeking to avoid disaffecting

white power in the South, it handed southern whites all the legal resources
they needed to maintain their oppression of African American pursuits of
social and economic equality. The landmark case legitimating these efforts
was *Plessy v. Ferguson* (1896), which rebuffed a request by black Americans to overturn the South's racial policies supporting segregation based
on Jim Crow legislation (Glasser, 1991, p. 201).[6] By 1894, the Democratic
controlled Congress had already capitulated to southern interests by repealing the remaining civil rights laws of the 1860s and 1870s. *Plessy v.
Ferguson* was an attempt on the part of the African American community
to stem the advance of Jim Crow legislation by challenging a recently
erected policy of segregation in railroad cars. By having Homer A. Plessy
sit in a railroad car reserved for whites, the African American community
hoped to precipitate a Court decision against that policy. So when Plessy
was arrested and convicted of violating state law segregating the races, he
appealed his conviction invoking his rights as guaranteed by the Thirteenth
and Fourteenth Amendments. But the Court ruled in favor of states rights,
claiming the purpose of the Fourteenth Amendment was "to enforce the
absolute equality of the two races before the law," and that legal distinctions based on color were not contrary to the Constitution given that the
separate facilities were equal (Glasser, 1991). This set back the cause for
equal rights for black Americans because it established a judicial precedent
subsequent courts would use to reaffirm again and again the rights of the
white majority in their oppression of the black minority. The injustice in
this ruling and what it did to the Court's reputation is expressed well by
Ira Glasser (1991) in the following:

> The cynicism of this decision seemed boundless. The Court argued that
> federal laws could not eradicate prejudice, yet ignored the plain fact that
> state laws had helped establish prejudice. It claimed that segregation
> actually enhanced the public good, because if the two races were allowed
> to mix freely, disorder would result. That racial discrimination itself was
> a disorder, and of the most pathological kind, was not considered. In what
> was perhaps the *Plessy* opinion's most cruel and gratuitous passage, the
> Court located the discriminatory nature of segregation not in segregation
> itself, but in the minds of blacks: If "the enforced separation of the two
> races stamps the colored race with a badge of inferiority," the Court
> scolded, "it is not by reason of anything found in this act, but solely
> because the colored race chooses to put that construction on it." (p. 202)

Of course, from the point of view offered by social selection theory,
what happened here is no surprise because the forces at work stripping

opportunity from the powerless to enhance the opportunity of the powerful *were no different* from the forces at work in other periods of history long before the birth of democracy and the promise of fairness in liberty for all. A social contract that promises fairness in the distribution of freedom means little when the power distribution necessary to make good on that promise is aligned against social redress for the least powerful. During the late 19th century, Congress and the courts were acting in accordance with the existing power structure that favored white interests in the South. Consequently, it is no surprise that during the final decades of that century, Congress dismantled the Civil Rights Acts of the 1860s and 1870s, the Supreme Court interpreted the Fourteenth Amendment narrowly, and the president enforced these policies and decisions. African Americans had no other choice but to battle the social, political, and economic oppression on their own, with virtually no help from the North or from the federal government. This meant that their prospects for improving their lot in life would become much worse before they would become much better.

As southern efforts to erect ever more rigid and secure systems of racial separation increased, prospects for living the self-determined life became ever more dismal and hopeless. Accumulated advantage charac- terized the life of the average white American in direct proportion to the accumulated disadvantage that characterized the life of the average black American. On nearly every occasion for securing a good in life, social advantage for a white person was erected by imposing a social disadvan- tage on a black person. And the mechanism for enforcing this ever expand- ing and oppressive caste system was violence and brutality supported by local law (Glasser, 1991). No enforcement of the federal social contract claiming fairness in liberty came to the rescue because there was no force to counter the will and determination of the white majority and its Jim Crow contract benefiting majority interests at the expense of minority rights. According to Glasser,

> Blacks were thus banished from Southern politics, as they had been during slavery, their right to vote denied both by state laws and by unbridled violence, which the states permitted and the Fifteenth Amendment was powerless to restrain. Black Americans were thus exiled, in effect, from their own communities, though often imprisoned there as well. Children learned, in ways they were likely never to forget, that they were inescap- ably inferior, and that their horizons were sharply limited. If any dared to dream, those dreams were quickly crushed. Economic opportunity was systematically cut off, at its roots. Poverty, subjugation, and dependence

were institutionalized. And at a time when men were expected to be able
to provide for their families and protect them, black men were allowed to
do neither. Emasculation became a condition of survival. (p. 204)

Judicial Redress

The sorry fact of this period in U.S. history is the failure of the federal
government to act on behalf of the rights of these least advantaged members
of society. The discrepancy between a right guaranteed by the Constitution
and the expression of that right by African Americans went unattended at
first, ignored later, and then it simply went unnoticed. For this group, there
was no redress because there was no collective will to redress the oppression that had become institutionalized through a grossly unfair distribution
of rights and responsibilities between white and black Americans. For
nearly a century, the Court was silent on the question of redress, justifying
its inaction as it did on the precedent set in *Plessy v. Ferguson.*

Add to this the difficulty in seeking redress through the Courts that can
rule only once complaints are filed and you have another hardship in seeking
redress for those who start out in life with few resources. Again, advantage
goes to the powerful who need only defend themselves after the Court agrees
to rule on a claim. Perhaps this explains why it took so long for the African
American community to mount a serious challenge to Jim Crow oppression
and consequently, why it took nearly a century before *Plessy* was finally
overturned and the equal opportunity principle was finally established. It took
that long for those seeking redress to acquire the social, economic, and
technical resources necessary to force a rewrite of the social contract favoring
an equal distribution of rights and responsibilities.

In fact, this is what happened. After W. E. B. Du Bois and a group of
intellectuals and reformers organized the National Association for the
Advancement of Colored People (NAACP), that organization pursued a
dogged, 50-year quest for social redress through the courts that led to a
final victory in *Brown v. Board of Education,* which overturned *Plessy v.
Ferguson* and established the equal opportunity principle. This long trek
began in 1917 when the NAACP won a decision in *Buchanan v. Warley,*
challenging a residential segregation ordinance in the city of Louisville.
From there, the NAACP gradually, painstakingly, amassed a succession of
favorable court rulings. For example, the *Nixon v. Herndon* decision in
1927 challenged a Texas statute declaring Negroes ineligible to participate
in the Democratic party primary; the *Missouri ex rel Gaines v. Canada*

decision in 1938 ruled against the University of Missouri's plan to prevent African American students from enrolling in law school until a separate facility was built; the *Morgan v. Virginia* decision in 1946 struck down a provision of the Virginia code requiring separation of the races on intrastate and interstate carriers; the *Henderson v. United States* decision in 1950 ruled against the interstate railroad for providing preferences for white passengers in dining cars; the *McLaurin v. Oklahoma State Regents* decision in 1950 rejected the University of Oklahoma's plan for a 68-year-old African American student to earn a doctoral degree in education by sitting in classroom rows assigned to black students; and, finally, the *Sweatt v. Painter* decision in 1950 permitted Heman Sweatt to attend the University of Texas Law School.

In 1954, this accumulation of judicial gains in defining fairness for the benefit of African Americans paid off. The Supreme Court overturned *Plessy v. Ferguson,* claiming that segregation itself produced an unfair disadvantage for black children. The Court claimed the following:

> There are findings below that the Negro and white schools involved have been equalized, or are being equalized, with respect to buildings, curricula, qualifications and salaries of teachers, and other "tangible" factors. Our decision, therefore, cannot turn on merely a comparison of these tangible factors in the Negro and white schools involved in each of these cases. We must look instead to the effect of segregation itself on public education.

According to evidence provided by psychologists, segregation affected the *capacity* of children to succeed in life by producing psychological conditions that debilitated their ability to compete in the modern world, and this violated the equal protection clause of the Fourteenth Amendment. The Court reasoned that an individual cannot prepare for a profession, become a good citizen, contribute to society, and succeed in life without an education. Achieving these ends in life requires an understanding of how to engage new opportunity. Therefore, education should be available equally to all:

> Today, education is perhaps the most important function of state and local governments. Compulsory school attendance laws and the great expenditures for education both demonstrate our recognition of the importance of education to our democratic society. It is required in the performance of our most basic public responsibilities, even service in the armed forces. It is the very foundation of good citizenship. Today it is the principal instrument in awakening the child to cultural values, in preparing him for

later professional training, and in helping him to adjust normally to his environment. In these days, it is doubtful that any child may reasonably be expected to succeed in life if he is denied the opportunity of an education. Such an opportunity, where the state has undertaken to provide it, is a right which must be made available to all on equal terms.

The Court concluded that segregation deprived minority children of an equal education opportunity. The *social conditions* of segregated schooling produced a *psychological effect* that depressed students' performance in school, and this, in turn, deprived them of *opportunity* to develop those talents and abilities they needed to participate fully in the modern world. In other words, segregated schooling decreased their prospects for enhancing their capacity for pursuing adult opportunity:

> Segregation of white and colored children in public schools has a detrimental effect on the colored children. The impact is greater when it has the sanction of the law; for the policy of separating the races is usually interpreted as denoting the inferiority of the Negro group. A sense of inferiority affects the motivation of a child to learn. Segregation with the sanction of law, therefore, has a tendency to retard the educational and mental development of Negro children and to deprive them of some of the benefits they would receive in a racially integrated school system. (pp. 257-258)[7]

Social Redress

The establishment of equal educational opportunity through judicial redress also came at a time when the resource position of African Americans had improved substantially in that, by the 1950s, African Americans had the *capacity* to take full advantage of the equal opportunity principle established in the *Brown* decision. Their improved condition was partly due to the robust economy the country experienced following World War II and partly due to the nondiscrimination clause in defense contracts during the Korean War, which decreased unemployment among blacks from 9.0% to 5.3% between 1950 and 1951 and increased median income levels of African American families from $1,615 in 1947 to $2,338 per year in 1950. African Americans also benefited from their increased membership in trade unions that went from 1.5 million in 1949 to 2.4 million in 1953. Their graduation rates from school and college also increased (Cashman, 1991).

All of this translated into greater access to the resources necessary to press the white majority to rewrite the social contract in the direction of fairness for all. In 1955, a year after *Brown,* the African American community in Montgomery, Alabama, initiated that press by challenging a Jim Crow law regulating black seating on buses in Montgomery (Cashman, 1991, p. 126). The challenge commenced when Rosa Parks got herself arrested for refusing to leave her seat in the white-only section of a Montgomery bus and the African American community, under the leadership of E. D. Nixon, Ralph S. Abernathy, H. H. Hubbard, and Martin Luther King Jr., initiated a bus boycott in protest, which lasted 381 days. The boycott and subsequent Supreme Court ruling that segregated busing was unconstitutional handed the African American community its first victory in its challenge of the Jim Crow social contract. And this victory, in turn, empowered African Americans to press for a complete rewrite of that contract, as J. Mills Thornton explains in the following:

> "What the boycott taught the city's black leaders as it dragged on was that their quarrel was—had to be—with the law. Compromise with segregation was impossible because segregation so forged and underlay social relationships that even the most modest reform of its requirements threatened—just as the white politicians claimed—the entire social fabric. In such a situation reform was impossible; only 'revolution' would do. The white response to the boycott revealed this truth forcefully to the blacks; that revelation is the boycott's supreme achievement, and it is something which no court suit could ever have accomplished." (quoted in Cashman, 1991, p. 129)

Legislative Redress

Two years after the Montgomery boycott, the rewriting of Jim Crow law commenced with the passage of the Civic Rights Act of 1957, which provided procedural civil rights protections through a Civil Rights Commission and through the Civil Rights Division of the Department of Justice (see Cashman, 1991, p. 136). This act was also empowering for African Americans because it was the first federal action on their behalf since Reconstruction, and, as Cashman points out, "it encouraged and legitimized aspirations among African-Americans in a way not observed in 20th-century America hitherto. Paradoxically, these moves increased African-American desire for change and justified its implementation" (Cashman, 1991, p. 137). Equally significant was that these federal actions *increased the experience self-determination:*

> They produced among blacks both soaring expectations that Jim Crow could soon be eliminated from American life and a growing rage toward

all temporizing. Cumulatively, they generated a *determination that segregation and discrimination, however wrong and unconstitutional, would cease only when blacks themselves acted massively and militantly enough to guarantee that end* [italics added]. (Cashman, 1991, p. 137)

The lesson worth remembering here is that social justice came about only *after* African Americans initiated action on their own behalf. It did not come about because the moral worth of their cause motivated others to act on their behalf, although this occurred later, after the movement was well underway. Then the moral claim helped to seal commitment and to extend the movement's influence when it was time to pass the Civil Rights Act of 1957 prohibiting discrimination in voting; the Civil Rights Act of 1960 authorizing federal judges to select "referees" to register African Americans to vote if local officials obstructed registrations; the Civil Rights Act of 1964 banning discrimination in business, trade unions, and public accommodations, and segregation in public schools, hospitals, libraries, and playgrounds; the Voting Rights Act of 1965 permitting federal action to enable African American citizens to vote (see Cashman, 1991, pp. 136-137, 166-168, 192); and finally, the Civil Rights Act of 1968 outlawing discrimination in housing (see Glasser, 1991, p. 223).

The Redress Principle

Another lesson worth noting is that the redress policy reflected in this redistribution of rights and responsibilities connecting black and white Americans was based on the equal opportunity principle. Consequently, the intent of legislative redress emanating from this principle was to correct injustices due to unequal opportunities in the social, educational, political, and economic domains of life. More than this even, the intent was to build capacity among the young so that they could take advantage of the opportunities and rights guaranteed by the new social contract. So in the decade following *Brown,* Congress set about determining the extent to which educational inequality in American schools affected the capacity of African American students to pursue adult opportunity. It authorized James Coleman to conduct an *Equality of Educational Opportunity* study that surveyed approximately 4,000 elementary and secondary schools to assess conditions of inequality of educational opportunity among African Americans, Puerto Ricans, American Indians, Mexican Americans, Oriental Americans, and whites.

After completing that study, Coleman (1990) found that, although the achievement for white and Asian American students was comparable across all grades, the achievement of other minority students was substantially lower, and the achievement of African American and Puerto Rican students was lowest of all. Moreover, he found that the achievement of African American students in schools in the South was lower than for similar students in the North. Coleman also found that family background, parental attitudes, and characteristics of the student body of the school explained more of the variance in student achievement than characteristics of teachers or the schools. Finally, and most important, Coleman concluded that the most robust predictors of student achievement were student attitudes toward school. Students' *interest* in school, their *self-concept,* and their *sense of control of the environment* were more powerful indicators of achievement than all the variables examined in the study. Coleman concluded the following:

> Taken alone, these attitudinal variables account for more of the variation in achievement than any other set of variables (all family background variables together, or all school variables together). When added to any other set of variables, they increase the accounted-for variation more than does any other set of variables. (p. 109)

Moreover, the variable reflecting student sense of control over the environment was the one most strongly related to achievement. It was even predictive in reverse comparisons between African American and white students, as Coleman (1990) explains in the following:

> Despite the very large achievement differences between whites and blacks at the 9th and 12th grades, those blacks who gave responses indicating a sense of control of their own fate achieved higher on the tests than those whites who gave the opposite responses. This attitude was more highly related to achievement than any other factor in the student's background or school. (p. 126)

Coleman's explanation for lowered achievement among African Americans was that these students were caught in a self-perpetuating cycle of declining performance in school, and that this cycle was due to three factors: (a) *segregated schooling,* which set up a self-perpetuating cycle of lowered expectations within the student body comprised of students from similarly disadvantaged backgrounds, (b) these *lowered expectations* depressed students' interest in school, their self-concept, and their sense of control over their environment, and (c) these *negative self-attitudes,* in turn, depressed students' achievement in school (Coleman, 1990, p. 64).[8] The redress suggested by this analysis of interaction between *student capacity* and *educational opportunity* was to build student capacity and to improve school opportunity by equalizing access to good schools. Coleman proposed, therefore, a policy of school desegregation to institute this redress.

REDRESS FOR PEOPLE WITH DISABILITIES

People with disabilities have also suffered long and hard from the discrimination and segregation associated with being classified as nonpersons. As with African Americans, they too were unable to obtain redress for their denial of equal rights simply because their claim was justified. Their redress also awaited two conditions before there would be any chance at improving their lot in life. First, there had to be a public recognition that being placed in institutions and being denied a public education was fundamentally wrong. This acknowledgment came about in the 1960s when Senator Robert Kennedy, who had a sister with mental retardation, visited an institution for people similar to his sister and discovered "overcrowded wards of patients, many naked and wandering about aimlessly or lying in their own feces and urine, and what he described as 'young children slipping into blankness and lifelong dependence' " (Shapiro, 1993, pp. 160-161). After that visit, documentaries of institutional life, similar to those published in *Christmas in Purgatory* by Burton Blatt and Fred Kaplan, highlighted the egregious treatment experienced by these forgotten people and suggested that segregated treatment constituted a denial of their basic human rights (see Shapiro, p. 196).

Social Redress

The second condition that was also necessary for social action on behalf of this least well situated group was, of course, a redistribution of power in favor of these people or in favor of their families and friends who were willing to advocate on their behalf. Fortunately, this shift in power had been in the making since the 1950s and accelerated in the 1960s when baby boomers became parents and their children enrolled in public school in record numbers. This new cohort of students also included children with disabilities whose demands for special education tripled enrollments in these programs. This created pressure on schools to improve services for these children and when appropriate educational services were not forthcoming, their well-educated middle class parents lobbied state legislatures and Congress for increased support for special education (see Lazerson, 1983, p. 39). They also joined forces with parents of minority students who wanted to end the second-class education their children received when they were placed in special education programs for scoring poorly on standardized intelligence tests.

This powerful parent group also sought redress through the courts, claiming that denying their children educational opportunity was unconstitutional, and the Court agreed in *Pennsylvania Association for Retarded Children v. Commonwealth of Pennsylvania* and *Mills v. DC Board of Education,* and it extended the equal opportunity principle to students with disabilities (see Rothstein, 1990, p. 2). The basic argument in these cases was that children with disabilities received unequal treatment because they were denied educational opportunities afforded nondisabled children. Also, given that segregated schooling was unequal for African American children, it was also unequal for children with disabilities. Both denials of equal opportunity were at variance with the equal protection clause of the Fourteenth Amendment (see Turnbull, 1993, p. 38).

The effect of the *Brown* decision and subsequent court rulings it influenced was to *operationalize* the equal opportunity principle through congressional acts that expanded educational access for students with disabilities at the same time it attempted to equalize educational opportunity for students of color. From the very first application of this principle of redress, federal legislation benefiting one group also provided assistance for the other group. For example, in the Elementary and Secondary Education Act of 1965 (P.L. 89-10), which set down a comprehensive plan for redressing inequalities in educational opportunity experienced by economically underprivileged children, Congress also provided services for children with disabilities. The act was primarily intended to provide financial support for schools with high concentrations of economically disadvantaged children and youth, but it also provided for the improvement of services for students with disabilities (see DeStefano & Snauwaert, 1989, p. 14).

Then, in 1965 Congress passed Public Law 89-313 that authorized grants to state-operated or state-supported schools devoted to the education of children with handicaps, which included students who were mentally retarded, hard of hearing, deaf, speech impaired, visually handicapped,

seriously emotionally disturbed, crippled, or other health impaired children
who by reason thereof require special education (see DeStefano & Snauwaert,
1989, p. 15). In the decade that followed, Congress focused exclusively on
the needs of disabled students by passing several other major pieces of
legislation before capping this initiative in educational redress by passing
the Education for All Handicapped Children Act in 1975.

The Redress Principle

By the time this precedent-setting act was in place to provide new
educational opportunities for children with disabilities, states and local
school districts throughout the nation had experienced a decade of preparation for meeting students' needs. Consequently, schools were in a position to comply with court mandates and with federal law articulating the
four principles of redress for this group of students. The first principle of
redress reaffirmed the primacy of the inclusive all in federal policy regarding access to public education. Public Law 94-142 stated that all children,
regardless of their handicapping condition, were to receive a public education, the assumption being that all children with disabilities could learn.
Consequently, they deserved access to educational opportunity just as their
nonhandicapped peers. No child could be denied access due to a disability.
The second principle of the act was that education was *free.* Public schools
were responsible for meeting educational needs of children with disabilities at no cost to their parents or guardians. Social redress on behalf of this
population was a *collective responsibility* (see Rothstein, 1990, p. 33). The
third principle reaffirmed the *Brown* decision that separate education was
not equal education. Consequently, instruction had to occur in the *least
restrictive* educational setting possible. The fourth principle of redress was
that the appropriate education students with disabilities were to receive
needed to be education so that it would optimally match their capacity to
learn. The expectation was that this condition would fully engage students
in learning new skills and building new capacities for the independence
and self-determination they would experience later in life. This principle
was a new addition to the redress package developed to equalize educational opportunity for African American students.

In sum, social redress for students with disabilities included the same
guarantees for a public education extended to students of color and then
some. Although both groups were assured opportunity for integrated school-

ing at public expense, desegregation for students of color and mainstreaming for students with disabilities, educational redress for students with disabilities went further. It attempted to mitigate obstacles to learning caused by various types of disabling conditions. In the process of redressing this problem, the new policy operationalized the optimal prospects principle, calling it *individualized instruction*. The optimal prospects principle was sensitive to the unique set of needs every child has that require individually designed instructional opportunities to optimize prospects for learning. The requirement that all students with disabilities have an individualized educational plan (IEPs) was an attempt to match student capacity with instructional opportunity to increase prospects for learning. This meant that this policy of redress also satisfied the ideal for fairness in liberty for all because it attempted to give students with disabilities an *optimal chance* of developing their capacity for pursuing adult opportunity after school. In other words, it attempted to optimize students' prospects for self-determination.

It is also worth noting what this optimal prospects principle *was not* intended to accomplish. It was not intended, for example, to guarantee maximum learning outcomes for each child. It was intended only to guarantee a fair chance for learning that was comparable to the fair chance afforded nondisabled children. To establish this fair chance, special education policy guaranteed access to a public education that was individualized according to the student's capacity and mainstreamed according to the least restrictive environment commensurate with that capacity. The intent was to provide an *optimal match* between learning capacity and educational opportunity so students would engage their minds and direct their behaviors to increase their capacity to choose and enact choice in pursuit of adult opportunity after school. In this sense, the principle conceived educational opportunity as a means for helping children with disabilities become self-determined in adult life.

The principle said nothing about guaranteed outcomes, however. It did not guarantee all students with disabilities would learn the same amount, at the same rate as other students, or that they would maximize their potential for learning. It guaranteed only a reasonable chance, a fair chance, a chance that was comparable to that afforded nondisabled students. This point was clarified in the Supreme Court decision in *Board of the Education v. Rowley* (1983) which overturned a lower court decision regarding a claim by Amy Rowley and her parents that she was not receiving a free and appropriate public education because there was a discrepancy between what she could have learned without her handicap and what she actually learned. Defining a free and appropriate public education as "an opportunity to achieve [her] full potential commensurate with the opportunity provided to other children," a lower court decided on her behalf citing that the standard " 'requires that the potential of the handicapped child be measured and compared to his or her performance, and that the remaining differential or "shortfall" be compared to the shortfall experienced by nonhandicapped children.' " The Supreme Court overturned this decision, citing the congressional intent of the Education for All Handicapped Children Act:

> "By passing the Act, Congress sought primarily to make public education available to handicapped children. But in seeking to provide such access to public education, Congress did not impose on the States any greater substantive educational standard than would be necessary to make such access meaningful. Indeed, Congress expressly recognize[d] that in many instances the process of providing special education and related services to handicapped children *is not guaranteed to produce any particular outcome*' S. Rep. No. 94-168, *supra,* at 11. Thus the intent of the act was more to open the door of public education to handicapped children on appropriate terms than to guarantee any particular level of education once inside [italics added]."[9] (quoted in Turnbull, 1993, p. 339)

The Court also countered the plaintiff's claim that " 'the goal of the Act is to provide each handicapped child with an equal educational opportunity' " by arguing this did not mean the act was to ensure some " 'absolute equality of opportunity regardless of capacity [of students]' " but rather it meant instead to guarantee a " 'basic floor of opportunity' " consistent with equal protection. Neither the history of the act nor Congress suggested that " 'equal protection required anything more than equal access' " (quoted in Turnbull, 1993, p. 341). The Court, therefore, ruled the following:

> "The District Court and the Court of Appeals thus erred when they held that the Act requires New York to maximize the potential of each handicapped child commensurate with the opportunity provided nonhandicapped children. Desirable though that goal might be, it is not the standard that Congress imposed on States which receive funding under the Act. Rather, Congress sought primarily to identify and evaluate handicapped children, and to provide them with access to a free public education." (quoted in Turnbull, 1993, p. 341)

Optimizing Prospects

According to equal opportunity theory, the basis for social redress in a democratic society is the social contract voluntarily negotiated by persons of equal power. When the contract specifies an agreed on distribution of rights and responsibilities, then the community has a moral obligation to live up to that agreement by providing redress when rights are violated or when responsibilities go unfulfilled. As indicated in this chapter, the problem with this basis for evoking social redress is that the power to enact that redress functions in accordance with existing distributions of social, economic, and technical power in the polity. Consequently, when these distributions change, prospects for altering the social contract also change in ways that benefit or deny redress for those most and least favored by the new distribution. Although this is a fundamental problem of all social contracts, it is an especially difficult problem in contracts claiming equal rights for all because here the powerless are legally but not socially included in the "all." And because they lack the necessary resources to enforce their claim for equal rights, their rights can be ignored by those who have greater resources. This creates a discrepancy between rights and experiences of freedom and provides the moral impetus for social redress.

This was not a significant problem early in the history of the United States because people of color and people with disabilities were not included in the all of the original contract. Consequently, there was no moral question precipitated by a discrepancy between the right to freedom and the fair distribution of that right among these left out groups. Moreover, several ideologies were available to justify their exclusion based, as they were, on narrow interpretations of what it meant to be human. This changed with the Emancipation Proclamation, the Thirteenth Amendment, and the Fourteenth Amendment which corrected the omission of people of color and people with disabilities from the constitutional all.

By the latter half of the 20th century, these corrections, together with a redistribution of social, economic, and technical resources that favored these left out groups, provided the occasion for the optimal prospects principle to evolve from the social redress policies constructed during this period. But it took considerable time for shifts in power to finally be aligned with the moral claim that justified redress. This is because it took that long for these disadvantaged groups to attain positions of power that would allow them to act on their own to seek redress from the courts and from Congress. In other words it took a *redistribution* of social, economic, and technical power in favor of those deserving redress for them to get what they deserved.

Today, redress along lines suggested by the optimal prospects principle is well established judicially, legally, and socially. The idea that *all persons* deserve a fair chance in life regardless of who they are is widespread. There is public support for justice as fairness as well. Should fairness be denied, then redress is required. It matters not whether the group of individuals being denied a fair chance is composed of people of color, people with disabilities, or people who are poor and destitute. If they do not receive a fair chance in life, then they deserve assistance so that they have that fair chance. The ideal that everyone deserves a fair chance is fundamental. It evokes willingness among the majority to act collectively on behalf of the deprived minority.

Given this ideal, it seems unfair that some individuals and groups have consistently better prospects of getting what they need and want in life than others. To the extent these conditions persist, it raises questions about the fairness of our institutions. Our ideal of social justice is threatened because we can see how those least advantaged in society might come to believe they would be better off in another society or in a reconstituted society—a society with rules that give everyone a fair chance. Our ideal of allocative justice is also threatened in that we can see how those least advantaged in society might compare the ratio of cost and gains they experience in pursuit of their ends in life with the cost-gain ratios of more advantaged members and believe other people are being treated more favorably than they are. So when prospects for pursuing the good in life are distributed unequally among individuals and groups, fairness conceived collectively and comparatively is threatened. This is troubling and is likely to provoke social change in the direction of fairness.

According to equal opportunity theory, this provocation for redress is stimulus for social change in the direction of the optimal prospects principle. This is what is happening today. Even in the midst of widespread disappointment about the pattern of social reform of past decades, there is the persistent, nagging reminder to be fair. This translates into increased clarity of purpose in recommending social redress. The issue today is one of fair chances, not one of equal outcomes. Policymakers are less likely to confuse a prospect or chance with a gain or an outcome because their focus is on *prospects* not gains. For students of color and students with disabilities, the expectation is for both to receive a fair chance at getting an education. It is not that they be guaranteed an educational outcome. No one deserves a guarantee. The same holds for people on welfare. The expectation for them is the same—to have a fair chance at pursuing opportunity for personal gain; it is not to receive a guaranteed level of support because no one in society deserves that. In other words, the focus on equal chances or equal prospects is a focus on the *means* individuals need to pursue opportunity that incurs a reasonable risk but promises a reasonable gain toward those ends in life they desire.

This book has argued that the chief determinant of the fair chance is the match between personal capacity and social opportunity. When the match is just right, when it is sufficient to engage Person in pursuit of opportunity, prospects for self-determination maximize. But when the match requires too great a cost for the gain promised, engagement of new opportunity is unlikely; when this condition persists, prospects for self-determination decline. Therefore, the problem of achieving fairness comes down to a problem of finding just-right matches between individuals of varying capacity and varying opportunity. In that when fairness is reflected in *equal probabilities* of engagement, then its realization is reflected in *equal experiences with just-right matches* between individual capacity with social opportunity.

This is based on what we know about how we regulate our resources to get what we need and want in life. When our capacity is limited and our opportunities are costly with respect to that capacity, we are unlikely to engage new opportunity because our prospects for success are unlikely. Only when our capacity and opportunity are optimally matched will we engage new opportunity. The difficulty, therefore, in finding adequate redress for the problem of unequal chances is one of finding the just-right connection between capacity and opportunity that engages the pursuit of new opportunity. When the connection is optimally challenging, Person is motivated to take control of her situation because she believes she can get what she wants in life through her own initiative. In this sense, Person becomes her own person; she becomes self-defining and self-determining. Person develops a sense of self-respect because she knows what she is capable of doing and perceives the environment in ways that will allow her to express what she is capable of doing.

This is what Coleman (1990) believed would result from school desegregation. He found that schooling had little influence on student achievement independent of family background and the context of schooling—segregated or integrated. His recommendation for policymakers, therefore, was to equalize educational opportunity by breaking the self-per-petuating cycle of underachievement promoted by segregated schooling. He believed that desegregation was a more potent policy option for im-proving school achievement than simply increasing school expenditures, which were weak correlates of achievement (Coleman, 1990, p. 74).

For decades following, schools across the nation commenced pro-grams of desegregation to correct inequities caused by the separate but equal doctrine. By the mid-1970s Coleman (1990) reevaluated the effects of desegregation and concluded,

> The current evidence indicates that the presumed benefits of school desegregation for black achievement are sometimes present, but not uniformly so, and are small when they are found. Thus the earlier hope that school desegregation would constitute a panacea for black achieve-ment, or contribute substantially to the goal of increasing black achieve-ment, appears to have been misplaced. (p. 201)

Moreover the effects of school desegregation on student attitudes were sometimes opposite from the hoped-for direction:

> Similarly, most of the studies mentioned earlier have found that the psychological effects (such as effects on self-esteem) and the attitudinal effects (such as interracial attitudes of school desegregation) are not uniformly in a positive directly, and are sometimes negative. Altogether, I believe we can say from the research results on the educational effects that school desegregation is seldom harmful, . . . sometimes beneficial, but not sufficiently so that school desegregation can be a major policy instrument for increasing black achievement and self-esteem. (p. 201)

In the 1980s, Gene Glass (1983) evaluated the effectiveness of special education made possible by the Education for All Handicapped Children Act of 1975, and he concluded that students enrolled in special classes failed to perform any better, on average, than students with disabilities enrolled in regular classrooms (see p. 68). Follow-up studies on the status of special education graduates also conducted in the 1980s found that most students were underemployed, underpaid, and overly dependent on parents and family (Mithaug & Horiuchi, 1983). These students were unable and perhaps unwilling to pursue their own ends in life. They lived at home awaiting direction from others about what to expect and what to do. Although their parents hoped they would become independent and em-ployed, they believed their children's lack of confidence, problem-solving skills, and awareness of their needs, interests, and abilities prevented them from doing so (Mithaug, Horiuchi, & McNulty, 1987).

By the 1990s, it was clear that access to public schooling, on its own, was insufficient to alter students' prospects for full engagement in adult opportunity after school. This is not surprising, given the initial focus of redress on increasing student capacity for academic performance, rather than on *using that capacity* to pursue *optimally challenging opportunity* at school, home, and in the community. What was missing in past policy was the optimally challenging connection between students' capacity and opportunities for learning and adjusting to school and community circumstance.

The focus of special education policy in the Individuals with Disabilities Education Act of 1990 (P.L. 101-476), which is a reauthorization of Public Law 94-142 (the Education for All Handicapped Children Act), has addressed this problem with its goal of improving student transitions from school to the community. This new policy requires that educational agencies (a) provide transition services that satisfy the needs, preferences, and interests of individual students; (b) ensure that students' individualized educational plans include statements of transition services beginning no later than age 16 and that it include a statement for each public agency's responsibilities or linkages (or both) before students leave school settings; (c) coordinate school and adult services to promote student transitions from school to postschool activities; (d) coordinate community-based experiences with instruction that includes the development of employment and other postschool adult living skills and where appropriate, the acquisition of daily living and functional vocational skills; (e) provide a full range of postschool engagement opportunities, including post-secondary education, vocational education, vocational training, integrated employment (including supported employment), continuing and adult education, adult services, independent living, and community participation; (f) define and evaluate student transitions in regard to expectations for student adjustments in the postschool, community environments; and (g) monitor the activities of various agencies obliged to deliver transition services.

It is hoped that the impact of this new policy will be to increase prospects for *experiencing the same freedom* of choice afforded persons without handicaps. To make this hope a reality, the U.S. Department of Education's Office of Special Education and Rehabilitative Services has supported research and demonstration projects throughout the country to demonstrate to states, local school districts, and classroom teachers how students with disabilities can acquire the attitudes, the skills, and experiences necessary for self-determination in adult life. The philosophy undergirding this federal initiative is consistent with the ideal of fair chances for liberty for all. This is also captured in the following statement by Michael Ward (1991), Chief of the Secondary Education and Transition Services Branch at the Office of Special Education Programs, U.S. Department of Education. Ward also uses a wheelchair and speaks from personal knowledge about the experience of self-determination:

> Skills necessary for self-determination must be taught to all children and youth; it is especially important for children and youth with disabilities. Expecting youth who have been overprotected and restricted in terms of self-determination to be functioning, independent adults is akin to expecting a nation that has lived under an oppressive, totalitarian system for centuries to govern by democratic principles immediately after a revolution. Self-Determination just doesn't happen; it requires a great deal of preparation and practice.
>
> Integrated education must be more than education in a regular setting; it must prepare youth to live and work in the community as independently as possible. Self-Determination must be an integral part of this education, with an ultimate goal of actualizing the old adage, "mother, father, please, I'd rather do it myself!" (p. 12)

Redress Through Equal Opportunity

According to the theory of social redress recommended in this book, policies that strive to increase levels of self-determination among least advantaged members of society should focus on *just-right matches* between capacity and opportunity because the *just-right condition* produces *optimal prospects for self-determination.* Consequently, when the optimal prospects principle guides social redress, the focus of reform is on providing all persons in society with the just-right challenge that encourages full engagement in opportunity that promises progress toward individually defined ends in life. Under these conditions, there is fairness in liberty for all.

The ideology of social redress based on equality of opportunity took root in *Brown v. Board of Education* and has evolved since then to influence old attitudes and to create new expectations about what redress is most likely to benefit people least likely to succeed in life. This evolution in attitudes and expectations has also been a consequence of major shifts in the distribution of sociopolitical power among different groups in society, which has provided the occasion for the equality of opportunity principle to influence the direction and content of social redress. The net effect has been a change in conceptions of what constitutes a person and what it means to have an opportunity. Now social redress on behalf of left out groups is based on ideas about *capacity* and *opportunity* that depart substantially from ancient conceptions of person and society on fundamental grounds. The new assumptions undergirding the optimal prospects principle, which captures the essence of social redress driven by the equality of value, are that (a) every person is an individual with a special set of talents, interests, and needs; (b) every person deserves a fair chance to express those unique attributes in pursuit of self-defined ends in life; and (c) as a consequence, there can be no overarching social mechanism for sorting individuals into categories of deserving and undeserving when it comes to distributing opportunities for the fair chance.

Notes

1. Patterson (1991) provides a detailed analysis of the evolution of freedom historically and suggests that in the earliest societies there was no such concept.

2. Lazerson is citing J. E. W. Wallin (1924). *The Education of Handicapped Children.* Boston: Houghton Mifflin.

3. Lazerson is quoting from L. M. Terman (1917, February). Feeble-minded children in the public schools of California. *School and Society, 5,* 161-165.

4. Lazerson is quoting from the White House Conference on Child Health and Project (1931). *Special Education.* New York: The Century Co.

5. Lazerson is citing Chicago Public Schools (1932). *Report of the Survey of the Schools of Chicago Illinois, 2.* New York: Columbia University, Teachers College.

6. Glasser claims that Jim Crow was a term used "after the title of a minstrel son that portrayed blacks as childlike and inferior."

7. All citations from *Brown v. Board of Education of Topeka* (1954) are from Adler (1987).

8. Coleman concluded that schooling was a means to improving adult opportunities: "What does appear achievable and attentive to results is the idea of effective public schooling that leads *in the direction of* equal adult opportunities. Such a formulation implies that public schooling is to reduce handicaps that children face as a function of their early environments, without committing the educational system to an unachievable end" (p. 64).

9. Turnbull's source of quotations is *Board of Education v. Rowley,* 458 U.S. 176, 102 S. Ct 3034, 73 L. Ed., 2d 690 (1982).

Conclusion

This book has addressed the problem created by the discrepancy between the right to self-determination and the expression of that right among persons least well situated in society. The explanation for the discrepancy was that circumstances beyond the control of those least advantaged in society contributed to their failure to engage opportunities leading to the self-determined life. Moreover, that similar circumstances have affected disadvantaged individuals in every society since the hunting and gathering era suggests the causal factors for the discrepancy to be social rather that moral. Consequently, the solution recommended was social redress rather than moral condemnation. The purpose of that redress was to *increase prospects* for self-determined pursuits by building capacity and improving opportunity for those least well situated in society.

The ultimate end of these social interventions was to equalize prospects for self-determination among all members of society rather than to make the beginning or end states of various self-determined pursuits equal.

Equalizing inputs and outcomes is not possible or practical because individuals have different needs, interests, and abilities; they have different approaches to optimizing opportunity; and they experience different outcomes as a consequence of their effort. The equal opportunity approach increases the probability individuals will engage opportunities leading to those ends in life that are consistent with their own needs, interests, and abilities.

The notion of fairness implied by this mode of social redress is consistent with both social and allocative versions of justice. It is consistent with the idea of fairness through *social justice* in that it increases the probability of my getting what I need and want in life by virtue of my membership in society, and it is consistent with the idea of fairness through *allocative justice* because it optimizes my prospects of my getting what I need and want just as it optimizes the prospects of others getting what they need and want in life. When prospects for self-determination are optimized for all, I am satisfied with the structure of society because it allows me a decent chance of pursuing what I want in life and I am satisfied with how my prospects compare with others who are seeking what they consider to be good in their life.

In the last few centuries, belief systems specifying collective preference for freedom for all have provoked a change in the direction of social selection toward redress on behalf of the least advantaged. What we can conclude from this is that this shift has yielded a less predictable set of circumstances than what we have contended with in the past. No longer do ideologies of "ought" consistently align themselves with existing distributions of power justifying the influence and advantage of the powerful. Now we are as likely to experience contradictions between what we believe is fair in a moral sense and what we experience as constituting fair treatment in a practical and social sense. The discrepancy between the right and the experience of self-determination is an example of what is more rather than less likely to trouble us now and in the future.

The emergence of ideologies of ought and their increased influence on social choice and action, therefore, are now positioned to function in ways never before envisioned in social life. The emergence of the rights movements reflective of these ideologies has the capacity of altering the distribution of power that can then feed back to accelerate the evolution and differentiation of the ideologies themselves. In countries with long-standing traditions valuing fair play, beliefs about what constitutes justice will become more influential in deciding social policy, and not because fairness derives from external authority in a metaphysical sense but because it influences the distribution of power that in turn affects the development of new ideologies and new social relationships. This pattern is most prevalent in democratic societies in which fairness in liberty for all is central to the ideologies justifying social institutions.

Chapter 5 described these evolutionary developments by tracing the idea of fairness from the 18th century when it meant *liberty for some* to the latter half of the 20th century when fairness came to mean *liberty for all*. To understand how this change occurred is to recognize the absence of a single precipitating event as being responsible for recent outcomes. This is because the evolutionary result was an emergent from interaction between an ideal of fairness, the collective's commitment to the ideal for all persons by virtue of their status as humans, and the self-determined pursuit of various groups of individuals claiming or disclaiming redress in accordance with various interpretations of this ideal. The point of this historical account was not that the result was predictable or inevitable given the high moral ground of the weak in their claim for social redress from the powerful. It was instead that the final outcome *contradicted* the prediction based on the initial power advantage of the better situated individuals and groups in society. Moreover, this contradiction was not the result of any change in social selection forces functioning differently from the past, either. It was instead due to the addition of new ideologies of ought in the interplay between various sources of social, economic, and technical influence exerted by different groups in society. No longer were the most persuasive ideologies of fairness ensured alignment with those in command of the greatest resources.

The upshot of these factors in social selectionism was less certainty in predicting who would benefit and who would not over the long term. Because trends in the accumulation and loss in advantage over time increasingly depended on (a) evolving belief systems regarding what is fair and who deserves consideration under its rule, (b) shifting power centers among groups claiming and refuting social redress according to these beliefs, and (c) changing environments of opportunity affecting the actual acquisition and loss of power among individuals and groups. As these factors influenced each other over time, they changed themselves as a function of this interdependence to create various power alignments unlike what could have been expected from any one factor influencing events on its own.

Given this analysis, it is not surprising the particular form social redress adopted in the latter half of the 20th century could not have been predicted a century ago, even though the social selection theory provided in this book to explain the development of an ideology of fairness in liberty for all was the same theory that explained the social forces responsible for the first social stratification system several millennia ago. What happened that was different in the modern period that accounts for the social drift toward fairness in liberty for all was a *decentralization* of power that affected the social system to such an extent it was no longer possible for the collective to develop an ideology that conveniently justified one group's power and control over all other groups. As a consequence, there was no assurance, over the long term, of conformity to the dictates of the powerful because there was no common allegiance to an ideology directing the distribution of opportunity and gain for all groups. Pluralism in ideologies of fairness came into play with the invention of the social contract, which guaranteed that basic set of rights all humans needed as means for securing their ends in life. The legitimization of this new instrument for social organization was based on what was common to all individuals rather than what was unique to a few—what was common to being human rather than what was unique about being connected with God, for example.

The problem with this institutional principle was that it tended to be unstable. The claim for natural rights afforded all by virtue of a common humanity gave all sorts of individuals the right to demand fairness, including those least powerful and well situated in society. The yawning crevice of opportunity along the conceptual fault line of the natural rights doctrine invited strangers to the party of political influence and these newcomers lacked the standard set of credentials based on social, economic, and technical advantage. This created the discrepancy between the right and the experience of self-determination.

But this discrepancy condition was by itself insufficient to blunt the force of social selection and its differentiation of opportunity and outcome along lines of an existing power distribution, as history shows. After the Civil War, the South rebuilt a class system excluding African Americans from mainstream social contact similar to what had existed before the Emancipation Proclamation, and after the initial inclusion of children with disabilities in regular classrooms at the turn of the century, school systems throughout the country constructed new sorting mechanisms to exclude disabled students from mainstream school contact similar to what had existed before compulsory school attendance came into effect. Social selection functioned as effectively at that time as at any other time in human history, again by advantaging those with power and disadvantaging those without power.

The difference here, however, was that the decentralization of power that began 300 years ago continued through that period when African Americans gained sufficient social, economic, and technical resources to enhance their capacity to seek redress on behalf of their own needs and interests. They built one ideological gain on another to advance their cause for social redress through the courts and then through the Congress until fairness in liberty for all became an enforceable claim on their behalf. Parents of children and youth with disabilities pursued a similar strategy, although they began with substantial advantages initially denied African Americans. As members of majority white populations, they had access to substantial social, economic, and technical resources when they made their claim. They also benefited from the ideological shift in the conception of a fair chance that resulted from *Brown v. Board of Education,* which established education as a necessary means for success in life. What remained for this new group of advocates was to demonstrate to the courts and to Congress that children with disabilities had the capacity to benefit from a public education and as a consequence, were as deserving as any other children for access to that resource.

What we have learned from this social evolution toward redress on behalf of least advantaged groups is that it is a function of the dynamic created when belief systems, collective commitment to act on those beliefs, and changing environmental circumstances interact to reduce the discrepancy between a right and its expression. This explains how it was possible that children and youth with disabilities who were relegated to institutional life less that half a century ago are now entitled to a free and appropriate public education regardless of their level or type of disability.

Measuring Progress Toward Fairness

The challenge of the coming millennia is qualitatively different from that of previous millennia in that the development of knowledge-based means of producing gain is less predictable, depending as it does on interaction between belief systems about what is (truth) and what ought to be (good) on the one hand and the social processes that derive from and affect those beliefs on the other hand. Whereas in the past, social process interacted with the physical environment to determine beliefs about the truth and the good, now belief systems are powerful influences on their own and they interact with social process and environmental circumstance to create new beliefs, social relations, and environmental circumstances. The net effect is that outcomes are less predictable. Our theories about what we think to be true and what we think to be good interact with the choices and actions we make in social life and the results we produce in turn affect subsequent beliefs and subsequent opportunities based on those beliefs.

Although the interaction between beliefs about the truth and the good, the social selection process, and the mechanisms of natural selection have always influenced the stratification of opportunity and outcome in human life, it is only recently that belief systems about truth and good have evolved and differentiated to function as *determinant* rather than simply as *consequent* factors in social life. It is this change in the human condition that has caused confusion about the course human adjustment will take into the next millennia. This new causal antecedent is on the one hand liberating but on the other hand constraining because of its threat to stability in social life. We can see the consequences of this change in the increase in ideological pluralism attached to increasingly differentiated centers of power that define various ends for directing the self-determined pursuit. The result is that on the one hand there are increasingly different ideals about what is desirable and good in life, and on the other hand, there is sufficient social, economic, and technical power attached to those different belief systems to create conditions necessary for rewriting the social contract to dissolve and then reunite the polity in various ways.

In the past, this was not a problem because diversification of belief and decentralization of power did not exist. The powerful imposed ideologies on the powerless to define institutional arrangements for social and allocative justice. But as we have seen in the past several centuries, this is no longer the case. The decentralization of power and the emergence of new ideologies of fairness have forced democratically based societies to respond to the needs and interests of previously left out groups. The source of this fundamental shift in social evolution is that access to the means of securing resources necessary for reaching desirable ends in life is no longer protected by a monopoly of control.

The implication for the evolution of social institutions is that they will be constructed, implemented, evaluated, and reconstructed based on their service to some end in life—to the extent they serve an ideology of what is and what ought to be. Social institutions will be constructed, implemented, evaluated, and reconstructed to *reduce various discrepancies* between how individuals perceive their world to be in the present and how they want their world to be in the future. Increasingly, individuals will perceive their social institutions to be means to various ideological ends that will themselves undergo evolution about what is truth and what is good. Social institutions will be reinvented repeatedly as individuals reinvent themselves repeatedly through adjustments in how they think, what they believe, what they expect, and what they do. This process of change through institutional reconstruction will be continuous, functioning as it does on theories of interdependent cause and effect.

THE CONCEPT OF "PERSON"

The upshot of all of this is a shift in locus of control over social life from external factors anchored in stable institutions representing universal constants of a static universe to internal factors embodied in the expansive and contracting capacity of individuals adjusting to a dynamic and fluid present. More fundamentally, this shift from the cosmic to the personal is a shift in conception of what it means to be a person. In the past, *person* was defined at birth as attached to a station in the social structure specifying a lifetime of fixed opportunity and outcome. *Capacity* was a constant fused with fixed opportunity and outcome to define what it was to be a person. To know one's social position was to know everything else about that person. To some extent, this conception of the fixed self has endured to this day. Even though this conception conflicts with the belief that humans have unlimited potential for growth and accomplishment, it retains a use in social theories of opportunity perhaps because of its longtime association with turn-of-the-century social science and the development of psychometrics, the measurement of cognitive ability, and the popularization of the intelligence scores.

Nevertheless, today we entertain conceptions of the self more in keeping with what we know about social life and about the sociopolitical process affecting opportunity for self-direction in that life. Contemporary views of intelligence such as those reported in Sternberg's *The Triarchic Mind: A New Theory of Human Intelligence* and Howard Gardner's *Frames of Mind: The Theory of Multiple Intelligences* remind us that, stripped of its psychometric manifestations, intelligence is still reflective of adaptive functioning through self-regulated problem solving. It is intelligent adaptation

to environmental circumstance that differentiates humans from each other
and from other species; this capacity is not easily captured in a single
psychometric score of mental ability. Contrary to popular claims that
intelligence scores are genetic markers for position in the social structure
(Herrnstein & Murray, 1994), IQ correlates poorly with real-life problem
solving required in adapting to life's circumstances, as Sternberg (1988)
points out in the following:

> That "academic" intelligence is insufficient for successful performance in
> real-world settings is suggested by the low typical correlations (about .2
> on a scale from 0 to 1) between occupational performance and perfor-
> mance on either IQ or employment tests reported by several researchers.
> Correlations of this magnitude indicate that hardly any variance (*only
> about 4 percent*) in occupational performance is accounted for by IQ Level
> [italics added]. (p. 211)

The reason for these weak associations between intelligence test scores
and human accomplishment is that intelligence is *more than* what can be
measured by a single psychometric test. Human intelligence is, according to
Sternberg (1988), a kind of "mental self-management of one's life in a
constructive, purposeful way" (pp. 16-17). It is management of one's personal,
social, economic, and technical resources that affects the pursuit of opportunity
to secure from the environment those means that are necessary for reaching
desirable ends in life. Human intelligence is the capacity to act and react to
opportunity in ways that yield beneficial gain. According to Sternberg,

> Intelligence involves the shaping of, adaptation to, and selection of your
> environment . . . *there may be no single set of behaviors that is intelligent
> for everyone*. . . . What does appear to be common among *successful
> people is the ability to capitalize on their strengths and compensate for
> their weaknesses.* Successful people are not only able to adapt well to their
> environment but also to modify this environment to increase the fit between
> the environment and their adaptive skills [italics added]. (pp. 16-17)

The reason psychometric scores on intelligence fail to fully reflect the
range and variety of human engagement in opportunity for self-determined
pursuits is that individuals vary in their capacity and in how they employ
that capacity to determine their own ends in life. The failure of psychometric measures to assess this capacity should not suggest that such assess-

ments are not possible because this is not the case. In fact, we can track variation in a person's capacity to self-determine in several ways.

First, we can consider an individual's level of *self-knowledge* and *self-awareness* of personal needs, interests, and abilities because individuals vary in how acutely aware they are of themselves and, as a consequence, how effectively they will act in engaging opportunity to advance pursuits that are consistent with this awareness of self. Moreover, this variation in their sense of self affects their motivation to pursue self-directed capacity building in accordance with their self-knowledge and self-awareness. This view is consistent with Nathan Branden's (1994) definition of self-esteem as "confidence in our ability to think, confidence in our ability to cope with the basic challenges of life, and confidence in our right to be successful and happy, the feelings of being worthy, deserving, entitled to assert our needs and wants, achieve our values, and enjoy the fruits of our efforts" (p. 4). It is also consistent with the Supreme Court's decision in *Brown v. Board of Education* regarding the effects of segregated schooling on the self-esteem of black children and how lowered self-esteem diminishes their capacity to benefit from schooling.

A second way we can track variation in capacity is by assessing the skills, knowledge, and motivation individuals use to manage their resources effectively and efficiently to get what they need and want in life. Those who are skilled self-managers, who have acquired information about when and how to use their skills effectively, and who are motivated to apply those skills and knowledge persistently and continuously are usually more successful than those deficient in these respects. People in business and industry have recognized the importance of these skills since Napoleon Hill (1960) first described them more than half a century ago in *Think and Grow Rich,* which identified five steps to securing desirable ends in life:

1. Choose a definite goal to be obtained
2. Develop sufficient power to attain that goal
3. Perfect a practical plan for attaining the goal
4. Accumulate specialized knowledge necessary for attaining the goal
5. Persist in carrying out the plan (p. 157)

Sternberg's (1988) research identified a similar set of self-management skills as essential for success in life:

[My] own research and that of others suggests that they are among the most important, because they must be used in the solution of almost every real-world problem. The processes are: recognizing the existence of the problem, defining the nature of the problem, generating the set of sets needed to solve the problem, combining these steps into a workable strategy for problem solution, deciding how to represent information about the problem, allocating mental and physical resources to solving the problem and monitoring the solution to the problem. (p. 79)

The third way of tracking variation in capacity is by assessing the resources available to Person for engaging different opportunities. These resources can be classified as personal, social, economic, and technical. *Personal resources* include the excess time, energy, and behavior Person has to engage a given opportunity; *social resources* are the time, energy, and behavior of other people that are available to Person; *economic resources* are the exchangeable currency and capital Person has at her disposal to access resources she is lacking; and *technical resources* are the specific means over which Person has personal control for engaging specific types of opportunities.

Individuals with sufficient personal resources to engage specific opportunities have the time and behavior necessary to alter social and physical circumstances defined by that opportunity in ways that increase their chances of getting what they need and want. Individuals with social resources have access to other people's resources in altering environmental circumstances for their own benefit. Individuals who have economic resources can purchase resources they lack but must have to optimize environmental circumstance for a given pursuit; and individuals who have technical resources have personal control over the means of changing an environmental circumstance simply by applying their knowledge, skills, behaviors, and time to get the results they want when they want them.

By tracking these three dimensions of capacity—self-knowledge, self-management, and resource access—we can assess how different patterns of growth and constraint can affect and be affected by changes in environmental circumstance at any point in time. Variation in capacity will occur within and across the three domains according to the level and type of capability present: Different individuals will have different interests, needs and abilities, different strategies for managing themselves, and different resources for engaging opportunity. They will also have different experiences of empowerment due to variation in interaction among these dimensions and with those changing environmental circumstance we call opportunity.

This conception of Person suggests a different strategy for measuring capacity to self-determine. It suggests an approach that assesses an individual's self-knowledge, self-management, and resource availability. It also suggests a method that determines how these three domains interact to produce an effect on the environment—a change in the favorableness or optimality of opportunity for producing a desirable gain. Finally, this conception of Person suggests a different conception of "opportunity" to self-determine.

THE CONCEPT OF "OPPORTUNITY"

According to this analysis, opportunity is an occasion in time and space that is more or less favorable for pursuit of a given end. The degree of this favorableness is expressed as an *optimality*. Hence, the greater the optimality of opportunity for a given pursuit contemplated by an actor, then the more favorable the environmental circumstance for producing gain by engaging that opportunity with action on those circumstances. Optimalities of opportunity are simply probabilities of success inferred by actors evaluating the circumstances surrounding the actions they plan to take to reach a desirable end. Person infers this prospect or probability by assessing her capacity for effective action based on her self-knowledge, self-management, and resource availability and by evaluating the favorableness (optimality) of her social and physical circumstances. The inference drawn from these assessments of capacity and circumstance constitutes the optimality of opportunity that will affect Person's decision to act or not to act on that set of circumstances.

If Person decides to act, she will attempt to alter those social and physical circumstance so she can reach her own ends and, depending on the consequences of her actions, Person will have altered the probability of success for subsequent endeavors. Person will have changed the optimalities of opportunity by making her circumstances more favorable for subsequent action, or she will have failed to produce the desired effect and perhaps made subsequent opportunity less favorable. From one engagement episode to another, therefore, Person's optimalities of opportunity will change, reflecting as they will different conditions of capacity and different conditions of environmental demand.

According to this conception of opportunity, it is difficult logically and empirically to separate the conception of Person from the conception of opportunity because the two are interdependent. Person's self-knowledge, self-management, and resource access affect her inferences about environmental circumstances, and the optimalities of opportunity he or she infers from assessing those circumstances affect Person's decisions to act in pursuit of various ends in life. Moreover, Person's success or failure in changing environmental circumstance to improve her chances—to increase optimalities of opportunity—will feed back to affect her subsequent levels of self-knowledge, self-management, and resource availability. In other words, Person's capacity and opportunity interact in various ways to expand capacity and optimize opportunity or to contract capacity and suboptimize opportunity. The only way for knowing what is cause and consequence is by knowing Person's capacity and inferred opportunity because it is Person and no one else who assesses the favorableness of a given opportunity prior to engaging those circumstances that lead to a self-determined end in life.

To claim opportunities among a population of actors should be equal at some imaginary starting point or that they should yield equal outcomes at some imaginary ending point is to ignore the empirical and contingent reality that there is no basis for equivalence. Every individual has a different capacity and every opportunity a different inference of optimality because optimalities of opportunity depend on an *individual*'s assessments of capacity, circumstance, and the correspondence between the two. To expect equivalence in capacity and opportunity is to expect individuals to be identical and to expect the circumstances for their actions to be equivalent. All we can expect by way of equality, then, is that *prospects* or *probabilities* for self-determined action to be roughly equivalent across individuals.

The phrase "equality of opportunity" often obfuscates this essential meaning of opportunity. Viewed simply as favorable occasions for action, opportunities can be equal only if they are equally favorable for the pursuits envisioned, only if the opportunities for engagement have comparable optimalities. They are comparable but not equivalent in that each opportunity depends on the purpose Person has in mind for altering circumstances to achieve some end. Opportunities for one purpose, therefore, may have one optimality valence, whereas opportunities for another purpose will have a different optimality valence. The idea of equal opportunity is meaningless without some consideration of the optimality Person has inferred after examining a set of circumstances and after evaluating her capacity to deal with those circumstances to produce the desired outcome.

The conclusion to draw from this analysis is that an individual's prospects for living the self-determined life are specific to that individual depending as they do on that person's capacity to self-determine and the optimalities of opportunity one believes will affect one's capacity to be successful. Therefore, given that (a) individuals vary in their capacity to self-determine and (b) individuals vary in their judgment about the favorableness of opportunity for the expression of that capacity, then (c) individuals vary in their prospects or chances of engaging in self-determined pursuits. As capacity to self-determine declines, Person's assessments of her optimalities of opportunity may decline as well, and as these two condition become suboptimal, Person becomes less likely to self-determine; she is less likely to engage opportunities and initiate pursuits of her own choosing. The converse relationship is also possible, as are many other combinations of capacity-opportunity interaction. The point is that when the same people repeatedly experience declining prospects for self-determination, then there is justification for social redress to improve their prospects, to make their chances comparable to the optimalities of opportunity other people experience.

The focus of social redress suggested for this problem of declining prospects for self-determination is twofold—to increase Person's capacity and to improve Person's opportunities. The likely method of pursuing these policy objectives to reverse the declining prospects of the least advantaged members in society is through educational interventions that build capacity to optimize opportunity. To be effective, these interventions will have to accomplish three objectives. First, they will have to improve Person's understanding of her own needs, interests, and abilities so she will be able to pursue opportunities consistent with those needs, interests, and abilities. Second, they must provide Person with the specific personal, social, and technical knowledge and skills required to optimize a full range of opportunities in the social and physical world. Third, they must help Person learn to manage those resources effectively and efficiently when she engages opportunity to achieve her own ends in life.

The expected outcome of these educational interventions is increased engagement in self-determined pursuits. As Person engages opportunity more frequently, she is more likely to improve her social and physical circumstances for action leading to ends in life she values. As these increased engagements succeed in improving Person's circumstances, they also enhance her capacity to engage more challenging opportunity. This, in turn, improves Person's chances of becoming a lifelong learner as she adjusts more optimally to given circumstances, making them more favorable for her own pursuits wherever and whenever she can. In this sense, Person experiences self-determination.

LEVELS OF SELF-DETERMINATION

The implication of this analysis for measuring progress toward fairness in liberty for all is that the process by which Person becomes self-determining is as important for assessing prospects for self-determination as are any outcomes produced by various pursuits. In that for prospects of self-determination to improve, capacity must increase, opportunity must become more favorable, and Person must engage that opportunity. Indicators of progress toward fairness would, therefore, include (a) measures of individual capacity, (b) measures of the optimalities of social opportunity with respect to an individual's capacity, and (c) measures of the individual's engagement of opportunity for self-determined ends. These three variables provide a yardstick for monitoring progress toward fairness. When capacity indicators indicate growth over time, when optimalities of opportunity are judged to be increasing by those in need of social redress, and when engagement in personal pursuits is increasing for those least likely to succeed in life, then the discrepancy between the right and the experience of self-determination is declining for individuals least well situated in society.

These measures of freedom depart from those used by the United Nations that focus on the sociopolitical circumstances or rights guaranteeing opportunity in an array of domains defining social life in different countries around the world, and they are different from measures of socioeconomic gain associated with different groups and reflected in income gaps between the most and least advantaged in society. Although these traditional measures of inequality validate the existence of the problem of unequal prospects for freedom by describing the discrepancy between the right and the experience of self-determination, they do not measure the process by which individuals gain and lose capacity and opportunity for self-determination, nor do they measure how these variations affect the engagement of opportunity and the pursuit of self-defined ends in life. The process indicators of freedom—capacity, opportunity, and engagement—reflect the means of producing the self-determination experience, whereas the outcome indicators used by the United Nations reflect the distribution of advantages and disadvantages among different members who vary in their experience of freedom. In this sense, the process indicators of freedom provide an answer to some of the major measurement problems Tim Gray (1991) identified in his book *Freedom:*

> Another conclusion is that more research is required if we are to make progress in applying the concept of freedom. In particular, considerable analytical and empirical work is necessary to clarify and refine our understanding of the ways in which freedom can be measured and distributed. The current literature abounds with discussion (though sometimes aridly combative in nature) of the meaning of freedom, and there is increasing interest in the subject of the justification of freedom. But precious little effort has been devoted to the issues of the measurement and distribution of freedom. Yet comparative judgements concerning both the extent of freedom in different countries and the impact of governmental intervention on the overall level of freedom and its distribution within a society are made confidently day after day, with little real grasp of the complexity of some of the issues involved. Since it seems that these judgements do play a role in important domestic and foreign policy decisions made by governments, it is a matter of some urgency that research is undertaken to place such judgements on a sounder footing than at present. (p. 173)

The process indicators are also similar to those employed in research projects funded by the U.S. Department of Education's Office of Special Education Programs and charged with developing a definition and measure of self-determination appropriate for use with children and youth with disabilities. The working definition of self-determination agreed to by those projects was "choosing and enacting choice to control one's life to the maximum extent possible, based on knowing and valuing one's self and in pursuit of one's needs, interests, and values."[1] The assumption undergirding this initiative to assess levels of self-determination was that students with disabilities needed to be more self-determined if they were to achieve their goals in life. Some of the projects that developed measures of self-determination included a school component for *capacity building* through more effective self-regulated problem solving to meet personal goals in life as well as an *opportunity* component for the expression of that capacity through pursuit of vocational training, job placement, and independent living.

The intended use of the self-determination data produced by these instruments was to guide educators in teaching the skills and behaviors necessary for students to become more self-determined at school, home, and in their community. The assessment instrument developed by the American Institutes for Research and Teachers College, Columbia University assessed students' capacity and opportunity to self-determine, with scores on these two dimensions indicating the students' levels of self-determination. This approach permitted variations in capacity and opportunity to yield comparable levels of (prospects for) self-determination across different students. For example, some students with greater capacity and lesser opportunity than other students scoring lower on capacity but more favorable on opportunity could have *equivalent* levels of (prospects for) self-determination.

The capacity component of the AIR-TC instrument focused only on two of the three domains—*self-knowledge* and *self-management*. The *resource* component was not included. The self-knowledge and self-management components included items on thinking, acting, and adjusting to opportunity for self-determined pursuits. Students responded to the items by indicating how often they

1. identified and expressed their own needs, interests, and abilities;
2. set expectations and goals to meet those needs and interests;
3. made choices and plans to meet goals and expectations;
4. took actions to complete plans;
5. evaluated the results of actions; and
6. altered plans and actions as necessary to meet goals more effectively.

The opportunity component of the assessment required students to indicate how often and to what extent they experienced circumstances at home and at school that permitted or encouraged them to perform each of these six behaviors.[2]

This research suggests a fruitful way of assessing the long-term benefits of educational intervention on behalf of capacity and opportunity. The idea that if schools do not improve students' academic achievement they have failed may be misleading in that access to mainstreamed, public education can produce other capacity enhancements not evident in achievement scores. One of these enhancements is socialization and networking that occurs as a consequence of attending mainstreamed, desegregated schools. Amy Wells and Robert Crain (1995), for example, report a study on the long-term effects of school desegregation that suggests that attending desegregated schools helps break the perpetual cycle of segregation and isolation by providing black students with social contacts with white students that predispose them to access similar social networks when they seek to advance themselves after they leave school. Wells and Crain conclude the following: "There is a strong possibility . . . that when occupational attainment is dependent on knowing the right people and being in the right place at the right time, school desegregation assists black students in gaining access to traditionally 'white' jobs" (p. 552). In other words, attending desegregated school functions to expand the social resource base of minority students for later use. This, in turn, improves their prospects for self-determination later in life.

A complete assessment of an individual's capacity to self-determine would include information on the range and depth of one's resources—personal, social, economic, and technical. This information, combined with assessments of the individual's self-knowledge and self-management skills, would provide a substantial basis for determining an individual's capacity to self-determine. It would also provide a basis for identifying the range of options—those just-right opportunities—that are most likely to engage Person in a self-determined pursuit. In other words, information on capacity and just-right opportunity based on assessed capacity would identify the optimal prospects condition most likely to engage Person in the self-determination experience—the pursuit of desirable ends that are consistent with Person's needs, interests, and abilities.

Although nothing like this now exists, the parts to the puzzle are known and are available for assembly for this purpose. For example, the AIR-TC instrument has demonstrated an approach to gathering information of self-knowledge and self-management but not on resource access, whereas efforts such as Michael Sherraden's (1991) "assets approach" offer guidelines for assessing Person's resources. In *Assets and the Poor: A New American Welfare Policy,* Sherraden uses the term *asset* instead of *resource* to evaluate Person's capacity for preparing for future action. His "theory suggests that assets are not simply nice to have, but yield various behavioral consequences such as enabling people to focus their efforts, allowing people to take risks, creating an orientation toward the future, and encouraging the development of human capital" (p. xiv).

Included in his assessment of a person's tangible and intangible assets are examples of the personal, social, economic, and technical resources described in this chapter. Sherraden's *tangible assets* include the following:

1. Money savings
2. Stocks and bonds
3. Real property, earnings from capital gains
4. Hard assets other than real estates with earnings in the form of capital gains (or losses)
5. Machines, equipment, and other tangible components of production with earnings in the form of profits on the sale of products plus capital gains (or losses)
6. Durable household goods with earnings in the form of increased efficiency of household tasks
7. Natural resources such as farmland, oil, minerals, and timber with earnings in the form of profit on sale of crops or extracted commodities plus capital gains (or losses)
8. Copyrights and patents, and earnings in the form of royalties and other user fees

His *intangible assets* include the following:

1. Access to credit
2. Human capital such as intelligence, educational background, work experience, knowledge, skill, and health (also energy, vision, hope, and imagination)
3. Cultural capital in the form of knowledge of culturally significant subjects and cues, ability to cope with social situations and formal bureaucracies, including vocabulary, accent, dress, and appearance
4. Informal social capital in the form of family, friends, contacts, and connections sometimes referred to as a "social network"
5. Formal social capital or organization capital, which refers to the structure and techniques of formal organization applied to tangible capital
6. Political capital in the form of participation, power, and influence, with earnings in the form of favorable rules and decisions on the part of the state and local government (see Sherraden, 1991, pp. 128-152)

Given this array of indicators, it is reasonable to expect substantial differences in resource-capacity among any population of actors and it is reasonable to expect that these differences will explain why some members have better prospects for pursuing what they need and want in life than others. When resource indicators are combined with indicators of self-knowledge and self-management, it is reasonable to expect that enhancement or contraction of Person's overall capacity to self-determine will function according to (a) Person's *understanding* of her needs, interests, and abilities at any point in time; (b) the *availability of resources* (or assets) to pursue ends that are consistent with those needs, interests, and abilities; and (c) Person's ability to manage those resources effectively and efficiently to expand her capacity to control the means of production necessary and sufficient to reach ends in life that are most desirable.

Measures of progress toward fairness in liberty for all that reflect these three capacity indicators will provide information for social redress for the purpose of *empowering* those least well situated in life by building their capacity to self-determine. Capacity indicators of self-determination provide information on individual baselines for self-determination that indicate the just-right opportunities that will engage them toward increasing their own capacity either through improved self-knowledge, increased self-management, or enhanced personal, social, economic, or technical resources. Individualized capacity-indicator information permits those responsible for authorizing social redress to construct just-right opportunities that provoke the desire as well as the experience of self-determination. It guides intervention according to the optimal prospects principle.

Seeking Fairness With Excellence

The policy debates that have confronted us in the last half of this century are likely to continue into the next. Then, as now, these debates will force us to reconcile our desire for freedom in pursuit of excellence on the one hand and our desire for equality in pursuit of fairness on the other. It is hoped that by such time the paradox between equality and freedom will be better understood and this understanding will help us resolve apparent contradictions between fairness and excellence. Because today, the prevailing assumption is that realizing one value will require sacrifice in pursuit of the other—choosing equality will sacrifice freedom or excellence, and choosing excellence will sacrifice equality or freedom.

Equal opportunity theory challenges this view that freedom, equality, and excellence are incompatible values in social life. It claims the conflict experienced is not due to values but due to the psychological and social processes that differentiate activities and outcomes in social life. We *feel* a moral conflict when our pursuits create discrepancies between rights and experiences. This feeling of distress and disharmony in our moral life causes us to see values in conflict when the fundamental problem has little to do with the values that motivate what we do or how we justify what we have done. The cause of our moral distress is the *discrepancy* between rights and experiences. The apparent values conflict between freedom, equality, and excellence is in fact a reflection of interaction between the capacity and opportunity causing social *drift* toward accumulated advantage for some and accumulated disadvantage for others. When this creates a discrepancy between rights and experience, we feel moral distress and then label that distress a values conflict. But it is not. It is a failure of our social relationships to live up to our expectations for fairness, however we have defined fairness. Because, as we have seen, our beliefs about fairness interact with the social selection mechanisms to influence distributions of opportunities and outcomes in society. Depending on how this interaction proceeds, prospects for adjusting to life's circumstances vary from individual to individual and from group to group.

An example of an apparent values conflict is ongoing between proponents of fairness and proponents of excellence. Depending on how the belief systems surrounding these values are expressed, there will be different outcomes favoring various groups. Proponents of fairness worry that focusing on excellence to increase competitiveness in the global economy will channel scarce resources toward more capable people at the expense of less capable individuals. On the other hand, proponents of excellence worry that focusing on equality will waste limited resources on individuals least able to contribute to national competitiveness. This illustrates how thinking about fairness and excellence determines how we argue for or against a given policy for social action. It also illustrates how social theory linking these values coherently toward desirable ends can assist in resolving debates about what actions will benefit the collective in its quest for competitive advantage in the global economy and, at the same time, benefit all members of the collective who are striving for a meaningful and worthwhile life. Equal opportunity theory offers this needed coherence by claiming equality and freedom are means rather than ends when they are linked together according to the optimal prospects principle, which gives all members of society an equal chance of thinking and acting in pursuit of their own ends in life.

When the optimal prospects principle is operative in society, every member of society will be fully engaged in pursuit of self-defined ends.

When individuals are fully engaged in pursuit of their own ends in life, they are self-determining. In the previous section, we saw that the best indicator of this experience of self-determination is *engagement* in the pursuit of one's ends; hence, the greater the engagement of opportunity leading to one's own ends in life, the greater one's experience of self-determination and the more likely fairness in liberty for all is achieved. This analysis applies to the excellence question as well, because during optimal prospects for self-determination, excellence in outcomes of self-determined pursuits also maximizes. Moreover, this is perhaps the only condition under which excellence in human activity maintains because only in this condition are individuals fully motivated and fully engaged in *optimally challenging* circumstance.

This observation is consistent with the restructuring taking place in business and industry today. Nevertheless, policymakers often presume achieving excellence means jeopardizing equality or guaranteeing equality and expanding liberty means sacrificing excellence. These contradictions are not logical necessities, however, at least when social and economic reform is guided by the optimal prospects principle. Whereas the notion that *setting high expectations* for the activities of government, business, and education may regulate toward the ideal of excellence of results, the notion of *empowering individuals* for excellent effort and performance through application of the optimal prospects principle captures the ideal fairness in liberty for all.

The apparent incompatibility between equality, liberty, and excellence dissolves when we understand that fairness in liberty for all is a *means* for self-determination and that excellence is an *outcome* of that self-determination. To understand how this relationship functions, we must understand that the condition necessary for achieving fairness in liberty for all is the same as the condition that promotes excellence. Fairness in liberty for all is present when all persons are fully engaged in optimal opportunity for pursuing desirable ends in life and this condition is most likely when the prospects for self-defining pursuits are optimally challenging for all. Excellence is also most prevalent in a population of actors fully engaged in optimally challenging opportunity for pursuing desirable ends in life. Because during these conditions, they are fully involved in determining how to reduce discrepancies between what they want and what they have, in solving difficult problems and overcoming difficult obstacles impeding the reduction of those discrepancies, in implementing plans that resolve those difficulties, and in evaluating results to improve their next attempt should they fail or in setting higher expectations for themselves should they succeed. This process of improving next time based on performance of the previous time and of setting higher expectations should success obtain is the same process restructuring advocates call for in reinventing government and reforming education. The optimal prospects condition stimulating this process of productive engagement produces excellence in human performance as well as excellence in institutional and organizational outcome in that it presents optimally challenging opportunity that fully energizes individuals and organizations to persevere in the pursuit of desirable ends in life.

Notes

1. Definition was developed at a Washington DC meeting sponsored by the Department of Education, Office of Special Education Program and attended by directors of five research projects charged with developing and validating methods and materials for assessing levels of self-determination in children and youth with disabilities. The five grantees conducting this research were the American Institutions of Research and Teachers College, Columbia University, the University of Minnesota, the Virginia Commonwealth University, Wayne State University, and the Association for Retarded Citizens-Texas.

2. The AIR-TC Project tested and validated this self-determination instrument on 484 students with and without disabilities ranging in age from 6 to 25 years. The results indicated that (1) male and female students did not have significantly different scores on levels of self-determination; (2) students who were African American, Hispanic, and white did not have significantly different scores on self-determination; (3) economically disadvantaged students (i.e., those enrolled in free-lunch programs) had significantly lower scores on self-determination than other students; (4) students enrolled in special education programs had significantly lower scores on self-determination than students not enrolled in special education; and (5) students with mild disabilities had significantly higher scores on self-determination than students with moderate to severe disabilities.

Although the results yielded expected differences between advantaged and disadvantaged students and between students with and without disabilities, an additional finding indicated that older students with disabilities had higher scores on self-determination than younger students with disabilities. This finding is consistent with the claim articulated earlier that capacity and opportunity to self-determine are not fixed entities functioning like psychometric measures of intelligence. Instead they interact to produce different prospects for self-determination. Gain toward the self-determined life is not simply a function of academic performance, although improvements here will undoubtedly have positive effects later.

Still, academic gain is but one of several areas of capacity enhancement that help students optimize opportunity to get what they need and want in life. Also, the fact that the AIR-TC instrument only measured two of the three capacity domains—self-knowledge and self-management—limits its ability to accurately reflect a student's prospects for self-determination. Were data collected on resource availability in terms of students' personal, social, economic, and technical assets then estimates of prospects for self-determination would have been based upon the relationship between all three capacity components—self-knowledge, self-management, and resource access.

References

Adler, M. J. (1987). *We hold these truths: Understanding the ideas and ideals of the Constitution.* New York: Collier.

Allen, J. (1989). *As a man thinketh.* Philadelphia: Running Press.

Beauchamp, T. L. (1980). Distributive justice and the difference principle. In H. G. Blocker & E. Smith (Eds.), *John Rawls' theory of social justice: An introduction* (pp. 132-137). Athens: Ohio University Press.

Bentham, J. (1961). An introduction to the principles of morals and legislation. In *The utilitarians.* Garden City, NJ: Doubleday. (original publication 1789)

Blocker, H. G., & Smith, E. H. (Eds.). (1980). *John Rawls' theory of social justice: An introduction.* Athens: Ohio University Press.

Branden, N. (1994). *The six pillars of self-esteem.* New York: Bantam.

Brim, G. (1992). *Ambition: How we manage success and failure throughout our lives.* New York: Basic Books.

Buchanan, A. (1980). A critical interaction to Rawls' theory of justice. In H. G. Blocker & E. Smith (Eds.), *John Rawls' theory of social justice: An introduction.* Athens: Ohio University Press.

Cashman, S. D. (1991). *African-Americans and the quest for civil rights: 1900-1990.* New York: New York University Press.

Chambers J. G., & Hartman, W. T. (Eds.). (1983). *Special education policies.* Philadelphia: Temple University Press.

Coleman, J. S. (1990). *Equality and achievement in education.* Boulder, CO: Westview.

Coughlin, E. K. (1994, August 3). Experts add their voices to welfare-reform debate. *Chronicle of Higher Education,* pp. A6-A7.

Csikszentmihalyi, M. (1990). *Flow: The psychology of optimal experience.* New York: Harper & Row.

DeStefano, L., & Snauwaert, D. (1989). *A value-critical approach to transition policy analysis.* Champaign, IL: Transition Institute at Illinois.

Foucault, M. (1965). *Madness and civilization: A history of insanity in the Age of Reason.* New York: Vintage.

Galbraith, J. K. (1987). *Economics in perspective: A critical history.* Boston: Houghton Mifflin.

Gans, H. J. (1988). *Middle American individualism: The future of liberal democracy.* New York: Oxford University Press.

Garraty, J. A., & Gay, P. (Eds.). (1981). *The Columbia history of the world.* New York: Harper & Row.

Glass, G. V. (1983). Effectiveness of special education. *Policy Studies Review, 2*(1), 65-78.

Glasser, I. (1991). *Visions of liberty: The Bill of Rights for all Americans.* New York: Arcade.

Gray, T. (1991). *Freedom.* Atlantic Highlands, NJ: Humanities Press.

Gutek, G. L. (1988). *Education and schooling in America.* Englewood Cliffs, NJ: Prentice Hall.

Herrnstein, R. J., & Murray, C. (1994). *The bell curve: Intelligence and class structure in American life.* New York: Free Press.

Hill, N. (1960). *Think and grow rich.* New York: Fawcett Crest.

Humana, C. (1992). *World human rights guide.* New York: Oxford University Press.

Jackson, D. W. (1992). *Even the children of strangers: Equality under the U.S. Constitution.* Lawrence: University of Kansas Press.

Lasch, C. (1979). *The culture of narcissism: American life in an age of diminishing expectations.* New York: Warner.

Lazerson, M. (1983). The origins of special education. In J. G. Chambers & W. T. Hartman (Eds.), *Special education policies.* Philadelphia: Temple University Press.

Lenski, G., & Lenski, J. (1974). *Human societies: An introduction to macrosociology.* New York: McGraw-Hill.

Levins, R., & Lewontin, R. (1985). *The dialectical biologist.* Cambridge, MA: Harvard University Press.

Lewis, P. (1994, June 2). U.S. lists four nations at risk because of wide income gaps. *New York Times,* p. A6.

Mann, M. (1986). *The sources of social power: Vol. 1. A history of power from the beginning to A.D. 1760.* New York: Cambridge University Press.

Marx, K., & Engels, F. (1955). *The communist manifesto* (S. H. Beer, Ed.). New York: Appleton-Century-Crofts.

Maryanski, A., & Turner, J. H. (1992). *The social cage: Human nature and the evolution of society.* Stanford, CA: Stanford University Press.

Meltzer, M. (1993). *Slavery: A world history.* New York: DaCapo.

Microsoft Encarta. (1993a). *Feudalism.* Bellevue, WA: Microsoft Corporation.

Microsoft Encarta. (1993b). *Slavery.* Bellevue, WA: Microsoft Corporation.

Mithaug, D. E. (1993). *Self-regulation theory: How optimal adjustment maximizes gain.* Westport, CT: Praeger.

Mithaug, D. E., & Horiuchi, C. N. (1983). *Colorado statewide follow-up survey of special education students.* Denver: Colorado Department of Education.

Mithaug, D. E., Horiuchi, C. N., & McNulty, B. A. (1987). *Parent reports on the transition of students graduating from Colorado special education programs in 1978 and 1979.* Denver: Colorado Department of Education.

Myers, D. G. (1992). *The pursuit of happiness: Who is happy and why.* New York: William Morrow.

Newell, A., & Simon, H. A. (1972). *Human problem solving.* Englewood Cliffs, NJ: Prentice Hall.

Nietzsche, F. (1957). The good as power. In M. Mandlebaum, F. W. Gramlich, & R. Anderson (Eds.), *Philosophic problems: An introductory book of readings.* New York: Macmillan.

Nozick, R. (1974). *Anarchy, state and utopia.* New York: Basic Books.

Palmer, R. R. (1963). *A history of the modern world.* New York: Knopf.

Patterson, O. (1991). *Freedom: Vol. 1. Freedom in the making of Western culture.* New York: Basic Books.

Rawls, J. (1971). *A theory of justice.* Cambridge, MA: Belknap.

Roberts, J. H. (1993). *History of the world.* New York: Oxford University Press.

Rothman, R. A. (1993). *Inequality and stratification: Class, color, and gender.* Englewood Cliffs, NJ: Prentice Hall.

Rothstein, L. F. (1990). *Special education law.* New York: Longman.

Rousseau, J. J. (1962). The social contract. In Sir E. Barker (Ed.), *Social contract: Essays by Locke, Hume, and Rousseau* (Introduction by Sir Ernest Barker). New York: Oxford University Press. (original publication 1762; first published in this volume in 1947)

Routh, G. (1989). *The origin of economic ideas.* Dobbs Ferry, NY: Sheridan House.

Scheerenberger, R. C. (1983). *A history of mental retardation.* Baltimore, MD: Paul Brookes.

Schwarz, J. E., & Volgy, T. J. (1992). *The forgotten Americans: Thirty million working poor in the land of opportunity.* New York: Norton.

Sen, A. (1992). *Inequality reexamined.* Cambridge, MA: Harvard University Press.

Shapiro, J. P. (1993). *No pity: People with disabilities forging a new civil rights movement.* New York: Times Books.

Sherraden, M. (1991). *Assets and the poor: A new American welfare policy.* Armonk, NY: M. E. Sharpe.

Shields, C. V. (1955). The political thought of the British utilitarians. In *James Mill, an essay on government.* New York: Liberal Arts Press.

Simon, H. (1960). *The new science of management decision.* New York: Harper & Row.

Sternberg, R. J. (1988). *The triarchic mind: A new theory of human intelligence.* New York: Penguin.

Stone, D. A. (1988). *Policy paradox and political reason.* New York: HarperCollins.

Sumner, W. G. (1961). *What social classes owe to each other.* Caldwell, ID: Caxton Printers. (original publication 1883)

Turnbull, H. R., III. (1993). *Free appropriate public education: The law and children with disabilities* (4th ed.). Denver, CO: Love Publishing.

Ward, M. J. (1991). Self-determination revisited: Going beyond expectations. *NICHCY Transition Summary, 7,* 1-12.

Weinreb, L. L. (1987). *Natural law and justice.* Cambridge, MA: Harvard University Press.

Weinreb, L. L. (1994). *Oedipus at Fenway Park: What rights are and why there are any.* Cambridge, MA: Harvard University Press.

Wells, A. S., & Crain, R. L. (1995). Perpetuation theory and the long-term effects of school desegregation. *Review of Educational Research, 64,*(4), 531-555.

Wilkinson, J. H., III. (1979). *From Brown to Bakke—The Supreme Court and school integration: 1954-1978.* New York: Oxford University Press.

William T. Grant Foundation Commission on Work, Family and Citizenship. (1988). *The forgotten half: Non-college youth in America, an interim report on the school-to-work transition.* Washington, DC: Author.

Wolff, M., Rutten, P., & Bayers III, A. F. (1992). *Where we stand: Can America make it in the global race for wealth, health, and happiness?* New York: Bantam Books, 202-215.

Wolman, J. M., Campeau, P. L., DuBois, P. A., Mithaug, D. E., & Stolarski, V. S. (1995). *AIR self-determination scale and user guide.* Palo Alto, CA: American Institutes for Research.

Wright, J. W. (Ed.). (1990). *The universal almanac, 1990.* New York: Andrews & McMeel.

Yolton, J. W. (1985). John Locke (1632-1704). In A. Kuper & J. Kuper (Eds.), *The social science encyclopedia.* New York: Routledge.

Index

About the Author

Dennis E. Mithaug is Professor and Chair of the Department of Special Education at Teachers College, Columbia University. He received a BA in Psychology from Dartmouth College, an MA and PhD in Sociology and an MEd in Special Education from the University of Washington. He has authored many journal articles, chapters, and books that include *Self-Regulation Theory: How Optimal Adjustment Maximizes Gain* (1993), *Self-Determinated Kids: Raising Satisfied and Successful Children* (1991), *Prevocational Training for Retarded Students* (1981), and *Vocational Training for Mentally Retarded Adults* (1980).